ASPEN PUBLISHERS

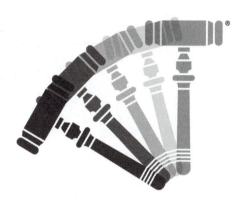

Casenote™ Legal Briefs

ANTITRUST

Keyed to Courses Using

Sullivan, Hovenkamp and Shelanski's
Antitrust Law, Policy and Procedure

Sixth Edition

AUSTIN   BOSTON   CHICAGO   NEW YORK   THE NETHERLANDS

This publication is designed to provide accurate and authoritative information in regard to the subject matter covered. It is sold with the understanding that the publisher is not engaged in rendering legal, accounting, or other professional services. If legal advice or other expert assistance is required, the services of a competent professional person should be sought.

> — From a Declaration of Principles adopted jointly
> by a Committee of the American Bar Association
> and a Committee of Publishers and Associates

Aspen Publishers
Attn: Permissions Dept.
76 Ninth Avenue, 7th Floor
New York, NY 10011-5201

To contact Customer Care, e-mail customer.service@aspenpublishers.com, call 1-800-234-1660, fax 1-800-901-9075, or mail correspondence to:

Aspen Publishers
Attn: Order Department
P.O. Box 990
Frederick, MD 21705

Printed in the United States of America.

1 2 3 4 5 6 7 8 9 0

ISBN 978-0-7355-9901-7

About Wolters Kluwer Law & Business

Wolters Kluwer Law & Business is a leading provider of research information and workflow solutions in key specialty areas. The strengths of the individual brands of Aspen Publishers, CCH, Kluwer Law International and Loislaw are aligned within Wolters Kluwer Law & Business to provide comprehensive, in-depth solutions and expert-authored content for the legal, professional and education markets.

CCH was founded in 1913 and has served more than four generations of business professionals and their clients. The CCH products in the Wolters Kluwer Law & Business group are highly regarded electronic and print resources for legal, securities, antitrust and trade regulation, government contracting, banking, pension, payroll, employment and labor, and health-care reimbursement and compliance professionals.

Aspen Publishers is a leading information provider for attorneys, business professionals and law students. Written by preeminent authorities, Aspen products offer analytical and practical information in a range of specialty practice areas from securities law and intellectual property to mergers and acquisitions and pension/benefits. Aspen's trusted legal education resources provide professors and students with high-quality, up-to-date and effective resources for successful instruction and study in all areas of the law.

Kluwer Law International supplies the global business community with comprehensive English-language international legal information. Legal practitioners, corporate counsel and business executives around the world rely on the Kluwer Law International journals, loose-leafs, books and electronic products for authoritative information in many areas of international legal practice.

Loislaw is a premier provider of digitized legal content to small law firm practitioners of various specializations. Loislaw provides attorneys with the ability to quickly and efficiently find the necessary legal information they need, when and where they need it, by facilitating access to primary law as well as state-specific law, records, forms and treatises.

Wolters Kluwer Law & Business, a unit of Wolters Kluwer, is headquartered in New York and Riverwoods, Illinois. Wolters Kluwer is a leading multinational publisher and information services company.

Format for the Casenote Legal Brief

Nature of Case: This section identifies the form of action (e.g., breach of contract, negligence, battery), the type of proceeding (e.g., demurrer, appeal from trial court's jury instructions), or the relief sought (e.g., damages, injunction, criminal sanctions).

Fact Summary: This is included to refresh your memory and can be used as a quick reminder of the facts.

Rule of Law: Summarizes the general principle of law that the case illustrates. It may be used for instant recall of the court's holding and for classroom discussion or home review.

Facts: This section contains all relevant facts of the case, including the contentions of the parties and the lower court holdings. It is written in a logical order to give the student a clear understanding of the case. The plaintiff and defendant are identified by their proper names throughout and are always labeled with a (P) or (D).

Palsgraf v. Long Island R.R. Co.

Injured bystander (P) v. Railroad company (D)

N.Y. Ct. App., 248 N.Y. 339, 162 N.E. 99 (1928).

NATURE OF CASE: Appeal from judgment affirming verdict for plaintiff seeking damages for personal injury.

FACT SUMMARY: Helen Palsgraf (P) was injured on R.R.'s (D) train platform when R.R.'s (D) guard helped a passenger aboard a moving train, causing his package to fall on the tracks. The package contained fireworks which exploded, creating a shock that tipped a scale onto Palsgraf (P).

🏛 RULE OF LAW
The risk reasonably to be perceived defines the duty to be obeyed.

FACTS: Helen Palsgraf (P) purchased a ticket to Rockaway Beach from R.R. (D) and was waiting on the train platform. As she waited, two men ran to catch a train that was pulling out from the platform. The first man jumped aboard, but the second man, who appeared as if he might fall, was helped aboard by the guard on the train who had kept the door open so they could jump aboard. A guard on the platform also helped by pushing him onto the train. The man was carrying a package wrapped in newspaper. In the process, the man dropped his package, which fell on the tracks. The package contained fireworks and exploded. The shock of the explosion was apparently of great enough strength to tip over some scales at the other end of the platform, which fell on Palsgraf (P) and injured her. A jury awarded her damages, and R.R. (D) appealed.

ISSUE: Does the risk reasonably to be perceived define the duty to be obeyed?

HOLDING AND DECISION: (Cardozo, C.J.) Yes. The risk reasonably to be perceived defines the duty to be obeyed. If there is no foreseeable hazard to the injured party as the result of a seemingly innocent act, the act does not become a tort because it happened to be a wrong as to another. If the wrong was not willful, the plaintiff must show that the act as to her had such great and apparent possibilities of danger as to entitle her to protection. Negligence in the abstract is not enough upon which to base liability. Negligence is a relative concept, evolving out of the common law doctrine of trespass on the case. To establish liability, the defendant must owe a legal duty of reasonable care to the injured party. A cause of action in tort will lie where harm,

though unintended, could have been averted or avoided by observance of such a duty. The scope of the duty is limited by the range of danger that a reasonable person could foresee. In this case, there was nothing to suggest from the appearance of the parcel or otherwise that the parcel contained fireworks. The guard could not reasonably have had any warning of a threat to Palsgraf (P), and R.R. (D) therefore cannot be held liable. Judgment is reversed in favor of R.R. (D).

DISSENT: (Andrews, J.) The concept that there is no negligence unless R.R. (D) owes a legal duty to take care as to Palsgraf (P) herself is too narrow. Everyone owes to the world at large the duty of refraining from those acts that may unreasonably threaten the safety of others. If the guard's action was negligent as to those nearby, it was also negligent as to those outside what might be termed the "danger zone." For Palsgraf (P) to recover, R.R.'s (D) negligence must have been the proximate cause of her injury, a question of fact for the jury.

▶ ANALYSIS
The majority defined the limit of the defendant's liability in terms of the danger that a reasonable person in defendant's situation would have perceived. The dissent argued that the limitation should not be placed on liability, but rather on damages. Judge Andrews suggested that only injuries that would not have happened but for R.R.'s (D) negligence should be compensable. Both the majority and dissent recognized the policy-driven need to limit liability for negligent acts, seeking, in the words of Judge Andrews, to define a framework "that will be practical and in keeping with the general understanding of mankind." The Restatement (Second) of Torts has accepted Judge Cardozo's view.

Quicknotes

FORESEEABILITY A reasonable expectation that change is the probable result of certain acts or omissions.

NEGLIGENCE Conduct falling below the standard of care that a reasonable person would demonstrate under similar conditions.

PROXIMATE CAUSE The natural sequence of events without which an injury would not have been sustained.

Party ID: Quick identification of the relationship between the parties.

Concurrence/Dissent: All concurrences and dissents are briefed whenever they are included by the casebook editor.

Analysis: This last paragraph gives you a broad understanding of where the case "fits in" with other cases in the section of the book and with the entire course. It is a hornbook-style discussion indicating whether the case is a majority or minority opinion and comparing the principal case with other cases in the casebook. It may also provide analysis from restatements, uniform codes, and law review articles. The analysis will prove to be invaluable to classroom discussion.

Issue: The issue is a concise question that brings out the essence of the opinion as it relates to the section of the casebook in which the case appears. Both substantive and procedural issues are included if relevant to the decision.

Holding and Decision: This section offers a clear and in-depth discussion of the rule of the case and the court's rationale. It is written in easy-to-understand language and answers the issue presented by applying the law to the facts of the case. When relevant, it includes a thorough discussion of the exceptions to the case as listed by the court, any major cites to the other cases on point, and the names of the judges who wrote the decisions.

Quicknotes: Conveniently defines legal terms found in the case and summarizes the nature of any statutes, codes, or rules referred to in the text.

Aspen Publishers is proud to offer *Casenote Legal Briefs*—continuing thirty years of publishing America's best-selling legal briefs.

Casenote Legal Briefs are designed to help you save time when briefing assigned cases. Organized under convenient headings, they show you how to abstract the basic facts and holdings from the text of the actual opinions handed down by the courts. Used as part of a rigorous study regimen, they can help you spend more time analyzing and critiquing points of law than on copying bits and pieces of judicial opinions into your notebook or outline.

Casenote Legal Briefs should never be used as a substitute for assigned casebook readings. They work best when read as a follow-up to reviewing the underlying opinions themselves. Students who try to avoid reading and digesting the judicial opinions in their casebooks or online sources will end up shortchanging themselves in the long run. The ability to absorb, critique, and restate the dynamic and complex elements of case law decisions is crucial to your success in law school and beyond. It cannot be developed vicariously.

Casenote Legal Briefs represents but one of the many offerings in Aspen's Study Aid Timeline, which includes:

- *Casenote Legal Briefs*
- *Emanuel Law Outlines*
- *Examples & Explanations* Series
- *Introduction to Law* Series
- Emanuel *Law in a Flash* Flash Cards
- Emanuel *CrunchTime* Series

Each of these series is designed to provide you with easy-to-understand explanations of complex points of law. Each volume offers guidance on the principles of legal analysis and, consulted regularly, will hone your ability to spot relevant issues. We have titles that will help you prepare for class, prepare for your exams, and enhance your general comprehension of the law along the way.

To find out more about Aspen Study Aid publications, visit us online at *www.AspenLaw.com* or email us at *legaledu@wolterskluwer.com*. We'll be happy to assist you.

Get this Casenote Legal Brief as an AspenLaw Studydesk eBook today!

By returning this form to Aspen Publishers, you will receive a complimentary eBook download of this Casenote Legal Brief and AspenLaw Studydesk productivity software.* Learn more about AspenLaw Studydesk today at *www.AspenLaw.com/Studydesk.*

Name	Phone ( )	
Address		Apt. No.
City	State	ZIP Code
Law School	Graduation Date Month _____ Year _____	

Cut out the UPC found on the lower left corner of the back cover of this book. Staple the UPC inside this box. Only the original UPC from the book cover will be accepted. (No photocopies or store stickers are allowed.)

Attach UPC inside this box.

Email (Print legibly or you may not get access!)

Title of this book (course subject)

ISBN of this book (10- or 13-digit number on the UPC)

Used with which casebook (provide author's name)

Mail the completed form to:

Aspen Publishers, Inc.
Legal Education Division
130 Turner Street, Bldg 3, 4th Floor
Waltham, MA 02453-8901

* Upon receipt of this completed form, you will be emailed a code for the digital download of this book in AspenLaw Studydesk eBook format and a free copy of the software application, which is required to read the eBook.

For a full list of eBook study aids available for AspenLaw Studydesk software and other resources that will help you with your law school studies, visit *www.AspenLaw.com.*

Make a photocopy of this form and your UPC for your records.

For detailed information on the use of the information you provide on this form, please see the PRIVACY POLICY at *www.AspenLaw.com.*

How to Brief a Case

A. Decide on a Format and Stick to It

Structure is essential to a good brief. It enables you to arrange systematically the related parts that are scattered throughout most cases, thus making manageable and understandable what might otherwise seem to be an endless and unfathomable sea of information. There are, of course, an unlimited number of formats that can be utilized. However, it is best to find one that suits your needs and stick to it. Consistency breeds both efficiency and the security that when called upon you will know where to look in your brief for the information you are asked to give.

Any format, as long as it presents the essential elements of a case in an organized fashion, can be used. Experience, however, has led *Casenotes* to develop and utilize the following format because of its logical flow and universal applicability.

NATURE OF CASE: This is a brief statement of the legal character and procedural status of the case (e.g., "Appeal of a burglary conviction").

There are many different alternatives open to a litigant dissatisfied with a court ruling. The key to determining which one has been used is to discover *who is asking this court for what.*

This first entry in the brief should be kept as *short as possible.* Use the court's terminology if you understand it. But since jurisdictions vary as to the titles of pleadings, the best entry is the one that addresses who wants what in this proceeding, not the one that sounds most like the court's language.

RULE OF LAW: A statement of the general principle of law that the case illustrates (e.g., "An acceptance that varies any term of the offer is considered a rejection and counteroffer").

Determining the rule of law of a case is a procedure similar to determining the issue of the case. Avoid being fooled by red herrings; there may be a few rules of law mentioned in the case excerpt, but usually only one is *the* rule with which the casebook editor is concerned. The techniques used to locate the issue, described below, may also be utilized to find the rule of law. Generally, your best guide is simply the chapter heading. It is a clue to the point the casebook editor seeks to make and should be kept in mind when reading every case in the respective section.

FACTS: A synopsis of only the essential facts of the case, i.e., those bearing upon or leading up to the issue.

The facts entry should be a short statement of the events and transactions that led one party to initiate legal proceedings against another in the first place. While some cases conveniently state the salient facts at the beginning of the decision, in other instances they will have to be culled from hiding places throughout the text, even from concurring and dissenting opinions. Some of the "facts" will often be in dispute and should be so noted. Conflicting evidence may be briefly pointed up. "Hard" facts must be included. Both must be *relevant* in order to be listed in the facts entry. It is impossible to tell what is relevant until the entire case is read, as the ultimate determination of the rights and liabilities of the parties may turn on something buried deep in the opinion.

Generally, the facts entry should not be longer than three to five *short* sentences.

It is often helpful to identify the role played by a party in a given context. For example, in a construction contract case the identification of a party as the "contractor" or "builder" alleviates the need to tell that that party was the one who was supposed to have built the house.

It is always helpful, and a good general practice, to identify the "plaintiff" and the "defendant." This may seem elementary and uncomplicated, but, especially in view of the creative editing practiced by some casebook editors, it is sometimes a difficult or even impossible task. Bear in mind that the *party presently* seeking something from this court may not be the plaintiff, and that sometimes only the cross-claim of a defendant is treated in the excerpt. Confusing or misaligning the parties can ruin your analysis and understanding of the case.

ISSUE: A statement of the general legal question answered by or illustrated in the case. For clarity, the issue is best put in the form of a question capable of a "yes" or "no" answer. In reality, the issue is simply the Rule of Law put in the form of a question (e.g., "May an offer be accepted by performance?").

The major problem presented in discerning what is *the* issue in the case is that an opinion usually purports to raise and answer several questions. However, except for rare cases, only one such question is really the issue in the case. Collateral issues not necessary to the resolution of the matter in controversy are handled by the court by language known as *"obiter dictum"* or merely *"dictum."* While dicta may be included later in the brief, they have no place under the issue heading.

To find the issue, ask *who wants what* and then go on to ask *why did that party succeed or fail in getting it.* Once this is determined, the "why" should be turned into a question.

The complexity of the issues in the cases will vary, but in all cases a single-sentence question should sum up the issue. *In a few cases,* there will be two, or even more rarely, three issues of equal importance to the resolution of the case. Each should be expressed in a single-sentence question.

Since many issues are resolved by a court in coming to a final disposition of a case, the casebook editor will reproduce the portion of the opinion containing the issue or issues most relevant to the area of law under scrutiny. A noted law professor gave this advice: "Close the book; look at the title on the cover." Chances are, if it is Property, you need not concern yourself with whether, for example, the federal government's treatment of the plaintiff's land really raises a federal question sufficient to support jurisdiction on this ground in federal court.

The same rule applies to chapter headings designating sub-areas within the subjects. They tip you off as to what the text is designed to teach. The cases are arranged in a casebook to show a progression or development of the law, so that the preceding cases may also help.

It is also most important to remember to *read the notes and questions* at the end of a case to determine what the editors wanted you to have gleaned from it.

HOLDING AND DECISION: This section should succinctly explain the rationale of the court in arriving at its decision. In capsulizing the "reasoning" of the court, it should always include an application of the general rule or rules of law to the specific facts of the case. Hidden justifications come to light in this entry: the reasons for the state of the law, the public policies, the biases and prejudices, those considerations that influence the justices' thinking and, ultimately, the outcome of the case. At the end, there should be a short indication of the disposition or procedural resolution of the case (e.g., "Decision of the trial court for Mr. Smith (P) reversed").

The foregoing format is designed to help you "digest" the reams of case material with which you will be faced in your law school career. Once mastered by practice, it will place at your fingertips the information the authors of your casebooks have sought to impart to you in case-by-case illustration and analysis.

B. Be as Economical as Possible in Briefing Cases

Once armed with a format that encourages succinctness, it is as important to be economical with regard to the time spent on the actual reading of the case as it is to be economical in the writing of the brief itself. This does not mean "skimming" a case. Rather, it means reading the case with an "eye" trained to recognize into which "section" of your brief a particular passage or line fits and having a system for quickly and precisely marking the case so that the passages fitting any one particular part of

the brief can be easily identified and brought together in a concise and accurate manner when the brief is actually written.

It is of no use to simply repeat everything in the opinion of the court; record only enough information to trigger your recollection of what the court said. Nevertheless, an accurate statement of the "law of the case," i.e., the legal principle applied to the facts, is absolutely essential to class preparation and to learning the law under the case method.

To that end, it is important to develop a "shorthand" that you can use to make marginal notations. These notations will tell you at a glance in which section of the brief you will be placing that particular passage or portion of the opinion.

Some students prefer to underline all the salient portions of the opinion (with a pencil or colored underliner marker), making marginal notations as they go along. Others prefer the color-coded method of underlining, utilizing different colors of markers to underline the salient portions of the case, each separate color being used to represent a different section of the brief. For example, blue underlining could be used for passages relating to the rule of law, yellow for those relating to the issue, and green for those relating to the holding and decision, etc. While it has its advocates, the color-coded method can be confusing and time-consuming (all that time spent on changing colored markers). Furthermore, it can interfere with the continuity and concentration many students deem essential to the reading of a case for maximum comprehension. In the end, however, it is a matter of personal preference and style. Just remember, whatever method you use, underlining must be used sparingly or its value is lost.

If you take the marginal notation route, an efficient and easy method is to go along underlining the key portions of the case and placing in the margin alongside them the following "markers" to indicate where a particular passage or line "belongs" in the brief you will write:

N   (NATURE OF CASE)

RL   (RULE OF LAW)

I   (ISSUE)

HL   (HOLDING AND DECISION, relates to the RULE OF LAW behind the decision)

HR   (HOLDING AND DECISION, gives the RATIONALE or reasoning behind the decision)

HA   (HOLDING AND DECISION, APPLIES the general principle(s) of law to the facts of the case to arrive at the decision)

Remember that a particular passage may well contain information necessary to more than one part of your brief, in which case you simply note that in the margin. If you are using the color-coded underlining method instead of marginal notation, simply make asterisks or checks in the margin next to the passage in question in the colors that indicate the additional sections of the brief where it might be utilized.

The economy of utilizing "shorthand" in marking cases for briefing can be maintained in the actual brief writing process itself by utilizing "law student shorthand" within the brief. There are many commonly used words and phrases for which abbreviations can be substituted in your briefs (and in your class notes also). You can develop abbreviations that are personal to you and which will save you a lot of time. A reference list of briefing abbreviations can be found on page xii of this book.

C. Use Both the Briefing Process and the Brief as a Learning Tool

Now that you have a format and the tools for briefing cases efficiently, the most important thing is to make the time spent in briefing profitable to you and to make the most advantageous use of the briefs you create. Of course, the briefs are invaluable for classroom reference when you are called upon to explain or analyze a particular case. However, they are also useful in reviewing for exams. A quick glance at the fact summary should bring the case to mind, and a rereading of the rule of law should enable you to go over the underlying legal concept in your mind, how it was applied in that particular case, and how it might apply in other factual settings.

As to the value to be derived from engaging in the briefing process itself, there is an immediate benefit that arises from being forced to sift through the essential facts and reasoning from the court's opinion and to succinctly express them in your own words in your brief. The process ensures that you understand the case and the point that it illustrates, and that means you will be ready to absorb further analysis and information brought forth in class. It also ensures you will have something to say when called upon in class. The briefing process helps develop a mental agility for getting to the *gist* of a case and for identifying, expounding on, and applying the legal concepts and issues found there. The briefing process is the mental process on which you must rely in taking law school examinations; it is also the mental process upon which a lawyer relies in serving his clients and in making his living.

acceptance	acp	offer	O
affirmed	aff	offeree	OE
answer	ans	offeror	OR
assumption of risk	a/r	ordinance	ord
attorney	atty	pain and suffering	p/s
beyond a reasonable doubt	b/r/d	parol evidence	p/e
bona fide purchaser	BFP	plaintiff	P
breach of contract	br/k	prima facie	p/f
cause of action	c/a	probable cause	p/c
common law	c/l	proximate cause	px/c
Constitution	Con	real property	r/p
constitutional	con	reasonable doubt	r/d
contract	K	reasonable man	r/m
contributory negligence	c/n	rebuttable presumption	rb/p
cross	x	remanded	rem
cross-complaint	x/c	res ipsa loquitur	RIL
cross-examination	x/ex	respondeat superior	r/s
cruel and unusual punishment	c/u/p	Restatement	RS
defendant	D	reversed	rev
dismissed	dis	Rule Against Perpetuities	RAP
double jeopardy	d/j	search and seizure	s/s
due process	d/p	search warrant	s/w
equal protection	e/p	self-defense	s/d
equity	eq	specific performance	s/p
evidence	ev	statute	S
exclude	exc	statute of frauds	S/F
exclusionary rule	exc/r	statute of limitations	S/L
felony	f/n	summary judgment	s/j
freedom of speech	f/s	tenancy at will	t/w
good faith	g/f	tenancy in common	t/c
habeas corpus	h/c	tenant	t
hearsay	hr	third party	TP
husband	H	third party beneficiary	TPB
injunction	inj	transferred intent	TI
in loco parentis	ILP	unconscionable	uncon
inter vivos	I/v	unconstitutional	unconst
joint tenancy	j/t	undue influence	u/e
judgment	judgt	Uniform Commercial Code	UCC
jurisdiction	jur	unilateral	uni
last clear chance	LCC	vendee	VE
long-arm statute	LAS	vendor	VR
majority view	maj	versus	v
meeting of minds	MOM	void for vagueness	VFV
minority view	min	weight of authority	w/a
Miranda rule	Mir/r	weight of the evidence	w/e
Miranda warnings	Mir/w	wife	W
negligence	neg	with	w/
notice	ntc	within	w/i
nuisance	nus	without	w/o
obligation	ob	without prejudice	w/o/p
obscene	obs	wrongful death	wr/d

Table of Cases

Introduction

Quick Reference Rules of Law

United States v. Trans-Missouri Freight Assn.

Federal government (P) v. Cartel (D)

166 U.S. 290 (1897).

NATURE OF CASE: Review of dismissal of antitrust enforcement action.

FACT SUMMARY: Trans-Missouri Freight Association (D) contended that the Sherman Act prohibited contracts in restraint of competition if they were unreviewable.

RULE OF LAW
The Sherman Act's prohibition on agreements in restraint of trade is not limited to unreasonable restraints.

FACTS: Eighteen western railroads created a cartel, the Trans-Missouri Freight Association (Trans-Missouri) (D), in order to set fixed rates. The federal government (P) instituted an action under the Sherman Act contending that Trans-Missouri (D) had entered into an agreement in restraint of competition. Trans-Missouri (D) moved to dismiss on the grounds that its rates were reasonable and therefore its agreement was not unlawful at common law or under the Sherman Act. The motion was granted, and the U.S. Supreme Court granted review.

ISSUE: Is the Sherman Act's prohibition on agreements in restraint of trade limited to unreasonable restraints?

HOLDING AND DECISION: (Peckham, J.) No. The Sherman Act's prohibition on agreements in restraint of trade is not limited to unreasonable restraints. The words used in the Act are clear and unambiguous; the Act prohibits "contracts in restraint of trade." Congress included no limiting or qualifying language with respect to reasonableness. A contract may be in restraint of trade and still be valid at common law yet be in violation of the Act. In this case, Trans-Missouri (D) does not have the right to enter into a combination with competing railroads to maintain fixed rates, no matter how reasonable those rates may be or what the intent of the railroads may have been. Reversed.

ANALYSIS

This case represents the most expansive interpretation ever given as to the reach of the Sherman Act. It interpreted the Act as reaching much further than common law antitrust rules, which only prohibited unreasonable restraints. Today, antitrust law voids some types of agreements categorically, while other types are subject to a reasonableness analysis.

Quicknotes

ANTITRUST LAW Body of federal law prohibiting business conduct that constitutes a restraint on trade.

COMBINATION (ANTITRUST DEFINITION) Alliance of entities, for the purpose of impeding free trade, that results in a monopoly, suppression of competition, or affecting prices.

RESTRAINT OF TRADE Agreement between entities, for the purpose of impeding free trade, that results in a monopoly, suppression of competition, or affecting prices.

SHERMAN ACT Makes every contract or conspiracy in unreasonable restraint of commerce illegal.

United States v. Addyston Pipe & Steel Co.

Federal government (P) v. Manufacturing company (D)

85 F. 271 (6th Cir. 1898), *aff'd*, 175 U.S. 211 (1899).

NATURE OF CASE: Action to dissolve a combination which sought to regulate the price of pipe.

FACT SUMMARY: Addyston Pipe & Steel Co. (D) and other pipe manufacturers entered into an agreement to artificially raise the price of pipe.

🏛 RULE OF LAW
A combination with the sole purpose to regulate price is violative of both public policy and the Sherman Act.

FACTS: A majority of pipe manufacturers in the U.S. entered into an agreement to artificially regulate the price of caste-iron pipe. The federal government (P) sought to dissolve this agreement as violative of the Sherman Act's prohibition against combinations in restraint of interstate commerce. Addyston Pipe and Steel Co. (D), the named representative of this combination, argued that they still had to meet the price set by their competition and lacked the power to absolutely fix prices. The price charged was fair, they argued, and competition was not restrained.

ISSUE: Is an agreement to set prices violative of the Sherman Act?

HOLDING AND DECISION: (Taft, J.) Yes. An agreement with the sole purpose to artificially set prices violates the Sherman Act. It is a combination in restraint of trade or commerce. Such agreements were also illegal at common law. It is immaterial whether the combination can actually affect prices or whether the prices charged are fair. It is sufficient that the sole purpose of the combination is to attempt to fix prices. A complete monopoly is not required. The impermissible purpose of the combination is sufficient to violate § 1 of the Sherman Act. It is a combination in restraint of trade or commerce. The combination is ordered dissolved. Reversed.

▌ ANALYSIS

In *U.S. v. American Tobacco Co.*, 221 U.S. 106 (1911), the Court held that not all combinations violated the Sherman Act. It held that only those acts or contracts which operated to the prejudice of the public interest by unduly restricting competition or trade were violative of § 1 of the Sherman Act. The exact amount and nature of such restrictions on competition or restraints on trade must be handled on a case-by-case basis.

Quicknotes

COMBINATION (ANTITRUST DEFINITION) Alliance of entities, for the purpose of impeding free trade, that results in a monopoly, suppression of competition, or affecting prices.

MONOPOLY A privilege or right conferred upon an individual or entity granting it the exclusive power to manufacture, sell and distribute a particular service or commodity; a market condition in which one or a few companies control the sale of a product or service thereby restraining competition in respect to that article or service.

PUBLIC POLICY Policy administered by the state with respect to the health, safety and morals of its people in accordance with common notions of fairness and decency.

RESTRAINT OF TRADE Agreement between entities, for the purpose of impeding free trade, that results in a monopoly, suppression of competition, or affecting prices.

SHERMAN ACT Makes every contract or conspiracy in unreasonable restraint of commerce illegal.

■■■

Enforcement

Quick Reference Rules of Law

Summit Health, Ltd. v. Pinhas

Health care operator (D) v. Physician (P)

500 U.S. 322 (1991).

NATURE OF CASE: Appeal from order reversing dismissal of antitrust action.

FACT SUMMARY: Pinhas (P), a physician, alleged that Summit Health, Ltd. (D) conspired with several doctors (D) to drive him out of practice after he refused to pad the cost of eye surgery by requiring a useless second surgeon to be present during surgery.

> **🏛 RULE OF LAW**
> Violation of the Sherman Act is determined by the potential harm that would ensue if a conspiracy were successful, not by actual occurrences.

FACTS: Pinhas (P) was an ophthalmologist employed at Midway Hospital (Midway) (D) operated by Summit Health, Ltd. (Summit) (D), which operated numerous medical facilities in the western United States. Pinhas (P) objected to Midway's (D) requirement that a second surgeon assist during all eye surgeries. In response, Midway (D) instituted a biased peer-review process that resulted in his termination. Midway (D) also planned to disseminate defamatory material concerning Pinhas (P) to other potential employers, with the intent of driving him out of practice. Pinhas (P) filed an action under the Sherman Act, alleging restraint of trade on the practice of ophthalmological services. Summit (D) moved to dismiss, contending that because the boycott of a single surgeon does not affect the adequate supply of surgeons market-wide, interstate commerce had not been implicated. The district court granted the motion, but the Ninth Circuit reversed, reinstating the claim. The U.S. Supreme Court granted review.

ISSUE: Is violation of the Sherman Act to be determined by the potential harm that would ensue if a conspiracy were successful?

HOLDING AND DECISION: (Stevens, J.) Yes. Violation of the Sherman Act is to be determined by the potential harm that would ensue if a conspiracy were successful. Thus, an attempt by a medical group to drive a physician out of practice may create a claim under the Sherman Act. An activity or set of activities has a sufficient nexus with interstate commerce so as to implicate the Sherman Act if it has an effect on interstate commerce, even if the activity itself is local in character. The provision of ophthalmological services affects interstate commerce because physicians perform services on out-of-state patients and receive payment from out-of-state Medicare sources. In this case, the exclusion of Pinhas (P) from the Los Angeles market would impact interstate commerce by reducing the provision of ophthalmological services there. Thus, Pinhas's

(P) claim that Midway (D) conspired with others to abuse the peer-review process and deny him access to the Los Angeles market for ophthalmological services has a sufficient nexus with interstate commerce to invoke Sherman Act jurisdiction. Affirmed.

DISSENT: (Scalia, J.) Because the economic effects of "blackballing" a single service provider like Pinhas (P) would not be felt throughout the Los Angeles market, the boycott alleged here does not substantially affect interstate commerce by restricting competition. At most, the conspiracy involved one hospital; the only anticompetitive scheme was the price "padding" that Pinhas (P) initially opposed.

▶ ANALYSIS

A defendant arguing against Sherman Act jurisdiction today has a hard row to hoe. All that is required is some effect on interstate commerce. With today's economic globalization, it is questionable if any economic activity can truly be characterized as local.

■=■

Quicknotes

BOYCOTT A concerted effort to refrain from doing business with a particular person or entity.

INTERSTATE COMMERCE Commercial dealings between two parties located in different states or located in one state and accomplished through a point in another state or a foreign country; commercial dealings transacted between two states.

RESTRAINT OF TRADE Agreement between entities, for the purpose of impeding free trade, that results in a monopoly, suppression of competition, or affecting prices.

SHERMAN ACT Makes every contract or conspiracy in unreasonable restraint of commerce illegal.

■=■

Illinois Brick Co. v. Illinois

Manufacturer (D) v. State (P)

431 U.S. 720 (1977).

NATURE OF CASE: Damage action under § 4 of the Clayton Act.

FACT SUMMARY: It was alleged that manufacturers of concrete blocks conspired to fix prices to distributors who, in turn, passed on these price increases to customers.

🏛 RULE OF LAW
Only direct purchasers from those engaged in unlawful price-fixing at the manufacturing level may seek damages for antitrust violations.

FACTS: Illinois (P) and various governmental entities brought a private damage action under § 4 of the Clayton Act. It was alleged that the manufacturers of concrete blocks in the State (P) had engaged in price-fixing activities. The blocks were sold to distributors who, in turn, sold them to general contractors. Ultimately, the increased prices were passed on to consumers such as the State of Illinois (P). Illinois Brick Co. (D) and the other manufacturers (D) alleged that even if they had conspired to fix prices, the indirect damages suffered by those not purchasing from the manufacturers could not be used as a measure of damages in an antitrust action.

ISSUE: May all parties in a distribution chain who are injured by price-fixing at any level maintain a damage action under antitrust law?

HOLDING AND DECISION: (White, J.) No. We find that only direct purchasers of those engaged in price-fixing at any level of the distribution chain should be allowed to seek damages for the antitrust violations. Unless a pass-on theory can be used both offensively and defensively, inequitable results subjecting parties to multiple liability would occur. We declared in *Hanover Shoe v. United Shoe Mach. Corp.*, 392 U.S. 481 (1968), a pass-on defense was generally unavailable to those charged with price-fixing by direct purchasers. Where the defense is not available, we must deny offensive use of the pass-on theory. We decide in this manner because of considerations of stare decisis, i.e., Congress has not amended § 4 even though it was aware of our decision in *Hanover Shoe*. Moreover, permitting damage actions predicated on a pass-on theory would require an apportionment of damages all along the distribution chain. It would create an almost unworkable analysis of the component parts of the chain to determine what percentage of markup was associated with the price-fixing activity. It would subject all members of the distribution chain to multiple litigation, and joinder of all claimants would be difficult, if not impossible, to achieve. Purchasers would be involved in suits between middlemen and manufacturers or between contractors and middlemen or manufacturers, etc. We reject attempts in suits between middlemen and manufacturers or between contractors and middlemen or manufacturers, etc. We reject attempts to carve out numerous exceptions to the pass-on theory. For all of these reasons we must reject the pass-on theory. Reversed.

▶ ANALYSIS

A pass-on defense is permitted where the direct purchaser is owned or controlled by its customer, *Perkins v. Standard Oil Co.*, 395 U.S. 642 (1969). Another exception is found where the overcharge is essentially determined in advance and is not dependent on the interaction of supply and demand, *In re Western Liquid Asphalt Cases*, 487 F.2d 191 (1973).

Quicknotes

CLAYTON ACT Legislation passed by the U.S. Congress in 1914 as an amendment to clarify and supplement the Sherman Antitrust Act of 1890. The act prohibited various anti-competitive business practices and gave labor certain rights in disputes with management. It declared that "the labor of a human being is not a commodity or article of commerce."

PRICE-FIXING An illegal combination in violation of the Sherman Act entered into for the purpose of setting prices below the natural market rate.

STARE DECISIS Doctrine whereby courts follow legal precedent unless there is good cause for departure.

Reiter v. Sonotone Corp.

Consumer (P) v. Manufacturer (D)

442 U.S. 330 (1979).

NATURE OF CASE: Appeal from interlocutory review of standing in action seeking damages under the Clayton Act.

FACT SUMMARY: Reiter (P), a consumer, sought damages under the Clayton Act for alleged price-fixing among hearing aid manufacturers (D).

🏛 RULE OF LAW
A consumer of retail goods and services has standing to sue for damages for price-fixing under § 4 of the Clayton Act.

FACTS: Reiter (P) brought a class-action suit in favor of purchasers of certain types of hearing aids against five corporations (D), including Sonotone Corp. (D), who manufactured the products. The complaint alleged price-fixing prohibited by the Clayton Act. The Ninth Circuit held that Reiter (P) did not have standing to sue for damages under the Act because she had not been injured in her "business or property," as required by § 4 of the Act. The U.S. Supreme Court granted review.

ISSUE: Does a consumer have standing to sue for damages under antitrust laws for price-fixing?

HOLDING AND DECISION: (Burger, C.J.) Yes. A consumer has standing to sue for damages under antitrust laws for price-fixing. The Clayton Act gives standing to anyone who is damaged in his "business or property." The court of appeals held this to refer only to those whose commercial interests were damaged. However, such a construction would render "business" synonymous with "property." Statutes will not be construed so as to make their terms redundant. "Property" is a different concept than "business" and encompasses a different category of items, including, as relevant to this case, money. Consequently, the statute is broad enough to include consumers within its protections. A consumer whose money has been diminished by reason of an antitrust violation has been injured "in his . . . property" within the meaning of § 4. Reversed.

▶ ANALYSIS

The present case was preceded by *Goldfarb v. Virginia State Bar*, 421 U.S. 773 (1975). In that case, aggrieved legal clients were allowed to sue a state bar association for treble damages under § 4. As a client is a "consumer" of legal services, that case impliedly approved consumer standing.

■=■

Quicknotes

CLAYTON ACT Legislation passed by the U.S. Congress in 1914 as an amendment to clarify and supplement the Sherman Antitrust Act of 1890. The act prohibited various anti-competitive business practices and gave labor certain rights in disputes with management. It declared that "the labor of a human being is not a commodity or article of commerce."

DAMAGES Monetary compensation that may be awarded by the court to a party who has sustained injury or loss to his or her person, property or rights due to another party's unlawful act, omission or negligence.

INTERLOCUTORY Intervening; temporary; refers to an issue that is determined during the course of a proceeding and which does not constitute a final judgment on the merits.

PRICE-FIXING An illegal combination in violation of the Sherman Act entered into for the purpose of setting prices below the natural market rate.

■=■

Brunswick Corp. v. Pueblo Bowl-O-Mat, Inc.

Manufacturer (D) v. Bowling alley (P)

429 U.S. 477 (1977).

NATURE OF CASE: Review of judgment awarding damages for antitrust violations.

FACT SUMMARY: Brunswick Corp. (D) engaged in the practice of buying and operating failing competitors of local bowling alleys, thereby preventing the local alleys from enjoying increased market share.

🏛 RULE OF LAW
Antitrust damages are not available when the sole injury alleged by the plaintiff is that the defendant's conduct allowed a competitor of the plaintiff to remain in business.

FACTS: Brunswick Corp. (D) was a large manufacturer of bowling equipment. Starting in the 1960s, Brunswick (D) began acquiring defaulting bowling alleys which purchased its equipment and operating them, thus preventing them from going out of business. Over the years, Brunswick (D), as a result of these acquisitions, became far and away the nation's largest owner of bowling alleys. When Brunswick (D) acquired several bowling centers in the same market as Pueblo Bowl-O-Mat, Inc. (Pueblo) (P), the latter brought an action under the Clayton Act, seeking damages and injunctive relief. The district court, following a jury verdict, awarded treble damages and injunctive relief to Pueblo (P), and the court of appeals affirmed. Brunswick (D) appealed the award, and the U.S. Supreme Court granted review.

ISSUE: Are antitrust damages available when the sole injury alleged by the plaintiff is that the defendant's conduct allowed a competitor of the plaintiff to remain in business?

HOLDING AND DECISION: (Marshall, J.) No. Antitrust damages are not available when the sole injury alleged by the plaintiff is that the defendant's conduct allowed a competitor of the plaintiff to remain in business. Antitrust law does not prohibit mergers and vertical integration per se; rather, it addresses only anticompetitive conduct. Antitrust law protects competition, not individual competitors. Section 4 of the Clayton Act provides treble damages to any "person who shall be injured in his business or property by reason of anything forbidden in the antitrust laws." Here, when Brunswick (D) acquired the defaulting alleys, Pueblo (P) lost the windfall profits it would have received had the alleys failed. This is not an "injury" within the meaning of § 4. Nor did Pueblo's (P) loss occur "by reason of" the antitrust violation that made Brunswick's (D) acquisitions unlawful. Pueblo (P) has not proven an "antitrust injury," that is, an actual decrease in competition caused by an antitrust violation. Treble damages are therefore denied. Reversed.

▶ ANALYSIS

One commentator has argued persuasively that Brunswick (D) was entitled to the "failing company" defense. See Areeda, 89 *Harv. L. Rev.* 1127 (1976). That defense holds that the acquisition of one company by another does not substantially lessen competition if the acquired company is on the brink of collapse and the acquiring company is the only available purchaser. In the case above, Pueblo (P) claimed that the acquired companies would have failed without the challenged merger. Therefore, Brunswick (D) did not violate the antitrust laws because it was the only available purchaser of a failing company.

Quicknotes

ANTITRUST LAW Body of federal law prohibiting business conduct that constitutes a restraint on trade.

CLAYTON ACT Legislation passed by the U.S. Congress in 1914 as an amendment to clarify and supplement the Sherman Antitrust Act of 1890. The act prohibited various anti-competitive business practices and gave labor certain rights in disputes with management. It declared that "the labor of a human being is not a commodity or article of commerce."

INJUNCTIVE RELIEF A court order issued as a remedy, requiring a person to do, or prohibiting that person from doing, a specific act.

TREBLE DAMAGES An award of damages triple of the amount awarded by the jury and provided for by statute for violation of certain offenses.

Cargill, Inc. v. Monfort of Colorado, Inc.

Meat-packing plant (D) v. Meat-packing plant (P)

479 U.S. 104 (1986).

NATURE OF CASE: Review of injunction prohibiting a merger.

FACT SUMMARY: Monfort of Colorado, Inc. (P) sought to enjoin a proposed merger by Excel (D), a larger competitor, on the ground that its potential for increased market share violated the Clayton Act.

> 🏛 **RULE OF LAW**
> A plaintiff seeking injunctive relief under § 16 of the Clayton Act must show an injury of the type the antitrust laws were designed to prevent.

FACTS: Monfort of Colorado, Inc. (Monfort) (P) operated three beef-packing plants. A competitor was Excel Corp. (D), which operated five beef-packing plants. Excel (D) signed a merger agreement with Spencer Beef, another meat-packing concern. Monfort (P) brought an injunctive action under § 16 of the Clayton Act, alleging that the merger would give Excel (D) and its owner, Cargill, Inc. (D), a larger market share, which would impair Monfort's (P) ability to compete. The district court granted the injunction, and the court of appeals affirmed. The U.S. Supreme Court granted review.

ISSUE: Must a plaintiff seeking injunctive relief under § 16 of the Clayton Act show an injury of the type that the antitrust laws were designed to prevent?

HOLDING AND DECISION: (Brennan, J.) Yes. A plaintiff seeking injunctive relief under § 16 of the Clayton Act must show an injury of the type that the antitrust laws were designed to prevent. A showing of loss or damage due merely to increased competition does not constitute such injury. In other words, injunctive relief is not available under the Clayton Act for activities by a competitor that increases its market share. Antitrust laws are intended to prevent threats to competition. Acts by a company to increase its market share are not inimical to competition; indeed, they represent vigorous competition and are not prohibited under the Clayton Act. Moreover, the threat of loss of profits due to possible price competition following a merger like Excel's (D) does not constitute a threat of "antitrust injury." On the other hand, predatory pricing, which means using greater resources to drive competition out of business, is actionable under antitrust law. However, Monfort (P) neither properly alleged nor proved predatory pricing threats in the proceedings below. Reversed and remanded.

▶ **ANALYSIS**

As stated in the opinion, § 4 of the Clayton Act provides money damages and § 16 provides injunctive relief. The

Court, in *Brunswick Corp. v. Pueblo Bowl-O-Mat, Inc.*, 429 U.S. 477 (1977), had already held that a § 4 remedy existed for diminution of competition flowing from an antitrust violation. To have held otherwise with respect to § 16 would have created an illogical asymmetry in the Clayton Act.

■=∎

Quicknotes

CLAYTON ACT Legislation passed by the U.S. Congress in 1914 as an amendment to clarify and supplement the Sherman Antitrust Act of 1890. The act prohibited various anti-competitive business practices and gave labor certain rights in disputes with management. It declared that "the labor of a human being is not a commodity or article of commerce."

INJUNCTION A court order requiring a person to do or prohibiting that person from doing a specific act.

MERGER The acquisition of one company by another, after which the acquired company ceases to exist as an independent entity.

■=∎

Blue Shield of Virginia v. McCready

Group health plan (D) v. Plan subscriber (P)

457 U.S. 465 (1982).

NATURE OF CASE: Appeal from award of treble damages under § 4 of the Clayton Act for antitrust violations in a class action.

FACT SUMMARY: McCready (P), a Blue Shield (D) subscriber, sought treble damages under § 4 of the Clayton Act when Blue Shield (D) refused to reimburse her for psychological consultations.

🏛 **RULE OF LAW**
▥ Standing to maintain an action under § 4 of the Clayton Act is limited to those plaintiffs who can show a physical and economic nexus between the antitrust violation and their injury, as well as a relationship between their injury and the type of injury § 4 was designed to remedy.

FACTS: Blue Shield of Virginia (Blue Shield) (D) wrote a plan of medical insurance coverage that provided reimbursement for psychiatric care but not for treatment by a psychologist. McCready (P), a Blue Shield (D) subscriber who had submitted psychological treatment bills and had been denied benefits, sued for treble damages under § 4 of the Clayton Act, alleging a conspiracy between Blue Shield (D) and the psychiatric community to boycott psychological care providers. The court of appeals ruled that McCready (P) had standing to seek damages under § 4. The U.S. Supreme Court granted review.

ISSUE: Is standing to maintain an action under § 4 of the Clayton Act limited to those plaintiffs who can show a physical and economic nexus between the antitrust violation and their injury, as well as a relationship between their injury and the type of injury § 4 was designed to remedy?

HOLDING AND DECISION: (Brennan, J.) Yes. Standing to maintain an action under § 4 of the Clayton Act is limited to those plaintiffs who can show a physical and economic nexus between the antitrust violation and their injury, as well as a relationship between their injury and the type of injury § 4 was designed to remedy. Section 4 of the Clayton Act provided a remedy to "any person" injured "by reason of" anything prohibited in the antitrust laws. The two-pronged inquiry stated above focuses on the remoteness of the plaintiff's injuries from an antitrust violation. In this case, the § 4 remedy cannot reasonably be restricted only to psychologists whom the conspirators sought to eliminate from the market. As a medical plan purchaser who uses the services of a psychologist, a plaintiff such as McCready is clearly within the area of the economy endangered by a breakdown of competitive conditions caused by the alleged conspiracy. Since McCready (P) had to pay more for her

psychologist's therapy due to Blue Shield's (D) coercive pressure, she suffered an injury due to an anticompetitive scheme. Her injury thus appears to be the type Congress had in mind when enacting a § 4 private remedy, so she enjoys standing under that section. Affirmed.

▶ **ANALYSIS**

The present decision represents a rejection of the "target area" theory of § 4 standing. Under that analysis, only a person targeted by anticompetitive activities (here, for instance, psychological care providers) were granted standing. This had been the rule, prior to this decision, in three of the federal circuits.

▰▬▰

Quicknotes

BOYCOTT A concerted effort to refrain from doing business with a particular person or entity.

CLASS ACTION A suit commenced by a representative on behalf of an ascertainable group that is too large to appear in court, who shares a commonality of interests and who will benefit from a successful result.

CLAYTON ACT Legislation passed by the U.S. Congress in 1914 as an amendment to clarify and supplement the Sherman Antitrust Act of 1890. The act prohibited various anti-competitive business practices and gave labor certain rights in disputes with management. It declared that "the labor of a human being is not a commodity or article of commerce."

STANDING Whether a party possesses the right to commence suit against another party by having a personal stake in the resolution of the controversy.

TREBLE DAMAGES An award of damages triple of the amount awarded by the jury and provided for by statute for violation of certain offenses.

▰▬▰

Associated General Contractors v. California State Council of Carpenters

Employer's organization (D) v. Labor union (P)

459 U.S. 519 (1983).

NATURE OF CASE: Review of denial of motion to dismiss antitrust class action seeking treble damages.

FACT SUMMARY: The California State Council of Carpenters (the Union) (P), a labor union, contended that Associated General Contractors (D), an employer's organization, conspired to coerce builders and developers to use nonunion labor, hereby entitling the Union (P) to treble damages under § 4 of the Clayton Act.

> ## 🏛 RULE OF LAW
> Indirect, highly speculative damages that may not even be caused by the alleged antitrust violation are not cognizable under § 4 of the Clayton Act.

FACTS: The California State Council of Carpenters (the Union) (P) was an association of AFL-CIO locals representing unionized carpenters. The Union (P) brought an action under § 4 of the Clayton Act, alleging that Associated General Contractors (D), an organization composed of building contractors, coerced member and nonmember contractors, as well as developers, to hire nonunion subcontractors as a way of circumventing collective-bargaining agreements. The Ninth Circuit held that the Union (P) had standing under § 4, and the U.S. Supreme Court granted review.

ISSUE: Are indirect, highly speculative damages that may not even be caused by the alleged antitrust violation cognizable under § 4 of the Clayton Act?

HOLDING AND DECISION: (Stevens, J.) No. Indirect, highly speculative damages that may not even be caused by the alleged antitrust violation are not cognizable under § 4 of the Clayton Act. Congress did not intend for every interest potentially harmed by activities proscribed by antitrust law to be redressable by way of a private right of action under § 4 of the Clayton Act. Rather, only those injured by decreased competition have standing under the Act. Here, the Union (P) was neither a competitor nor a consumer in the market allegedly being restrained. Also, the alleged acts by Associated General Contractors (D) do not necessarily subvert competition, and antitrust law protects competition, not competitors. Finally, it is unclear whether it would be possible to quantify the Union's (P) damages; they are quite speculative. Consequently, the Union (P) lacks standing under § 4. Reversed.

▶ ANALYSIS

The textual scope of antitrust law is quite broad. If § 4 were literally interpreted, almost every person affected by an antitrust law violation would have standing to bring an action for damages. Such a broad rule has been uniformly rejected by the courts, which tend to look at congressional intent behind antitrust laws in deciding standing.

■■■■

Quicknotes

CLASS ACTION A suit commenced by a representative on behalf of an ascertainable group that is too large to appear in court, who shares a commonality of interests and who will benefit from a successful result.

CLAYTON ACT Legislation passed by the U.S. Congress in 1914 as an amendment to clarify and supplement the Sherman Antitrust Act of 1890. The act prohibited various anti-competitive business practices and gave labor certain rights in disputes with management. It declared that "the labor of a human being is not a commodity or article of commerce."

COLLECTIVE BARGAINING Negotiations between an employer and employee that are mediated by a specified third party.

STANDING Whether a party possesses the right to commence suit against another party by having a personal stake in the resolution of the controversy.

TREBLE DAMAGES An award of damages triple of the amount awarded by the jury and provided for by statute for violation of certain offenses.

■■■■

Concord Boat Corp. v. Brunswick Corp.

Boat builder (P) v. Boat engine maker (D)

207 F.3d 1039 (8th Cir. 2000), *cert. denied*, 531 U.S. 979 (2000).

NATURE OF CASE: Appeal from denial of motion for judgment.

FACT SUMMARY: Concord Boat Corp.'s (P) expert, Hall—using evidence that was contrary to the undisputed record evidence and was based on a theoretical economic model—testified that Brunswick Corp. (D) had monopoly power in the stern drive engine market and used this power to engage in anticompetitive behavior. The jury returned a verdict for Concord Boat (P), and Brunswick (D) moved for judgment.

🏛 RULE OF LAW
Expert opinion is inadmissible where it does not incorporate all aspects of the economic reality of a given market and where it does not separate lawful from unlawful conduct.

FACTS: Concord Boat Corp. (P), a boat manufacturer, brought suit against Brunswick Corp. (D), a manufacturer of stern drive engines used in boats, alleging anticompetitive conduct. Concord Boat's (P) expert, Hall, testified that Brunswick (D) had monopoly power in the stern drive engine market that enabled it to use its market share discount programs to penalize boat builders and dealers who chose to purchase engines from other manufacturers. He asserted that Brunswick (D) forced its competitors to charge substantially lower prices to convince customers to purchase from them and forgo Brunswick's (D) discount. However, he contended that because Brunswick (D) had captured 78 percent of the stern drive market, other manufacturers could not enter into the market, and, therefore, Brunswick's (D) program was anticompetitive. To determine damages, Hall relied on the Cournot model of economic theory, which posits that a firm maximizes its profits by assuming the observed output of other firms as a given, and then equating its own marginal revenue on that assumption. Based on this model, Hall postulated that a competitive (yet hypothetical) stern drive market would have two equal 50 percent market share holders, and he concluded that any market share over 50 percent had to be the result of anticompetitive conduct. Brunswick (D) argued that Hall's expert opinion should have been excluded because it was contrary to undisputed record evidence and because it did not separate lawful from unlawful conduct, and Brunswick (D) moved for judgment. The district court denied Brunswick's (D) motion, and the court of appeals granted review.

ISSUE: Is expert opinion admissible where it does not incorporate all aspects of the economic reality of a given market and where it does not separate lawful from unlawful conduct?

HOLDING AND DECISION: (Murphy, J.) No. Expert opinion is inadmissible where it does not incorporate all aspects of the economic reality of a given market and where it does not separate lawful from unlawful conduct. A thorough analysis of Hall's economic model and his proffered opinion was necessary, despite Concord Boat's (P) assurances that his model would reflect the reality of the market. Under *Daubert v. Merrell Dow Pharmaceuticqls, Inc.*, 509 U.S. 579, 583 (1993), the district court must determine whether the methodology underlying the expert opinion is scientifically valid and whether it can be applied to the facts in issue. Here, not all relevant circumstances were incorporated into Hall's analysis as it related to antitrust liability. His opinion was not supported by the fact that some boat builders chose to purchase 100 percent of their engines from Brunswick (D), even though they only needed 80 percent to qualify for the maximum discount, and other evidence showed that the boat builders had influence over Brunswick (D). Also, his model failed to account for the fact that Brunswick (D) achieved 75 percent market share before it started its discount program, and before it acquired other stern drive engine manufacturers. The model also failed to take into account market events, such as the recall of engines by other manufacturers. Accordingly, Hall's expert opinion should not have been admitted. Because the jury relied on his testimony when it assessed damages, it could not be said that the verdict would have been the same without his opinion. Therefore, Brunswick's (D) motion for judgment should have been granted. Reversed.

▶ ANALYSIS

A *Daubert* analysis assesses both the reliability and the relevance of the proposed expert testimony. In this case, expert Hall was a professor of economics at Stanford University. Also, Brunswick (D) did not challenge the Cournot model as a scientific theory. Thus, there was no issue as to the reliability of his testimony. The real issue was whether there was a "fit" with the facts of the case—which goes to relevance. Essentially, the court ruled that Hall's testimony and opinion did not fit with all the facts of the case—that it was not entirely relevant.

■=■

Quicknotes

EXPERT TESTIMONY Testimonial evidence about a complex area of subject matter relevant to trial, presented by a person competent to inform the trier of fact due to specialized knowledge or training.

Continued on next page.

MONOPOLY A privilege or right conferred upon an individual or entity granting it the exclusive power to manufacture, sell and distribute a particular service or commodity; a market condition in which one or a few companies control the sale of a product or service thereby restraining competition in respect to that article or service.

∎══∎

Perma Life Mufflers, Inc. v. International Parts Corp.

Franchisee (P) v. Parts distributor (D)

392 U.S. 134 (1968).

NATURE OF CASE: Review of order dismissing antitrust action seeking treble damages.

FACT SUMMARY: When International Parts Corp. (D) was sued for antitrust violations by Perma Life Mufflers (P) it raised the defense of *in pari delicto*, arguing the plaintiff voluntarily took part in the illegal scheme.

> 🏛 **RULE OF LAW**
> *In pari delicto* is not available as a defense to an action based on antitrust violations.

FACTS: International Parts Corp. (International) (D), through its subsidiary, Midas, Inc. (D), distributed its parts partially through franchise agreements. A franchisee, in exchange for the right to call itself a "Midas Muffler Shop" in order to benefit from corporate advertising, agreed to carry only Midas parts and not sell in the territory of other franchisees. Perma Life Mufflers, Inc. (Perma Life) (P), a dealer that had signed a franchise agreement, later brought an action seeking treble damages and injunctive relief, claiming that International's (D) restrictive agreements constituted illegal restraints of trade. The court of appeals held Perma Life (P) *in pari delicto*, that is, of equal fault, for voluntarily entering into the restrictive franchise agreement and dismissed. The U.S. Supreme Court granted review.

ISSUE: Is *in pari delicto* available as a defense to an action based on antitrust law violations?

HOLDING AND DECISION: (Black, J.) No. *In pari delicto* is not available as a defense to an action based on antitrust law violations. This common-law defense is largely limited to actions in equity when a plaintiff is as equally at fault as a defendant. When a private suit serves important public purposes, however, the defense is inappropriate because it can interfere with vindication of important public rights. There is an important public component to antitrust actions, and therefore, *in pari delicto* is an inappropriate defense. Moreover, since Perma Life (P) did not aggressively support the restrictions but was in fact forced to accept them in order to benefit from Midas' (D) offer, it was not at equal fault. Reversed.

▶ ANALYSIS

Antitrust actions often seek both legal and equitable relief. *In pari delicto* is an equitable defense. Logically, it should be applied if injunctive relief is sought. The court based its rejection on public policy rather than analytical grounds.

Quicknotes

EQUITABLE RELIEF A remedy that is based upon principles of fairness as opposed to rules of law.

INJUNCTIVE RELIEF A court order issued as a remedy, requiring a person to do, or prohibiting that person from doing, a specific act.

IN PARI DELICTO Doctrine that a court will not enforce an illegal contract in an action for losses incurred as a result of the breach of that contract.

PUBLIC POLICY Policy administered by the state with respect to the health, safety and morals of its people in accordance with common notions of fairness and decency.

RESTRAINT OF TRADE Agreement between entities, for the purpose of impeding free trade, that results in a monopoly, suppression of competition, or affecting prices.

TREBLE DAMAGES An award of damages triple of the amount awarded by the jury and provided for by statute for violation of certain offenses.

■═■

California v. American Stores Co.

State (P) v. Owner of supermarkets (D)

495 U.S. 271 (1990).

NATURE OF CASE: Review of order dissolving injunction issued pursuant to antitrust laws.

FACT SUMMARY: American Stores Co. (D) contended that a district court was not empowered under § 16 of the Clayton Act to order a company to divest itself of another.

🏛️ **RULE OF LAW**

A district court is empowered under § 16 of the Clayton Act to order a company to divest itself of another.

FACTS: American Stores Co. (American) (D) was the owner of the fourth largest chain of supermarkets in California. American (D) signed a merger agreement with Lucky Stores, Inc., the owner of the largest chain in the state, wherein the latter corporation would be merged into the former. The State of California (P) brought an action under § 16 of the Clayton Act, contending that the merger would be injurious to competition. The district court agreed and issued a preliminary injunction prohibiting integration of the corporations pending a final injunction ordering divestiture. The Ninth Circuit reversed, holding that § 16 did not authorize a divestiture order. The U.S. Supreme Court granted review.

ISSUE: Is a district court empowered under § 16 of the Clayton Act to order a company to divest itself of another?

HOLDING AND DECISION: (Stevens, J.) Yes. A district court is empowered under § 16 of the Clayton Act to order a company to divest itself of another. Section 16 empowers district courts, in suits by private litigants, to render "injunctive relief . . . against threatened loss or damage." This text represents a broad grant and when Congress gives the district court equitable powers in a statute, it is assumed that Congress intended to give the court its full range of authority. Beyond this, such a construction of § 16 is consistent with the other provisions of the Clayton Act. For example, § 11 of the Act gives the federal government, through the Federal Trade Commission, the power to issue cease-and-desist orders against violators; § 16 should be seen as a grant of power to allow private litigants to obtain the same relief in court when faced with an anticompetitive merger. Consequently, the Ninth Circuit's reading of the statute was too narrow. Reversed and remanded.

▶ *ANALYSIS*

Note that the plaintiff here was the State of California. A state government is not generally considered to be a "private litigant." However, in the context of the Clayton Act, a state may bring a suit under *parens patriae* theory on behalf of private consumers, thus becoming, in effect, a private litigant itself.

■▅■

Quicknotes

CLAYTON ACT Legislation passed by the U.S. Congress in 1914 as an amendment to clarify and supplement the Sherman Antitrust Act of 1890. The act prohibited various anti-competitive business practices and gave labor certain rights in disputes with management. It declared that "the labor of a human being is not a commodity or article of commerce."

DIVESTITURE The divestment of an interest in a corporation pursuant to court order.

INJUNCTION A court order requiring a person to do or prohibiting that person from doing a specific act.

PARENS PATRIAE Maxim that the government as sovereign is conferred with the duty to act as guardian on behalf of those citizens under legal disability.

■▅■

Cartels and Other Joint Conduct by Competitors

Quick Reference Rules of Law

Chicago Board of Trade v. United States

Trade organization (D) v. Federal government (P)

246 U.S. 231 (1918).

NATURE OF CASE: Antitrust action by the Government (P) to enjoin practice of limiting hours in which "arriving grain" deals could be made.

FACT SUMMARY: The Chicago Board of Trade (Board) (D) passed a rule that its members could not make deals on Chicago grain arrivals during periods in which the Board (D) was closed.

RULE OF LAW

Restrictions that merely regulate conduct by imposing minimal restraints for a reasonable purpose are lawful.

FACTS: To correct the monopolistic practices of some of its members, the Chicago Board of Trade (Board) (D) restricted deals on Chicago grain arrivals to hours during which the Board (D) was in operation. The Government (P) obtained an injunction against this practice on the basis that it was an impermissible restraint on competition. The Board (D) argued that the restraint was minimal; it only involved a small percentage of grain deals; it did not restrict the right to buy grain arriving in other cities; it aided free competition; it was only imposed to regulate prior impermissible conduct.

ISSUE: Is a minimal regulation of conduct for a legitimate purpose a violation of antitrust law?

HOLDING AND DECISION: (Brandeis, J.) No. The true test of legality is whether the restraint imposed is such as merely regulates, and perhaps thereby promotes competition or whether it is such as may suppress or destroy competition. Here, the restriction is minimal, merely a regulation of hours. It forces those who are dealing in arriving grain to abide by the final price quoted in the Board's (D) call at the end of the trading day. If a buyer wishes to pay less, he must wait until the next day when the optimum amount of free competition will set the market price. The amount of grain involved is minimal and only affects Chicago grain arrivals. It is imposed to eliminate sharp practices by some members. Under the circumstances, we do not see that the regulation is an improper restraint of trade or free competition. Judgment reversed.

▌ANALYSIS

Where an advertised price is not the result of free competition, an agreement to abide by the price violates antitrust law, *Vandervelde v. Put & Call Brokers & Dealers Association*, 344 F. Supp. 118 (S.D.N.Y. 1972). The key difference in the *Chicago Board of Trade* case is that prices fluctuated from day to day based on free-market pressures. The restraint only involved grain arriving after the Board (D) had closed

for the day. Members were free to wait until it reopened and could then obtain the grain for whatever price it commanded in a free and open market.

■■■

Quicknotes

INJUNCTION A court order requiring a person to do or prohibiting that person from doing a specific act.

RESTRAINT OF TRADE Agreement between entities, for the purpose of impeding free trade, that results in a monopoly, suppression of competition, or affecting prices.

■■■

United States v. Trenton Potteries Co.

Federal government (P) v. Pottery trade association (D)

273 U.S. 392 (1927).

NATURE OF CASE: Action against a combination engaged in price-fixing and limiting sales.

FACT SUMMARY: The trial judge withdrew from the jury the issue of whether restraints were reasonable.

RULE OF LAW

A combination to artificially set prices is a prima facie violation of the Sherman Act regardless of the reasonableness of the prices charged.

FACTS: Trenton Potteries Co. (Trenton) (D) and others entered into a combination to set prices for vitreous pottery and to limit sales. The Government (P) sought to dissolve the combination under § 1 of the Sherman Act. At trial, the judge removed from the jury's consideration the question of whether the restraint was reasonable. Trenton (D) appealed an adverse finding on this basis.

ISSUE: Are all price-fixing combinations illegal restraints on trade?

HOLDING AND DECISION: (Stone, J.) Yes. The Sherman Act was enacted to preserve our competitive economic society. Any agreement such as price-fixing which removes an element of pure competition is a per se violation of the Act. The fact that the price charged is reasonable today does not mean that it will continue to be reasonable. The reasonableness of the price charged is not a criterion as to whether the restraint is reasonable. The power to fix prices is one element of a monopoly. It is never a reasonable restraint on trade. It is an impermissible agreement which must be dissolved under the mandate of the Sherman Act. The trial judge correctly removed the question from the jury. Reversed.

▶ ANALYSIS

A cartel is a group of manufacturers who band together in an attempt to restrict the output of a given commodity in the hope that this will stimulate prices upwards. These groups are held to violate the Sherman Act for the same reasons that price-fixing combinations are violative. Other per se violative combinations are those which restrict entry into a given field or those which attempt to squeeze others out of the market.

Quicknotes

CARTEL An agreement between manufacturers or producers of the same product so as to form a monopoly.

COMBINATION (ANTITRUST DEFINITION) Alliance of entities, for the purpose of impeding free trade, that results in a monopoly, suppression of competition, or affecting prices.

MONOPOLY A privilege or right conferred upon an individual or entity granting it the exclusive power to manufacture, sell and distribute a particular service or commodity; a market condition in which one or a few companies control the sale of a product or service thereby restraining competition in respect to that article or service.

PER SE VIOLATION Business transactions that in themselves constitute restraints on trade, obviating the need to demonstrate an injury to competition in making out an antitrust case.

PRICE-FIXING An illegal combination in violation of the Sherman Act entered into for the purpose of setting prices below the natural market rate.

PRIMA FACIE VIOLATION Evidence presented by a party that is sufficient, in the absence of contradictory evidence, to support the fact or issue for which it is offered

RESTRAINT OF TRADE Agreement between entities, for the purpose of impeding free trade, that results in a monopoly, suppression of competition, or affecting prices.

SHERMAN ACT Makes every contract or conspiracy in unreasonable restraint of commerce illegal.

Appalachian Coals, Inc. v. United States

Selling agent (D) v. Federal government (P)

288 U.S. 344 (1933).

NATURE OF CASE: Review of order enjoining marketing arrangement.

FACT SUMMARY: When 137 coal companies pooled their resources to create an exclusive selling agent, the Justice Department (P) argued that the arrangement constituted a cartel that would fix prices.

🏛 RULE OF LAW
A cooperative enterprise that is neither an unreasonable restraint of trade nor an attempt to monopolize is permissible under the Sherman Act.

FACTS: In response to depressed conditions in the coal industry during the early stages of the Great Depression, 137 producers of coal created Appalachian Coals, Inc. (D), an exclusive selling agent for their products. The company's stated purpose was to organize and streamline the coal industry, thus avoiding over-expansion and wasteful trade practices. The Justice Department (P) filed an action under the Sherman Act, alleging that the coal companies were engaging in monopolistic behavior. A district court enjoined the operations of Appalachian Coals, Inc. (D), and the U.S. Supreme Court granted review.

ISSUE: Is a cooperative enterprise that is neither an unreasonable restraint of trade nor an attempt to monopolize, permissible under the Sherman Act?

HOLDING AND DECISION: (Hughes, C.J.) Yes. A cooperative enterprise that is neither an unreasonable restraint of trade nor an attempt to monopolize does not necessarily violate the Sherman Act. The purpose of the Sherman Act is to prevent undue restraints upon interstate commerce and to afford protection from monopolistic endeavors. The essential standard is reasonableness. The mere fact that an arrangement restrains competition is not sufficient to create a violation; every business agreement in some way restrains competition. Only those arrangements that, in the context of the relevant circumstances, unreasonably restrain competition are illegal. Intent, while not conclusive, is highly relevant. Here, the stated purpose behind the creation of Appalachian Coals (D) was greater efficiency in the production and distribution of the product of a troubled industry. There has been no showing that Appalachian Coals (D) will have monopoly control of any market, nor the power to fix monopoly prices, and therefore, no Sherman Act violation has occurred. Reversed and remanded.

▶ ANALYSIS

The present opinion represented an important shift in Sherman Act analysis. In *United States v. Trenton Potteries Co.*, 273 U.S. 392 (1927), the Court had applied a per se rule regarding horizontal integration rather than the "rule of reason" approach here. Prior to this case, all alleged antitrust violations were regarded as unlawful without regard to the "reasonableness" of, for example, a fixed price.

■■■

Quicknotes

CARTEL An agreement between manufacturers or producers of the same product so as to form a monopoly.

RULE OF REASON The standard for determining whether there has been a violation of § 1 of the Sherman Antitrust Act, requiring a determination of whether the activity unreasonably restrains competition as demonstrated by actual harm.

SHERMAN ACT Makes every contract or conspiracy in unreasonable restraint of commerce illegal.

■■■

United States v. Socony-Vacuum Oil Co.

Federal government (P) v. Oil company (D)

310 U.S. 150 (1940).

NATURE OF CASE: Review of order reversing convictions under the Sherman Act.

FACT SUMMARY: The Government (P) contended that a scheme to affect the flow of output and surplus of oil by a consortium of oil companies (D) was illegal per se.

🏛 RULE OF LAW
Price-fixing by a group of competitors in a market is illegal per se.

FACTS: Beginning around 1926, increased production in the oil industry resulted in falling prices. The National Industrial Recovery Act and regulations promulgated thereunder in 1933 proved unable to reverse the trend. Beginning in 1935, several oil companies (D), representing 83 percent of all oil sold in the Midwest, formed a gentleman's agreement whereby they would purchase oil and gasoline on the spot-market to prop up prices. A minimum price for spot-market purchases was established. The Government (P) charged the oil companies (D) with price-fixing in violation of the Sherman Act. A jury returned a guilty verdict. The court of appeals reversed and remanded, holding that a rule of reason should be applied to alleged price-fixing, rather than the per se rule applied by the district court. The oil companies' (D) activities were not unlawful, the court concluded, unless they constituted an unreasonable restraint of trade. The U.S. Supreme Court granted review.

ISSUE: Is price-fixing by a group of competitors in a market illegal per se?

HOLDING AND DECISION: (Douglas, J.) Yes. Price-fixing by a group of competitors in a market is per se illegal. This Court, in interpreting the clear wording of the Sherman Act, has held that any agreement among competitors to fix prices is illegal. Those cases that applied a rule of reason to anticompetitive conduct involved agreements that did not purport to fix prices. The mandate of the Sherman Act is clear, and the fact that competition may be ruinous to an industry is no justification for creating an exception to the per se rule. Because Congress has spoken on this matter, this is a congressional policy decision. Here, the agreement by oil companies (D) controlling the vast majority of the relevant market, although not an explicit price-fixing agreement, did affect price and therefore falls in the price-fixing category. Consequently, the agreement was per se illegal. Reversed.

▶ ANALYSIS

A general proposition can be divined from reading the present case, along with is predecessor, *Appalachian Coals, Inc. v. United States*, 288 U.S. 344 (1933). Agreements fixing prices are per se illegal, while agreements in restraint of trade that do not directly set prices are subject to a reasonableness test. The per se rule of illegality has been justified on two grounds: industries are on notice as to what constitutes unlawful conduct, and courts are spared from conducting expensive and time-consuming inquiries to determine whether schemes affecting prices are unreasonable.

Quicknotes

PER SE RULE OF VOIDABILITY Transactions by interested directors can be voided.

PRICE-FIXING An illegal combination in violation of the Sherman Act entered into for the purpose of setting prices below the natural market rate.

RESTRAINT OF TRADE Agreement between entities, for the purpose of impeding free trade, that results in a monopoly, suppression of competition, or affecting prices.

RULE OF REASON The standard for determining whether there has been a violation of § 1 of the Sherman Antitrust Act, requiring a determination of whether the activity unreasonably restrains competition as demonstrated by actual harm.

SHERMAN ACT Makes every contract or conspiracy in unreasonable restraint of commerce illegal.

SPOT MARKET In terms of the commodities market, refers to the immediate sale of the commodity as opposed to its future sale.

Maple Flooring Manufacturers Association v. United States

Association of manufacturers (D) v. Federal government (P)

268 U.S. 563 (1925).

NATURE OF CASE: Antitrust action for information dissemination.

FACT SUMMARY: The Maple Flooring Manufacturers Association (D) received voluntary information from a majority of hardwood flooring manufacturers and published a periodic summary of the information.

RULE OF LAW
Merely alleging that information dissemination has the potential to cause price regulation does not establish a Sherman Act violation.

FACTS: The Maple Flooring Manufacturers Association (Association) (D) contained 70 percent of the hardwood flooring manufacturers in its membership. Members were encouraged to submit information as to their stock, orders, and prices to the Association (D). This information was summarized to show average prices by grade, freight rates, and stock information. A periodic letter with this information was sent to members. The information was also published in trade journals and was sent to various governmental agencies for statistical compilation purposes. The Government (P) argued that the dissemination of such information, with or without an agreement between manufacturers, tended to stabilize and regulate prices. The direct and necessary result was to limit free competition. The district court found for the Government (P).

ISSUE: Is the dissemination of information which may tend to regulate or stabilize price a violation of the Sherman Act?

HOLDING AND DECISION: (Stone, J.) No. The information published by the Association (D) was not much different than that which could be found in trade journals or statistical publications. No agreement to set prices was either alleged or proved by the Government (P). The mere fact that the information tended to stabilize prices and made them more uniform is not a per se violation of the Sherman Act. Merely gathering and disseminating such information, without any agreement as to how it is to be used or some other factor indicating the presence of a conspiracy, is not an unlawful restraint on trade. Reversed.

ANALYSIS

An unlawful conspiracy to restrain trade may be established by showing the presence of one or more of the following factors: (1) an agreement to follow the reported prices; (2) excessive penalties for failure to report minute details of everyday transactions; (3) requirements that immediate notice must be given if there are departures from published prices; and/or (4) over-comprehensive information requirements, *American Linseed Oil Co. v. U.S.*, 262 U.S. 371 (1923).

Quicknotes

CONSPIRACY Concerted action by two or more persons to accomplish some unlawful purpose.

PER SE VIOLATION Business transactions that in themselves constitute restraints on trade, obviating the need to demonstrate an injury to competition in making out an antitrust case.

RESTRAINT OF TRADE Agreement between entities, for the purpose of impeding free trade, that results in a monopoly, suppression of competition, or affecting prices.

SHERMAN ACT Makes every contract or conspiracy in unreasonable restraint of commerce illegal.

United States v. Container Corp. of America

Federal government (P) v. Container manufacturer (D)

393 U.S. 333 (1969).

NATURE OF CASE: Antitrust action based on an alleged conspiracy to fix prices through the exchange of price information.

FACT SUMMARY: Container manufacturers (D) exchanged price information on requests from other manufacturers.

> 🏛 **RULE OF LAW**
> When the market is inelastic and the number in it is small, the exchange of price information tends to restrain trade and restrict competition.

FACTS: The Government (P) brought an antitrust action against container manufacturers, including Container Corporation of America (D), alleging that the manufacturers (D) freely exchanged price information on request with the expectation that there would be reciprocity when such information was needed. While the arrangement was informal and sporadic, the Government (P) established that the container market was inelastic, price being the basic variable. The manufacturers (D) tended to meet the price of their competitors, and the pricing exchange arrangement tended to reduce competition. The district court refused to enjoin the practice.

ISSUE: Is an informal exchange of price information in a small inelastic market violative of antitrust law?

HOLDING AND DECISION: (Douglas, J.) Yes. The exchange of the price information had the effect of keeping prices within a fairly narrow ambit. This resulted in price stabilization through the means of an informal agreement. Such an arrangement whereby price information was freely exchanged between competitors on request tended to restrain competition. In a small inelastic market where price is the determinative factor in most purchases, this practice lessened free competition. There is no justification for the practice except to regulate prices. This was an impermissible restraint and was properly enjoined. Reversed.

CONCURRENCE: (Fortas, J.) Merely exchanging price information is not a per se violation of antitrust law. It is only where, as here, it is used for an impermissible purpose which can be independently established that it becomes unlawful.

DISSENT: (Marshall, J.) This is a growing industry. Entry is relatively easy and the number of manufacturers has almost doubled in eight years. It is not so oligopolistic that the mere exchange of price information stifles free competition. There is no showing that it has been restricted and the natural pressures of a free market appear to be working here.

> ▶ **ANALYSIS**

In one case, buyers quoted false prices from other sources in an attempt to buy from manufacturers at lower prices. In order to avoid this, the manufacturers (D) agreed to inform each other of quoted public prices and to adhere to them. The court found that the exchange of presale prices to avoid fraud was reasonable, but the agreement to abide by these prices was an impermissible restraint on trade, *Wall Products Co. v. National Gypsum Co.*, 326 F. Supp. 295 (N.D. Cal. 1971).

■━■

Quicknotes

OLIGOPOLISTIC A market condition in which the industry for a particular product is dominated by only a few companies.

RESTRAINT OF TRADE Agreement between entities, for the purpose of impeding free trade, that results in a monopoly, suppression of competition, or affecting prices.

■━■

United States v. United States Gypsum Co.

Federal government (P) v. Gypsum board manufacturer (D)

438 U.S. 422 (1978).

NATURE OF CASE: Review of reversal of criminal antitrust convictions.

FACT SUMMARY: United States Gypsum Co. (D) and other companies in the gypsum board industry were convicted of antitrust violations by a jury that had been instructed that intent to violate the Sherman Act was to be conclusively presumed if price-fixing has occurred.

🏛 RULE OF LAW
For purposes of antitrust criminal prosecutions, intent to fix prices is a separate element of the offense.

FACTS: Gypsum board is a primary component of inner walls. In the 1960s and 1970s, the industry was very concentrated, consisting of no more than nine producers. Producers engaged in a practice of obtaining quotes from competitors before quoting prices to prospective customers. The Government (P) brought a criminal prosecution against these producers (D), alleging Sherman Act violations. The district court instructed the jury that if the producers' (D) conduct had the effect of fixing or maintaining prices, the intent to achieve that result should be conclusively presumed. The jury returned a guilty verdict. The court of appeals reversed, ruling that intent was an element requiring independent proof. The U.S. Supreme Court granted review.

ISSUE: For purposes of antitrust criminal prosecutions, is intent to fix prices a separate element of the offense?

HOLDING AND DECISION: (Burger, C.J.) Yes. For purposes of antitrust criminal prosecutions, intent to fix prices is a separate element of the offense. In Anglo-American jurisprudence, *mens rea* as a separate element of a criminal offense is the rule, not the exception. While the Government (P) may create strict liability offenses without offending the constitution, the presumption is that a criminal statute incorporates a *mens rea* element, and statutory language must clearly contravene this presumption if it is to create a strict liability. The Sherman Act contains no such contravening language. While it lists certain types of conduct as sanctionable, it says nothing of mental state. Consequently, *mens rea* will be required to be proven. While a jury is free to infer intent from result, it cannot be compelled to do so, as the district court did here. Affirmed.

▶ ANALYSIS

There are two basic approaches to evaluating potentially anticompetitive activities—the per se rule and the rule of reason. The latter analysis is used on less egregious forms of potentially anticompetitive activities. Since the exchange of price information, as seen in the case above does not necessarily tend to have anticompetitive effects, it is subject to the rule of reason analysis. If an action does not rise to the level of an unreasonable restraint of trade, then a civil defendant's bad intent is probably irrelevant.

■══■

Quicknotes

MENS REA Criminal intent.

PER SE RULE OF VOIDABILITY Transactions by interested directors can be voided.

PRICE-FIXING An illegal combination in violation of the Sherman Antitrust Act entered into for the purpose of setting prices below the natural market rate.

RULE OF REASON The standard for determining whether there has been a violation of § 1 of the Sherman Antitrust Act, requiring a determination of whether the activity unreasonably restrains competition as demonstrated by actual harm.

SHERMAN ACT Makes every contract or conspiracy in unreasonable restraint of commerce illegal.

■══■

National Society of Professional Engineers v. United States

Professional organization (D) v. Federal government (P)

435 U.S. 679 (1978).

NATURE OF CASE: Review of order enjoining enforcement of a private organization's canon of ethics in civil antitrust action.

FACT SUMMARY: The National Society of Professional Engineers (D) contended that its canon of ethics, prohibiting competitive bidding, survived a rule of reason analysis under the Sherman Act because it minimized the risk that competition would produce inferior engineering work, endangering the public's safety.

🏛 RULE OF LAW
A restraint on competition cannot survive a Sherman Act challenge on the basis that it promotes public safety.

FACTS: The National Society of Professional Engineers (Society) (D) was an organization composed of seasoned professionals in the engineering field. One of the provisions in the Society's (D) canon of ethics was a prohibition on competitive bidding by members. The stated rationale for this canon was that the bidding process would result in inferior work, which would present a public hazard. Instead, the Society (D) sought to preserve the traditional method of selecting an engineer, i.e., on the basis of background and reputation, not price. The Government (P) filed an action seeking to prohibit enforcement of the canon, contending that it violated the Sherman Act. The district court entered such an injunction, and the U.S. Supreme Court granted review.

ISSUE: Can a restraint on competition survive a Sherman Act challenge on the basis that it promotes public safety?

HOLDING AND DECISION: (Stevens, J.) No. A restraint on competition cannot survive a Sherman Act challenge on the basis that it promotes public safety. The Society (D) contended that a restraint is reasonable and legitimate if competition would be dangerous to public health, safety, and welfare. This is a serious misunderstanding of the rule of reason. The rule of reason is applied when a particular practice may or may not have an anticompetitive effect; the rule is applied to determine whether or not the effect is anticompetitive. In the case of a clearly anticompetitive practice, the per se rule is applied instead. Any argument that a practice promotes public benefit—its anticompetitive effects notwithstanding—must be addressed to Congress not the courts. Here, the Society's (D) canon is clearly anticompetitive, so the per se rule is to be applied. Affirmed.

▌ *ANALYSIS*

At various times, the learned professions have argued that antitrust law was created to regulate business and should

not apply to the professions. These protestations fall on deaf judicial ears. There is no such limitation in the statutes, and courts have refused to read one into them.

■—■

Quicknotes

PER SE RULE OF VOIDABILITY Transactions by interested directors can be voided.

RESTRAINT OF TRADE Agreement between entities, for the purpose of impeding free trade, that results in a monopoly, suppression of competition, or affecting prices.

RULE OF REASON The standard for determining whether there has been a violation of § 1 of the Sherman Antitrust Act, requiring a determination of whether the activity unreasonably restrains competition as demonstrated by actual harm.

SHERMAN ACT Makes every contract or conspiracy in unreasonable restraint of commerce illegal.

■—■

Broadcast Music, Inc. v. Columbia Broadcasting System

Clearinghouse (D) v. Television network (P)

441 U.S. 1 (1979).

NATURE OF CASE: Action charging violations of antitrust and copyright laws.

FACT SUMMARY: Columbia Broadcasting System (P) claimed that the issuance by ASCAP (D) and Broadcast Music, Inc. (D) of blanket licenses to copyrighted musical composition on behalf of their members constituted per se unlawful price-fixing.

🏛 RULE OF LAW
The blanket license is not a form of per se unlawful price-fixing.

FACTS: Both ASCAP (D) and Broadcast Music, Inc. (BMI) (D) function as "clearinghouses." Music copyright owners, composers, etc., grant them nonexclusive rights to license nondramatic performances of their works in return for royalties distributed in accordance with a schedule reflecting the nature and amount of the use of their music and other factors. Both organizations operate primarily through blanket licenses, which give the licensees the right to perform any and all of the compositions owned by the members or affiliates as often as the licensees desire for a stated term. Fees for blanket licenses are ordinarily a percentage of total revenues or a flat dollar amount and do not directly depend on the amount or type of music used. Columbia Broadcasting System (CBS) (P), which operates one of three national commercial television networks and which held blanket licenses from both organizations, filed a complaint alleging that the blanket license constitutes per se unlawful price-fixing. The district court ruled that the practice did not fall within the per se rule, but the court of appeals held that the blanket license was indeed a form of price-fixing illegal per se under the Sherman Act.

ISSUE: Is the blanket license a form of price-fixing illegal per se under the Sherman Act?

HOLDING AND DECISION: (White, J.) No. Certain agreements or practices are so "plainly anticompetitive" and so often "lack . . . any redeeming virtue" that they are conclusively presumed illegal without further examination under the Rule of Reason generally applied in Sherman Act cases, but the blanket license cannot be so characterized. It is not a naked restraint of trade, with no purpose except stifling of competition. Rather, it is a means by which individual composers and authors who are inherently unable to effectively compete on their own can band together to make a market for their collective works. It may well be that the blanket licensing arrangement at issue cannot survive scrutiny under the Rule of Reason, but that is not the issue before this court. Reversed and remanded for further proceedings.

▶ ANALYSIS

Not all courts were overly enthusiastic about this strict approach to the per se rule. For example, in *U.S. v. Southern Motor Carriers Rate Conference*, 1979 Trade Cas. 62931 (N.D. Ga.), the Court warned that "overly enthusiastic application of [this case] would abrogate the per se rule in its entirety."

■══■

Quicknotes

PER SE RULE OF VOIDABILITY Transactions by interested directors can be voided.

PRICE-FIXING An illegal combination in violation of the Sherman Act entered into for the purpose of setting prices below the natural market rate.

RULE OF REASON The standard for determining whether there has been a violation of § 1 of the Sherman Antitrust Act, requiring a determination of whether the activity unreasonably restrains competition as demonstrated by actual harm.

SHERMAN ACT Makes every contract or conspiracy in unreasonable restraint of commerce illegal.

■══■

Catalano, Inc. v. Target Sales, Inc.

Brewing retailers (P) v. Brewing wholesalers (D)

446 U.S. 643 (1980).

NATURE OF CASE: Review of ruling holding certain agreements among wholesalers not to be a per se antitrust violation.

FACT SUMMARY: Catalano, Inc. (P) contended that an agreement among wholesalers in its market not to extend credit to retailers was a per se Sherman Act violation.

🏛 RULE OF LAW
An agreement among wholesalers to eliminate credit to retailers is illegal per se without further examination under the rule of reason.

FACTS: Beginning in 1967, Target Sales, Inc. (D) and other brewing wholesalers (D) in the Fresno, California, area secretly agreed to cease the practice of extending credit to brew-retailers and instead demanded cash payment upon delivery. A class of brew-retailers (P) subsequently brought suit under federal antitrust laws and made a motion to declare the case one of per se illegality. The district court denied the motion and then certified a question to the Ninth Circuit as to whether the credit agreement was, if proven, unlawful on its face. The Ninth Circuit ruled that an agreement among competitors to fix credit terms did not violate the antitrust laws. The brew-retailers (P) appealed, and the U.S. Supreme Court granted review.

ISSUE: Is an agreement among wholesalers to eliminate credit to retailers illegal per se?

HOLDING AND DECISION: (Per curiam) Yes. An agreement among wholesalers to eliminate credit to retailers is illegal per se without further examination under the rule of reason. Agreements to fix prices are so plainly anticompetitive that they are conclusively presumed to be illegal under the Sherman Act; an agreement among wholesalers to refuse to sell to retailers unless given payment in cash is merely one form of price-fixing. Credit is part of the price of a good; it is the equivalent of a discount for the amount of time the good is held before payment. Therefore, an agreement not to extend credit is a method of raising prices as plainly anticompetitive as a direct agreement to raise prices. Such agreements are per se illegal, and no balancing of anticompetitive versus beneficial aspects of the agreement need be undertaken. Reversed and remanded.

▶ ANALYSIS

Horizontal agreements (agreements among competitors) tend to be given exacting scrutiny under the Sherman Act. Agreements involving prices are likewise closely scanned.

When the two are combined, as here, the agreement has little chance of surviving a challenge.

■■■

Quicknotes

HORIZONTAL AGREEMENTS Agreements entered into by entities at the same level of production for the purpose of restraining trade.

PER SE RULE OF VOIDABILITY Transactions by interested directors can be voided.

PRICE-FIXING An illegal combination in violation of the Sherman Act entered into for the purpose of setting prices below the natural market rate.

RULE OF REASON The standard for determining whether there has been a violation of § 1 of the Sherman Antitrust Act, requiring a determination of whether the activity unreasonably restrains competition as demonstrated by actual harm.

SHERMAN ACT Makes every contract or conspiracy in unreasonable restraint of commerce illegal.

■■■

Arizona v. Maricopa County Medical Society

State (P) v. Professional organization (D)

457 U.S. 332 (1982).

NATURE OF CASE: Review of decision ordering a trial in an antitrust action.

FACT SUMMARY: The practice of member physicians of Maricopa County Medical Society (D) of setting uniform maximum fees reimbursable by insurance was challenged as a Sherman Act violation.

RULE OF LAW
Price-fixing agreements are per se unlawful, even if they are horizontal, fix maximum prices, and are among members of a profession.

FACTS: The Maricopa County Medical Society (Society) (D) comprised 70 percent of the medical practitioners of Maricopa County, Arizona. Member physicians agreed to a schedule of maximum fees for particular services that could be charged back to various insurance carriers. Insurance agencies agreed to pay the Society (D) doctors' charges up to the maximum amounts, and in exchange, the doctors agreed to accept those payments as payments in full for their services. The State of Arizona (State) (P) brought an action challenging this practice as a violation of the Sherman Act. The Ninth Circuit held that triable issues of fact justifying a trial were present. The State (P) appealed, and the U.S. Supreme Court granted review.

ISSUE: Are price-fixing agreements per se unlawful, even if they are horizontal, fix maximum prices, and are among members of a profession?

HOLDING AND DECISION: (Stevens, J.) Yes. Price-fixing agreements are per se unlawful, even if they are horizontal, fix maximum prices, and are among members of a profession. Therefore, an agreement among physicians concerning a schedule of maximum fees reimbursable by insurance is per se illegal. The undisputed rule is that all price-fixing agreements among competitors are per se Sherman Act violations. The rule is violated by any price restraint that tends to reward all practitioners equally. This is no less true of maximum price-fixing then it is of minimum price-fixing. The setting of fixed maximum prices may prevent buyers from competing and surviving and may restrain sellers' abilities to sell in accordance with their own judgment. Also, the fact that, in this particular situation, a learned profession is involved is not relevant; the Society's (D) claim that their price restraint will make it easier for customers to pay does not distinguish the medical profession from any other provider of goods or services. Furthermore, the per se rule need not be rejustified for every industry and must be applied to all industries alike. Here, since a price-fixing agreement has been alleged and not disputed, no further factual development is necessary for the State (P) to prevail. Reversed.

DISSENT: (Powell, J.) On the bare record, the agreement in question gives each physician considerably more leeway in dealing with his patient than the classic cartel agreement allows cartel members. Application of the per se rule is inappropriate on such a record.

ANALYSIS

The potential costs to consumers of minimum price-fixing are obvious. The costs of maximum fixed prices are less readily discernible. Nonetheless, they are present. Suppliers of goods and services differ greatly in quality. The fixing of maximum prices may distort high-end competition and discourage innovation.

■==■

Quicknotes

CARTEL An agreement between manufacturers or producers of the same product so as to form a monopoly.

PER SE RULE Rule that business transactions which in themselves constitute restraints on trade obviate the need to demonstrate an injury to competition in making out an antitrust case.

PRICE-FIXING An illegal combination in violation of the Sherman Act entered into for the purpose of setting prices below the natural market rate.

SHERMAN ACT Makes every contract or conspiracy in unreasonable restraint of commerce illegal.

■==■

National Collegiate Athletic Assn. v. Board of Regents

Amateur collegiate sports association (D) v. College board of regents (P)

468 U.S. 85 (1984).

NATURE OF CASE: Appeal from grant of injunctive relief for violation of the Sherman Antitrust Act.

FACT SUMMARY: The district court held that the National Collegiate Athletic Assn. (D) regulation of television rights to college football games violated the Sherman Act.

🏛 RULE OF LAW
Limitations imposed upon members of a cooperative organization on the manner in which the product is marketed are not illegal per se, but if such limitations hamper competition, they violate the Sherman Act.

FACTS: The National Collegiate Athletic Assn. (the NCAA) (D) was an organization of colleges which regulated the conduct of sporting competition. In 1951 it implemented a plan to regulate the granting of television rights to member football games in order to alleviate the lost revenue from the decrease in attendance owing to television. The regulations limited who could broadcast, and it regulated the amount of times a particular school could be featured nationally. The plan also determined the amount each school would receive for national and regional broadcasts. The universities of Georgia and Oklahoma (Universities) (P) negotiated a television contract which fell outside the boundaries of the plan. In response to the NCAA's (D) threat to impose sanctions on them, they sued, contending the plan violated the Sherman Act. The district court held for the Universities (P), and the court of appeals affirmed. The U.S. Supreme Court granted certiorari.

ISSUE: Do limitations on the marketing of products by members of cooperative organizations which hamper competition among such members violate the Sherman Act?

HOLDING AND DECISION: (Stevens, J.) Yes. Limitations imposed upon members of a cooperative organization regulating the manner in which the product is marketed are not illegal per se, but if such limitations hamper competition among the members, they violate the Sherman Antitrust Act. The product marketed by the member schools is college sports competition. As such, some concerted action on the part of the members is necessary to perpetuate the integrity of the product. As a result, the regulation of television rights is not per se illegal. However, because the regulations hamper competition in that schools with greater popularity cannot negotiate more favorable television rights, they do violate the Sherman Act. Affirmed.

in regulating the activity of the members is to perpetuate the amateurism of college football. Limiting television exposure, it is argued, aids the association in limiting the corrupting influence of professionalism on the college football market.

■■■

Quicknotes

CERTIORARI A discretionary writ issued by a superior court to an inferior court in order to review the lower court's decisions; the Supreme Court's writ ordering such review.

INJUNCTIVE RELIEF A court order issued as a remedy, requiring a person to do, or prohibiting that person from doing, a specific act.

RULE OF REASON The standard for determining whether there has been a violation of § 1 of the Sherman Antitrust Act, requiring a determination of whether the activity unreasonably restrains competition as demonstrated by actual harm.

SHERMAN ACT Makes every contract or conspiracy in unreasonable restraint of commerce illegal.

■■■

▶ ANALYSIS

It has been argued that the majority in this case failed to give proper consideration to the fact that the NCAA's (D) purpose

California Dental Assn. v. FTC

Nonprofit association (D) v. Federal agency (P)

526 U.S. 756 (1999).

NATURE OF CASE: Appeal from decision affirming the FTC's jurisdiction and finding an antitrust violation.

FACT SUMMARY: The Federal Trade Commission (FTC) (P), claimed that the California Dental Assn. (CDA) (D), a voluntary nonprofit association that conferred significant economic benefits on its members, violated § 5 of the Federal Trade Commission Act in applying its guidelines so as to restrict two types of truthful, nondeceptive advertising. The CDA (D) argued the FTC (P) did not have jurisdiction, and that the CDA (D) had not violated any antitrust laws.

🏛 RULE OF LAW
(1) The Federal Trade Commission has jurisdiction over a nonprofit organization that confers substantial economic benefits on its for-profit members.
(2) Where any anticompetitive effects of given restraints are far from intuitively obvious, the rule of reason demands a more thorough inquiry into the consequences of those restraints than provided by a "quick-look," abbreviated analysis.

FACTS: The California Dental Assn. (CDA) (D), a voluntary nonprofit association of local dental societies to which about three-quarters of the State's dentists belonged, provided, through for-profit subsidiaries, desirable insurance and preferential financing arrangements for its members, and engaged in lobbying, litigation, marketing, and public relations for members' benefit. These services and programs had a value to each member of between $22,739 and $65,127. Members agreed to abide by the CDA's (D) Code of Ethics, which, *inter alia,* prohibited false or misleading advertising. The CDA (D) also issued interpretive advisory opinions and guidelines relating to advertising. The Federal Trade Commission (FTC) (P) brought a complaint, alleging that the CDA (D) violated § 5 of the Federal Trade Commission Act (Act), 15 U.S.C. § 45, in applying its guidelines so as to restrict two types of truthful, nondeceptive advertising: (1) price advertising, particularly discounted fees, and (2) advertising relating to the quality of dental services. An Administrative Law Judge (ALJ) held the FTC (P) had jurisdiction over the CDA (D) and found a § 5 violation. The FTC (P) held that the advertising restrictions violated the Act under an abbreviated rule-of-reason analysis. In affirming, the court of appeals sustained the FTC's (P) jurisdiction and concluded that an abbreviated or "quick look" rule-of-reason analysis was sufficient to justify certain advertising restrictions adopted by the CDA (D). The U.S. Supreme Court granted certiorari.

ISSUE:
(1) Does the Federal Trade Commission have jurisdiction over a nonprofit organization that confers substantial economic benefits on its for-profit members?
(2) Where any anticompetitive effects of given restraints are far from intuitively obvious, does the rule of reason demand a more thorough inquiry into the consequences of those restraints than provided by a "quick-look," abbreviated analysis?

HOLDING AND DECISION: (Souter, J.)
(1) Yes. The Federal Trade Commission has jurisdiction over a nonprofit organization that confers substantial economic benefits on its for-profit members. The Act gives the FTC (P) authority over any persons, partnerships, or corporation, company, or association organized to carry on business for its own profit or that of its members. The Act does not require that a supporting organization must devote itself entirely to its members' profits or say anything about how much of the entity's activities must go to raising the members' bottom lines. There is thus no apparent reason to let the Act's application turn on meeting some threshold percentage of activity for this purpose or even a softer formulation calling for a substantial part of the entity's total activities to be aimed at its members' pecuniary benefit. The Act does not cover all membership organizations of profit-making corporations without more. However, the economic benefits conferred upon CDA's (D) profit-seeking professionals plainly fall within the object of enhancing its members' "profit," which is the Act's jurisdictional touchstone.
(2) Yes. Where any anticompetitive effects of given restraints are far from intuitively obvious, the rule of reason demands a more thorough inquiry into the consequences of those restraints than provided by a "quick-look," abbreviated analysis. An abbreviated or "quick-look" analysis is appropriate when an observer with even a rudimentary understanding of economics could conclude that the arrangements in question have an anticompetitive effect on customers and markets. This case fails to present a situation in which the likelihood of anticompetitive effects is obvious, because the CDA's (D) advertising restrictions might plausibly be thought to have a net procompetitive effect or possibly no effect at all on competition. The discount and nondiscount advertising restrictions are, on their face, designed to avoid false or deceptive advertising in a market characterized by striking disparities between the information available to the professional and the patient. The existence of significant challenges to informed

Continued on next page.

decision making by the customer for professional services suggests that advertising restrictions arguably protecting patients from misleading or irrelevant advertising call for more than cursory treatment. In applying cursory review, the court of appeals brushed over the professional context and described no anticompetitive effects from the discount advertising bar. The CDA's (D) price advertising rule appears to reflect the prediction that any costs to competition associated with eliminating across-the-board advertising will be outweighed by gains to consumer information created by discount advertising that is exact, accurate, and more easily verifiable. This view may or may not be correct, but it is not implausible; and neither a court nor the FTC (P) may initially dismiss it as presumptively wrong. The CDA's (D) plausible explanation for its non-price advertising restrictions, namely that restricting un-verifiable quality claims would have a procompetitive effect by preventing misleading or false claims that distort the market, likewise rules out the use of abbreviated "quick-look" rule-of-reason analysis for those restrictions. The obvious anticompetitive effect that triggers such analysis has not been shown. However, requiring a more extended examination of the possible factual underpinnings than was given, is not necessarily to call for the fullest market analysis. Not every case attacking a restraint not obviously anticompetitive is a candidate for plenary market examination. There is generally no categorical line between restraints giving rise to an intuitively obvious inference of anticompetitive effect and those that call for more detailed treatment. What is required is an inquiry that matches the circumstances of the case, looking to a restraint's circumstances, details, and logic. Here, a less quick look was required for the initial assessment of the CDA's (D) advertising restrictions. Vacated and remanded.

CONCURRENCE AND DISSEENT: (Breyer, J.) The majority is correct that the FTC (P) has jurisdiction, and that more than a "quick-look" analysis is required in this case, but it is incorrect in its application of those principles. Instead, a traditional application of the rule of reason to the facts of the case requires affirming the FTC (P) on the merits, which is supported by "substantial evidence" as to each of the four traditional antitrust questions. The first of these classical questions is: what is the restraint at issue? Here, there are three restraints created by the CDA's (D) ethical rule relating to advertising: (1) preclusion of advertising that characterized a dentist's fees as being low, reasonable, or affordable; (2) preclusion of advertising of across the board discounts; and (3) prohibition of all quality claims. A review of the evidence before the FTC (P) and the court of appeals shows that intervention by this Court is not warranted, as the question of "substantial evidence" is a matter for the lower courts, unless the standard has been grossly misapplied or misapprehended. Thus, the second classical question is reached: what are the likely anticompetitive effects of the restraints? Here, the restraint of truthful advertising as to pricing and quality of

service will likely restrain competition in respect to price, which arguably is unlawful per se (as the FTC (P) found) and will restrain competition over the quality of service. Therefore, the restraints have anticompetitive tendencies. The third classical question is whether there are offsetting procompetitive justifications for the restraints or some other redeeming virtues. Here, arguably, the question is a close one as it is plausible as the CDA (D) held, that the restrictions are inextricably tied to a legitimate effort to prevent false or misleading advertising. However, such an argument is merely theoretical, and the CDA (D) has failed to support it with empirical evidence. In the usual Sherman Act § 1 case, the defendant bears the burden of establishing a procompetitive effect—here, the CDA (D) has failed to meet its burden. The final classical question that must be answered is whether the parties have sufficient market power to make a difference. Here, there was sufficient evidence to establish that the CDA (D) had enough market power to harm competition through its standard setting in the area of advertising. In some markets, the CDA's (D) members made up 90 percent of the marketplace, and on average, they accounted for 75 percent. This would likely make a difference because potential patients might not respond readily to discount advertising by a small number of dentists (e.g., 10%), leaving the remaining 90 percent less likely to engage in price competition. The majority contends that the analysis conducted by the court of appeals was inadequate, but a close look at the court of appeal's decision reveals that it did not fail to properly address or resolve each of the traditional antitrust questions. Applying ordinary antitrust principles, the court of appeals reached an unexceptional legal conclusion. Finally, the form of analysis presented here, and used by the court of appeals, should not be abandoned, as it represents an allocation of burdens that represents a careful blending of procompetitive objectives of the law with administrative necessity.

▌ *ANALYSIS*

On remand, the court of appeals held that the FTC (P) had failed to prove that the CDA's (D) restrictions had a net anticompetitive effect on price and quality of service. Arguably, the case should be read narrowly in the context not of any advertising, but of professional advertising—an issue a closely divided Court has been grappling with for over two decades. At a minimum, however, the case should be read to require plaintiffs in both professional and non-professional advertising cases to have an empirical basis for why a restraint harms consumers, but not more.

■▬■

Quicknotes

FEDERAL TRADE COMMISSION ACT Establishes the Federal Trade Commission for the purpose of preventing persons or entities from using unfair methods of competition in or

Continued on next page.

affecting commerce, and unfair or deceptive acts or practices in or affecting commerce.

RULE OF REASON The standard for determining whether there has been a violation of § 1 of the Sherman Antitrust Act, requiring a determination of whether the activity unreasonably restrains competition as demonstrated by actual harm.

■━■

Texaco, Inc. v. Dagher

Oil company (D) v. Service station owner (P)

126 S. Ct. 1276 (2006).

NATURE OF CASE: Appeal from reversal of summary judgment for defendants in price-fixing action.

FACT SUMMARY: Texaco, Inc. (D) and Shell Oil Co. (D), which had collaborated in a joint venture, Equilon Enterprises (Equilon), contended that it was not per se illegal under § 1 of the Sherman Act for Equilon to set the prices at which it sold gasoline to service station owners (P).

> 🏛 **RULE OF LAW**
> It is not per se illegal under § 1 of the Sherman Act for a lawful, economically integrated joint venture to set the prices at which the joint venture sells its products.

FACTS: Texaco, Inc. (D) and Shell Oil Co. (D) had been competitors in the oil and gasoline market. Then they formed a joint venture, Equilon Enterprises (Equilon), through which Equilon gasoline would be sold to downstream purchasers under the original Texaco (D) and Shell Oil (D) brand names. The companies agreed to pool their resources and share the risks of and profits from Equilon's activities, and Equilon's board of directors was comprised of representatives from each company. Equilon's formation was approved by the Federal Trade Commission (FTC) and state attorneys general. Service station owners (P) brought suit, alleging that by unifying gasoline prices under the two brands, Texaco (D) and Shell Oil (D) had violated the per se rule against price-fixing found in § 1 of the Sherman Act. Finding that the rule of reason, rather than the per se rule applied, the district court granted summary judgment to Texaco (D) and Shell Oil (D), but the court of appeals reversed. The U.S. Supreme Court granted certiorari.

ISSUE: Is it per se illegal under § 1 of the Sherman Act for a lawful, economically integrated joint venture to set the prices at which the joint venture sells its products?

HOLDING AND DECISION: (Thomas, J.) No. It is not per se illegal under § 1 of the Sherman Act for a lawful, economically integrated joint venture to set the prices at which the joint venture sells its products. Although § 1 prohibits "[e]very contract [or] combination . . . in restraint of trade," this Court has not taken a literal approach to that language, recognizing, instead, that Congress intended to outlaw only unreasonable restraints. Under rule of reason analysis, antitrust plaintiffs must demonstrate that a particular contract or combination is in fact unreasonable and anticompetitive. Per se liability is reserved for "plainly anticompetitive" agreements. While "horizontal" price-fixing agreements between two or more competitors are per se unlawful, this litigation does not present such an agreement,

because Texaco (D) and Shell Oil (D) did not compete with one another in the relevant market—i.e., gasoline sales to western service stations—but instead participated in that market jointly through Equilon. When those who would otherwise be competitors pool their capital and share the risks of loss and opportunities for profit, they are regarded as a single firm competing with other sellers in the market. As such, Equilon's pricing policy may be price-fixing in a literal sense, but it is not price-fixing in the antitrust sense. The court of appeals erred in reaching the opposite conclusion under the ancillary restraints doctrine, which governs the validity of restrictions imposed by a legitimate joint venture on nonventure activities. That doctrine has no application here, where the challenged business practice involves the core activity of the joint venture itself—the pricing of the very goods produced and sold by Equilon. Reversed.

▶ *ANALYSIS*

The ancillary restraints doctrine, invoked by the court of appeals, governs the validity of restrictions imposed by legitimate business collaboration, such as a business association or joint venture, on nonventure activities. Under the doctrine, courts must determine whether the nonventure restriction is a naked restraint on trade, and thus invalid, or one that is ancillary to the legitimate and competitive purposes of the business association, and thus valid. The court, which found the doctrine inapplicable to the facts presented, noted that even if it had permitted invocation of the doctrine, Equilon's pricing policy was clearly ancillary to the sale of its own products and would have been valid under the doctrine.

■═■

Quicknotes

JOINT VENTURE Venture undertaken based on an express or implied agreement among the members, with a common purpose and interest, and an equal power of control.

PER SE VIOLATION Business transaction that in itself constitutes restraint on trade, obviating the need to demonstrate an injury to competition in making out an antitrust case.

■═■

Interstate Circuit v. United States

Film distributors (D) v. Federal government (P)

306 U.S. 208 (1939).

NATURE OF CASE: Action against a conspiracy in restraint of trade.

FACT SUMMARY: Interstate Circuit (D) and other distributors conspired to force theater owners to set admission prices for the showing of first- and second-run films.

> 🏛 **RULE OF LAW**
> An unlawful conspiracy in restraint of trade may be inferred from the facts, such as concerted action departing from previous practices.

FACTS: Several national film distributors, including Interstate Circuit (Interstate) (D), agreed to impose price restrictions on local theater owners showing subsequent-run films. Interstate (D) and the others met with local distributors and convinced them to require theater owners to charge a minimum admission of at least $0.25. At the time the admission price for subsequent-run films was less than $0.25 at most theaters. The Government (P) brought an antitrust action against Interstate (D) and the others to enjoin this practice. The conspiracy was established by circumstantial evidence and inference. It was shown that after the alleged conspiracy was entered, all subsequent-run theaters raised their prices to $0.25. At trial, no officers or directors of Interstate (D) or the others testified that no agreement had been reached. They left such testimony to the local distributors that the decision had been independently reached. The court, based on the facts, found that an unlawful conspiracy in restraint of trade had been formed and enjoined the arrangement.

ISSUE: Does the existence of an agreement have to be definitely established to find a conspiracy in restraint of trade?

HOLDING AND DECISION: (Stone, J.) No. Often, in such situations, no formal agreement has been reached. To impose such a requirement would unduly restrict the enforcement of antitrust laws. It is sufficient to show that concerted action occurred that was an unusual departure from previous conduct. If this fact, if not explained away, is added to other factors from which a conspiracy may be inferred, an antitrust violation has been made. No formal plan or communication between competitors is even required. Where competitors learn of a plan to restrict competition and elect to join in it, they are guilty of participating in a conspiracy even if no formal agreement exists and even if their participation was unsolicited. It is sufficient that the overall result of the conspiracy is to restrain trade in violation of the Sherman Act. There was ample proof adduced at trial that the distributors, including Interstate (D), were aware that a plan was in operation to regulate the price charged by subsequent-run theaters. Having joined in its effectuation, they are guilty of a conspiracy. Affirmed.

DISSENT: (Roberts, J.) The majority was incorrect in finding a conspiracy under the stipulated facts. Earlier courts have not viewed the kinds of agreements at issue in this case as conspiracies under the Sherman Act.

▶ **ANALYSIS**

An individual manufacturer may, under certain circumstances, require retailers to adhere to price schedules on threat of no further dealings for violations. However, such practices are illegal where the manufacturer or distributor occupies a monopoly position in the market or conspires with others (including competitors) to effectuate the plan.

■■■

Quicknotes

CONSPIRACY Concerted action by two or more persons to accomplish some unlawful purpose.

RESTRAINT OF TRADE Agreement between entities, for the purpose of impeding free trade, that result in a monopoly, the suppression of competition, or affecting prices.

SHERMAN ACT Makes every contract or conspiracy in unreasonable restraint of commerce illegal.

■■■

Theatre Enterprises, Inc. v. Paramount Film Distributing Corp.

Theatre owner (P) v. Film distributor (D)

346 U.S. 537 (1954).

NATURE OF CASE: Action for damages for a conspiracy to restrict distribution.

FACT SUMMARY: Paramount Film Distributing Corp. (D) and other distributors refused to grant Theatre Enterprises, Inc. (P), a first-run license for one of its suburban theaters.

🏛 RULE OF LAW
A conspiracy is not established merely because a group of competitors act in a like manner.

FACTS: Theatre Enterprises, Inc. (P) owned a suburban theater, the Crest. It approached various film distributors for a license to show first-run pictures. All of the distributors refused. Reasons assigned were that the arrangement was economically unfeasible and the downtown Baltimore theaters were larger and appealed to a wider audience. The downtown theater owners had the contractual authority to require the distributor to refuse licensing to owners in the same competitive area. Theatre Enterprises (P) brought suit against the distributors (D) asking treble damages for restraint of trade. To bolster its case, Theatre Enterprises (P) made reference to a previous conspiracy in restraint of trade in which Paramount Film Distributing Corp. (D) and the others had been engaged. The court found that no conspiracy existed and denied relief.

ISSUE: Is evidence of parallel actions sufficient to establish a conspiracy?

HOLDING AND DECISION: (Clark, J.) No. The mere fact that competitors pursue similar courses of action does not establish a conspiracy. This is especially true when, as here, the practice is economically sound, is long-standing, and, at least in part, is compelled by contract. While conspiracies may be inferred from the facts and need not be shown by proving a formal agreement, mere parallelism of action is insufficient. The fact that previous unlawful restraints had been practiced by the parties does not establish a present conspiracy. Judgment affirmed.

▶ ANALYSIS

A conspiracy cannot be shown simply because a distributor refuses to deal with a prospective licensee unless others in the field agree to deal with him. In *Delaware Valley Marine Supply Co. v. American Tobacco Co.*, 297 F. 2d 199 (3rd Cir. 1961), the court held that the evidence of numerous refusals by competitors was sufficient to establish "conscious parallelism" but fell short of the minimum necessary to establish a

conspiracy. There must be sufficient evidence to allow the jury to reasonably infer the existence of a conspiracy.

■▬■

Quicknotes

CONSPIRACY Concerted action by two or more persons to accomplish some unlawful purpose.

RESTRAINT OF TRADE Agreement between entities, for the purpose of impeding free trade, that results in a monopoly, suppression of competition, or affecting prices.

TREBLE DAMAGES An award of damages triple of the amount awarded by the jury and provided for by statute for violation of certain offenses.

■▬■

Bell Atlantic Corp. v. Twombly

Local telephone and Internet service provider (D) v. Local telephone
and Internet service subscriber (P)

127 S. Ct. 1955 (2007).

NATURE OF CASE: Appeal from reversal of dismissal of complaint in action for antitrust conspiracy under § 1 of the Sherman Act.

FACT SUMMARY: Providers of local telephone and/or high speed Internet services (defendants) (D) contended that representatives of a class of subscribers of local telephone and/or high speed Internet services (plaintiffs) (P) had not stated a claim against the defendants (D) under § 1 of the Sherman Act by merely alleging parallel conduct and making a bald assertion of conspiracy, without more.

RULE OF LAW

Stating a claim under § 1 of the Sherman Act requires a complaint with enough factual matter to suggest that an agreement was made, so that an allegation of parallel conduct unfavorable to competition and a bare assertion of conspiracy without more are insufficient to make out such a claim.

FACTS: Representatives of a class of subscribers of local telephone and/or high speed Internet services (plaintiffs) (P) brought suit against certain providers of local telephone and/or high speed Internet services (defendants) (D) for claimed violations of § 1 of the Sherman Act, which prohibits "[e]very contract, combination in the form of trust or otherwise, or conspiracy, in restraint of trade or commerce among the several States, or with foreign nations." The complaint alleged that the defendants (D) conspired to restrain trade (1) by engaging in parallel conduct in their respective service areas to inhibit the growth of upstart competitive local exchange carriers (CLECs) (e.g., by making unfair agreements with the competitive carriers, by providing inferior connections to the networks, overcharging, and billing in ways designed to sabotage the upstarts' relations with their owns customers); and (2) by agreeing to refrain from competing against one another, as indicated by their common failure to pursue attractive business opportunities in contiguous markets. The district court dismissed the complaint, concluding that parallel business conduct allegations, taken alone, do not state a claim under § 1; the court ruled that plaintiffs must allege additional facts tending to exclude independent self-interested conduct as an explanation for the parallel actions. Reversing, the court of appeals held that the plaintiffs' (P) parallel conduct allegations were sufficient to withstand a motion to dismiss because the defendants (D) failed to show that there was no set of facts that would permit the plaintiffs (P) to demonstrate that the particular parallelism asserted was the product of collusion rather than coincidence. The U.S. Supreme Court granted certiorari.

ISSUE: Does stating a claim under § 1 of the Sherman Act require a complaint with enough factual matter to suggest that an agreement was made, so that an allegation of parallel conduct unfavorable to competition and a bare assertion of conspiracy without more are insufficient to make out such a claim?

HOLDING AND DECISION: (Souter, J.) Yes. Stating a claim under § 1 of the Sherman Act requires a complaint with enough factual matter to suggest that an agreement was made, so that an allegation of parallel conduct unfavorable to competition and a bare assertion of conspiracy without more are insufficient to make out such a claim. Because § 1 prohibits "only restraints effected by a contract, combination, or conspiracy," the key question is whether the challenged anticompetitive conduct stems from an independent decision or from an agreement. While a showing of parallel business behavior is admissible circumstantial evidence from which the requisite agreement may be inferred, it falls short of conclusively establishing such agreement or constituting a § 1 violation. This is true even where there is "conscious parallelism" by interdependent companies in a concentrated market. Therefore, courts avoid making false inferences from identical behavior at a number of points in the trial sequence, e.g., at the summary judgment stage, unless the plaintiff can show that the defendants were not acting independently. Under the Federal Rules of Civil Procedure, only a "short and plain statement of the claim showing that the pleader is entitled to relief" is required. While detailed factual allegations are not necessary, mere labels or conclusions are insufficient, as they do not provide a defendant with grounds for the plaintiff's entitlement to relief. Factual allegations must be enough to raise a right to relief above the speculative level on the assumption that all of the complaint's allegations are true. In the context of a § 1 claim, this means that a complaint must contain enough factual matter to suggest an agreement. Thus, because lawful parallel conduct fails to give rise to unlawful conspiracy or agreement, an allegation of parallel conduct and a bare assertion of conspiracy are insufficient. Instead, such allegations, to be plausible, must be made in a factual context that raises a suggestion of preceding agreement. Because antitrust discovery can be expensive and can cause defendants to settle even anemic claims, taking care to require allegations that reach the level suggesting conspiracy will help avoid the potentially enormous

Continued on next page.

expense of discovery in cases with no "reasonably founded hope that the [discovery] process will reveal relevant evidence" to support a § 1 claim. Applying these principles here, it is clear that the plaintiffs' (P) claim of conspiracy in restraint of trade comes up short. There is no allegation of actual agreement by the defendants (D); there are merely allegations of the absence of meaningful competition, followed by the assertion of parallel action, from which agreement is inferred. These allegations on their own do not invest the defendants' (D) actions or inactions with a plausible suggestion of conspiracy, since they can be construed as covering each defendant's (D) unilateral actions or reactions to the CLECs; there was just no need for joint encouragement for each defendant (D) to want to avoid dealing with the CLECs, and each defendant (D) had ample reasons for attempting to keep the CLECs out, regardless of the actions of the other defendants (D). Finally, the requirement of a factual context that supports conspiracy does not amount to a requirement of heightened fact pleading of specifics, but only enough facts to state a claim to relief that is plausible on its face. Because the plaintiffs (P) here have not nudged their claims across the line from conceivable to plausible, their complaint must be dismissed. Reversed and remanded.

DISSENT: (Stevens, J.) The plaintiffs (P) have alleged a horizontal agreement among potential competitors, and such allegation has not even been denied. The majority's charge that such an allegation is not "plausible" is not a legally acceptable reason to dismiss the complaint. The plaintiffs (P) describe a variety of circumstantial evidence that supports an allegation of a classic per se violation of the Sherman Act, and these factual allegations must be accepted as true. While the majority's concern for the enormous expense of antitrust litigation is valid, the answer is careful case management, not dismissal of an adequately pleaded complaint. The majority's decision is driven by its appraisal of the plausibility of the ultimate factual allegations rather than their legal sufficiency. In dismissing the complaint, the majority scraps the precedential "no set of facts" language, but this formulation has hitherto not been questioned and, contrary to the majority's assertion, it does mean that the Federal Rules of Civil Procedure require, or invite, the pleading of facts. Instead, the majority formulates an evidentiary standard that while appropriate for the summary judgment stage, is not appropriate at the pleading stage. Moreover, an antitrust case such as the one at bar is a poor vehicle for enunciating a new pleading rule, given that in antitrust cases, the proof is largely in the hands of the alleged conspirators, and dismissals prior to giving the plaintiff ample opportunity for discovery should be granted very sparingly. This principle is supported by the Sherman Act itself, which encourages the bringing of private enforcement actions through the recovery of treble damages and attorneys' fees for successful plaintiffs. Thus, the majority's rule marches contrary to congressional intent.

▶ ANALYSIS

The Court has declined to limit its holding in this case to antitrust cases, and has ruled that it applies in all civil actions. Thus, in all such cases, plaintiffs must now plead sufficient factual matter to state a claim to relief that is plausible on its face, which means that the facts must support more than a sheer possibility that a defendant has acted unlawfully. *Ashcroft v. Iqbal,* 129 S. Ct. 1937 (2009).

■ ■ ■

Quicknotes

COLLUSION An agreement between two or more parties to engage in unlawful conduct or in other activities with an unlawful goal, typically involving fraud.

HORIZONTAL AGREEMENTS Agreements entered into by entities at the same level of production for the purpose of restraining trade.

RESTRAINT OF TRADE Agreement between entities, for the purpose of impeding free trade, that results in a monopoly, suppression of competition, or affecting prices.

■ ■ ■

FTC v. Cement Institute

Federal agency (P) v. Trade association (D)

333 U.S. 683 (1948).

NATURE OF CASE: Review of order setting aside regulatory sanctions.

FACT SUMMARY: The Federal Trade Commission (P) contended that the cement industry (D) restrained competition by charging identical prices for cement no matter where the cement shipped from, a form of "base-point pricing."

🏛 RULE OF LAW
The use of a base-point delivered pricing system throughout an industry is an unfair trade practice.

FACTS: The Federal Trade Commission (FTC) (P) brought an enforcement action against the Cement Institute (D), a trade association composed of most companies involved in the U.S. cement industry. The FTC (P) alleged a decades-old practice of multiple basing point system of pricing. This system worked as follows: The seller fixed a price for goods that included the cost of delivery to the buyer, but the cost of delivery was always set relative to a location chosen by the Cement Institute (D) and not necessarily the location that the goods were actually sent from. The alleged effect was that the "delivered prices" of producers in every locality were always identical, regardless of the producers' actual freight costs. The FTC (P) determined a violation of the Federal Trade Act and issued sanctions. The court of appeals reversed, holding that an economist's testimony that uniform prices were the result of market forces was determinative. The U.S. Supreme Court granted review.

ISSUE: Is the use of a base-point delivered pricing system throughout an industry an unfair trade practice?

HOLDING AND DECISION: (Black, J.) Yes. The use of a base-point delivered pricing system throughout an industry is an unfair trade practice. It is well established that an industry practice may constitute a Sherman Act violation and still fall within the FTC's (P) jurisdiction. Indeed, a Sherman Act violation is probably per se an unfair trade practice. Consequently, if the FTC (P) finds an industry practice to constitute concerted action in restraint of trade, it is entitled to impose sanctions. Here the evidence was mixed, with economists hired by the Cement Institute (D) testifying that uniformity of prices was the result of competition. The FTC (P), however, was not compelled to accept this testimony, and its findings were supported by substantial evidence. Reversed.

▶ ANALYSIS

Antitrust violations are the province of the Department of Justice. Unfair trade practices are investigated by the FTC.

Early in its life, the argument was made that the FTC did not have jurisdiction over anticompetitive behavior, as such conduct was within the Justice Department's jurisdiction exclusively. Those arguments were uniformly rejected.

■■■

Quicknotes

COMBINATION (ANTITRUST DEFINITION) Alliance of entities, for the purpose of impeding free trade, that results in a monopoly, suppression of competition, or affecting prices.

FEDERAL TRADE COMMISSION ACT Establishes the Federal Trade Commission for the purpose of preventing persons or entities from using unfair methods of competition in or affecting commerce, and unfair or deceptive acts or practices in or affecting commerce.

■■■

E.I. du Pont de Nemours & Co. v. FTC

Manufacturer (D) v. Federal agency (P)

729 F.2d 128 (2d Cir. 1984).

NATURE OF CASE: Appeal from administrative cease-and-desist order.

FACT SUMMARY: The Federal Trade Commission (FTC) (P) ordered Ethyl Corp. (D) and E.I. du Pont de Nemours & Co. (D), the two main players in the oligopolistic gasoline antiknock compound industry, to cease certain practices, even though the practices were not concerted actions and were done for legitimate business reasons.

> ### 🏛 RULE OF LAW
> Before business conduct in an oligopolistic industry may be labeled "unfair," there must be proof of collusion, an anticompetitive purpose, or absence of an independent legitimate reason for the conduct.

FACTS: For much of the era of the automobile, lead antiknock compounds have been a regular additive to gasoline. The industry manufacturing antiknock compounds is oligopolistic, with less than a dozen companies supplying these products to gasoline refiners. In the early 1980s, the Federal Trade Commission (FTC) (P) began an investigation into certain industry practices, namely (1) sale of the product at a delivered price, i.e., including transportation costs; (2) lengthy advance notice to buyers of price increases; and (3) uniform sale pricing to all buyers. The FTC (P) was unable to find that these practices were the result of concerted action. Also, legitimate business reasons for the practices existed. Nonetheless, pursuant to § 5 of the Federal Trade Commission Act, the FTC (P) issued a cease-and-desist order, finding that the practices had the collective effect of lessening competition by removing price uncertainties. Ethyl (D) and E.I. du Pont de Nemours & Co. (du Pont) (D) appealed.

ISSUE: Before business conduct in an oligopolistic industry may be labeled "unfair," must there be proof of collusion, an anticompetitive purpose, or the absence of a legitimate reason for the conduct?

HOLDING AND DECISION: (Mansfield, J.) Yes. Before business conduct in an oligopolistic industry may be labeled "unfair," there must be proof of collusion, an anticompetitive purpose, or absence of an independent legitimate reason for the conduct. The FTC may not prohibit an arguably anticompetitive practice in an oligopolistic industry if each company undertakes it for legitimate business reasons. That an industry is oligopolistic does not mean that it is inherently suspect in terms of competitiveness; it may well be that the industry is oligopolistic as a result of competitive conditions. Without further evidence of collusion or the absence of legitimate business reasons for the challenged conduct, oligopoly parallel pricing by Ethyl (D) and du Pont (D) cannot be said to be "unfair" in the sense of FTC (P) § 5 sanctionability. To hold otherwise would be to invest the FTC (P) with such unbridled discretion that arbitrary decision-making would become a matter of course. Here, there was no evidence of industrywide collusion, and legitimate business reasons for all the challenged practices were offered. Consequently, the FTC (P) erred in its decision. Vacated.

> ### ▶ ANALYSIS
>
> Numerous reasons may exist to explain an industry's naturally oligopolistic tendencies, independent of anticompetitive practices by the market players. One reason is the prohibitive initial investment cost. However, even though a market may be not be influenced by anticompetitive behavior, suspicions are easily aroused in regulators when a market is as centralized as the antiknock additive market in this case.

Quicknotes

CEASE AND DESIST ORDER An order from a court or administrative agency prohibiting a person or business from continuing a particular course of conduct.

COLLUSION An agreement between two or more parties to engage in unlawful conduct or in other activities with an unlawful goal, typically involving fraud.

FEDERAL TRADE COMMISSION ACT Establishes the Federal Trade Commission for the purpose of preventing persons or entities from using unfair methods of competition in or affecting commerce, and unfair or deceptive acts or practices in or affecting commerce.

OLIGOPOLISTIC A market condition in which the industry for a particular product is dominated by only a few companies.

Copperweld Corp. v. Independence Tube Corp.

Steel tube manufacturer (D) v. Steel tube manufacturer (P)

467 U.S. 752 (1984).

NATURE OF CASE: Review of judgment awarding damages for Sherman Act violations.

FACT SUMMARY: Copperweld Corp. (D) and its wholly owned subsidiary were sued under § 1 of the Sherman Act for conspiracies in restraint of trade.

🏛 RULE OF LAW
A parent corporation and its wholly owned subsidiary are legally incapable of a § 1 Sherman Act conspiracy.

FACTS: Copperweld Corp. (D) was engaged in the steel tubing business. In 1972, it purchased the Regal Division of Lear Siegler, Inc., which it incorporated as a subsidiary, named Regal Tube Co. (D). Subsequent to this, the former head of the Regal Division (D) started another corporation, Independence Tube Corp. (Independence) (P), as a competitor to Copperweld (D). Copperweld (D) contended that Independence (P) and its principal were bound by agreements not to compete and actively discouraged potential customers and creditors of Independence (P) with legal threats. Independence (P) brought an action against Copperweld (D) and Regal Tube (D) under § 1 of the Sherman Act, alleging a conspiracy between them in restraint of competition. A jury awarded $2,499,009, which the court trebled to $7,497,027. The Seventh Circuit affirmed, and the U.S. Supreme Court granted review.

ISSUE: Are a parent corporation and its wholly owned subsidiary legally capable of a Sherman Act conspiracy?

HOLDING AND DECISION: (Burger, C.J.) No. A parent corporation and its wholly owned subsidiary are legally incapable of a § 1 Sherman Act conspiracy. Section 1 of the Sherman Act only applies to situations where two or more market players conspire to restrain trade. Efforts to do so by only one player are addressed in § 2. Section 1 of the Act clearly contemplates untoward cooperation between two entities who do not otherwise share an identity of interest. This is not the case with a parent and a subsidiary, as they already enjoy such an identity. It is well established that a company cannot conspire, for § 1 purposes, with one of its unincorporated divisions. To hold to the contrary with respect to a parent and a subsidiary would elevate form over substance. In essence, the anticompetitive threat that § 1 seeks to address does not exist between a parent and a subsidiary, and therefore § 1 will not be applied in such situations. Reversed.

▶ ANALYSIS

Section 1 of the Sherman Act deals with intercompany conspiracies while § 2 deals with monopolistic behavior

by a single player. Section 1 prohibits all agreements in restraint of trade; § 2 only deals with restraints of trade that become monopolistic. The reason that § 1 is more draconian than § 2 is that the drafters of the Act considered conspiracies in restraint of trade to be a bigger threat to competition than single-entity restraints.

■==■

Quicknotes

CONSPIRACY Concerted action by two or more persons to accomplish some unlawful purpose.

RESTRAINT OF TRADE Agreement between entities, for the purpose of impeding free trade, that results in a monopoly, suppression of competition, or affecting prices.

SHERMAN ACT Makes every contract or conspiracy in unreasonable restraint of commerce illegal.

TREBLE DAMAGES An award of damages triple of the amount awarded by the jury and provided for by statute for violation of certain offenses.

■==■

Matsushita Electric Industrial Co. v. Zenith Radio Corp.

Japanese electronics manufacturer (D) v. American electronics manufacturer (P)

475 U.S. 574 (1986).

NATURE OF CASE: Review of reversal of summary judgment dismissing antitrust action.

FACT SUMMARY: Zenith Radio Corp. (P), an American electronics manufacturer, brought an antitrust action against twenty-one Japanese manufacturers (D), but the district court denied summary judgment because it had no evidence of a motive and evidence of a conspiracy was ambiguous.

RULE OF LAW
To survive a defense motion for summary judgment, a plaintiff must show direct evidence of concert of an action, as well as a plausible motive to engage in predatory pricing.

FACTS: Zenith Radio Corp. (Zenith) (P) filed a § 1 Sherman Act action against twenty-one Japanese companies (D) involved in manufacturing consumer electronics, mostly televisions. The complaint alleged that the Japanese companies (D) had conspired for nearly twenty years to sell their products at artificially low prices in the United States, in an effort to drive U.S. companies out of the market. Zenith (P) alleged that this conspiracy was underwritten by the ability of the Japanese companies (D) to keep prices artificially high in Japan, due to government compliance. At the time the case was filed, Zenith (P) had a larger market share than any of its Japanese counterparts (D). The Japanese companies (D) collectively moved for summary judgment, which the district court granted. Finding direct evidence of conspiratorial behavior in Japan and inferences from this of conspiratorial behavior in the United States, the Third Circuit reversed. The U.S. Supreme Court granted review.

ISSUE: To survive a defense motion for summary judgment, must a plaintiff show direct evidence of concerted action and a plausible motive to engage in predatory pricing?

HOLDING AND DECISION: (Powell, J.) Yes. To survive a defense motion for summary judgment, a plaintiff must show direct evidence of concert of an action, as well as a plausible motive to engage in predatory pricing. To survive a motion for summary judgment, a plaintiff opposing it must put forth evidence that there are genuine issues of triable, controverted facts so as to negate the contention that the moving party is entitled to judgment as a matter of law. Factual inferences are allowable, but they must be reasonable; they cannot be mere speculation or allegations. In this case, the direct evidence cited by the Third Circuit in reversing the district court and declining summary judgment was the Japanese companies' (D) anticompetitive acts in Japan. However, a conspiracy to increase profits in one market does not tend to show a conspiracy to sustain losses in another. In light of the absence of any rational motive to conspire, neither the Japanese companies' (D) practices nor their conduct in the Japanese market nor their agreements regarding prices or distribution here in the United States are sufficient to create a "genuine issue for trial" under Fed. R. Civ. P. 56(e). Consequently, summary judgment in favor of the Japanese companies (D) was proper. Reversed and remanded.

DISSENT: (White, J.) The standard used by the court here seems to require that a judge hearing a defendant's motion for summary judgment in an antitrust case should go beyond the traditional summary judgment inquiry and decide for himself whether the weight of the evidence favors the plaintiff.

ANALYSIS

In federal court, a defendant can prevail in a summary judgment motion if he can produce evidence tending to show that the plaintiff cannot prove one or more elements of his cause of action. Upon such evidence, the plaintiff must put forth evidence showing that he can in fact prove the element. This standard should be compared to that still used in many states, which requires a defendant to actually disprove an element in order to prevail.

Quicknotes

CONSPIRACY Concerted action by two or more persons to accomplish some unlawful purpose.

SUMMARY JUDGMENT Judgment rendered by a court in response to a motion by one of the parties, claiming that the lack of a question of material fact in respect to an issue warrants disposition of the issue without consideration by the jury.

United States v. Topco Associates

Federal government (P) v. Independent grocers' cooperative (D)

405 U.S. 596 (1972).

NATURE OF CASE: Antitrust action under § 1 of the Sherman Act.

FACT SUMMARY: Topco Associates (D), a cooperative for grocers, assigned exclusive territories for the members' business.

RULE OF LAW

Exclusive territorial assignments to independent retailers by a cooperative is a horizontal restraint on competition which is per se unlawful.

FACTS: A number of independent grocers formed a cooperative called Topco Associates (Topco) (D). Topco (D) allowed members to purchase goods at the same price as chain stores. Topco (D) expanded into different areas as it grew in size. The low prices at which goods could be obtained from Topco (D) allowed its members to compete with the chain stores in these areas. Topco's (D) members were assigned exclusive territories so that they would not be competing with each other. The Government (P) brought an antitrust action under § 1 of the Sherman Act to enjoin these practices as an impermissible restraint on trade. The Government (P) alleged that the arrangement constituted a horizontal restraint to eliminate competition between the grocer members.

ISSUE: Is an exclusive territorial grant by a cooperative to its independent members a per se violation of the Sherman Act?

HOLDING AND DECISION: (Marshall, J.) Yes. Topco (D) members are all independent businessmen who would normally be in competition with each other. Any practice which would restrict or eliminate such potential competitors is an unlawful restraint on trade. Exclusive territorial assignments constitute a horizontal restraint, which is a per se violation of the Sherman Act. It is immaterial that the motive behind the exclusive territorial grant was not motivated by an impermissible purpose or that this is the only way in which the independents can successfully compete with the chain stores. Unless permitted by specific legislation, all horizontal restraints are unlawful per se. Reversed and remanded.

DISSENT: (Burger, C.J.) There was no agreement herein to restrain trade. Topco's (D) exclusive territorial grants had the purpose and effect of promoting competition rather than restraining it. A per se rule should not be automatically applied to all situations where the objective facts indicate that it is not applicable. It is only the majority's decision which creates an automatic application of a previously flexible per se rule. Where an arrangement does not have as its primary purpose and effect the reduction of competition, it should be allowed.

ANALYSIS

Certain practices such as price-fixing agreements and horizontal restraints have been deemed illegal per se. Their mere existence, regardless of the reason or justification, is deemed a violation of the Sherman Act. Most other arrangements are tested under a "rule of reason" and will only be found to be illegal based on the objective facts of the case. Where the Sherman Act's application diminishes competition and furthers monopolistic or oligopolistic tendencies, it is illogical to apply it.

Quicknotes

HORIZONTAL RESTRAINT ON COMPETITION Agreement entered into by entities at the same level of production for the purpose of restraining trade.

PER SE RULE Rule that business transactions which in themselves constitute restraints on trade obviate the need to demonstrate an injury to competition in making out an antitrust case.

RULE OF REASON The standard for determining whether there has been a violation of § 1 of the Sherman Antitrust Act, requiring a determination of whether the activity unreasonably restrains competition as demonstrated by actual harm.

SHERMAN ACT Makes every contract or conspiracy in unreasonable restraint of commerce illegal.

Polk Bros. v. Forest City Enterprises

Appliance store (P) v. Hardware store (D)

776 F.2d 185 (7th Cir. 1985).

NATURE OF CASE: Appeal from order invalidating restrictive covenant.

FACT SUMMARY: Forest City Enterprises (D), which had covenanted not to sell certain products in competition with cotenant Polk Bros. (P), contended that the covenant was an illegal restraint of trade.

🏛 RULE OF LAW
A covenant not to compete may be legal if ancillary to a productive venture.

FACTS: Polk Bros. (Polk) (P) and Forest City Enterprises (Forest City) (D) agreed to build a store large enough to house sales outlets for both companies. As part of the agreement, Polk (P) agreed not to sell Forest City's (D) type of merchandise, i.e., building materials, and Forest City (D) agreed not to sell appliances, which were part of Polk's (P) product line. Years later, Forest City's (D) desire to sell appliances compelled it to inform Polk (P) that it considered the covenant invalid. Polk (P) sued to enforce the covenant. The district court held that the covenant was an unlawful contract allocating products and markets under the antitrust laws. Polk (P) appealed.

ISSUE: May a covenant not to compete be evaluated under the rule of reason if ancillary to a productive venture?

HOLDING AND DECISION: (Easterbrook, J.) Yes. A covenant not to compete may be evaluated under the rule of reason if ancillary to a productive venture. The per se rule under antitrust law applies to "naked" restraints of trade, that is, restraints that serve no purpose other than to lessen competition. On the other hand, restraints that require extensive cooperation toward a mutual goal of productivity are termed "ancillary." These restraints, which serve the function of facilitating some productive purpose, would not be practical absent the restraint. Covenants not to compete are an example of this. Here, the agreement between Polk (P) and Forest City (D) clearly falls within the latter category. By agreeing not to directly compete with each other, Polk (P) and Forest City (D) were able to build a large sales outlet which would not have been profitable had they been competing against each other. This productive cooperation, and thus the restraint, was ancillary to the purpose of expansion and should have been subjected to the rule of reason, not to a per se analysis. Polk (P) is entitled to a permanent injunction. Reversed.

▶ ANALYSIS

Probably the most common type of agreement in this area is the employer-employee or vendor-vendee agreement not to compete. The paradigmatic situation is when a person buys a business and the vendor agrees not to compete against the vendee. Such an arrangement, if reasonable, does not violate antitrust.

■■■

Quicknotes

PER SE RULE Rule that business transactions which in themselves constitute restraints on trade obviate the need to demonstrate an injury to competition in making out an antitrust case.

PERMANENT INJUNCTION A remedy imposed by the court ordering a party to cease the conduct of a specific activity until the final disposition of the cause of action.

RESTRICTIVE COVENANT A promise contained in a deed to limit the uses to which the property will be made.

RULE OF REASON The standard for determining whether there has been a violation of § 1 of the Sherman Antitrust Act, requiring a determination of whether the activity unreasonably restrains competition as demonstrated by actual harm.

■■■

Eastern States Retail Lumber Dealers' Assn. v. United States

Lumber trade association (D) v. Federal government (P)

234 U.S. 600 (1914).

NATURE OF CASE: Appeal from conviction of conspiracy under the Sherman Act.

FACT SUMMARY: The Government (P) challenged, as an antitrust violation, the practice of members of Eastern States Retail Lumber Dealers' Association (D), a retail trade association, of compiling and circulating a list of wholesalers who sold lumber retail directly to consumers.

> ## RULE OF LAW
> Compiling and circulating a list of undesirable wholesalers is an antitrust violation, if done to obstruct interstate trade and to unduly suppress competition.

FACTS: The Eastern States Retail Lumber Dealers' Association (Association) (D) was a trade association composed of lumber retailers. The Association (D) habitually circulated a list of "undesirable" wholesalers. These were wholesalers who sold lumber directly to the public as well as to the retailers; the Association (D) considered this an invasion of their domain. Although there was no official boycott of the wholesalers found on the "blacklist," in practice, most Association (D) members refused to deal with these wholesalers. The Government (P) brought an antitrust prosecution against the Association (D). The Association (D) was convicted and appealed.

ISSUE: Is circulating a list of undesirable wholesalers an antitrust violation if done to obstruct trade and unduly suppress competition?

HOLDING AND DECISION: (Day, J.) Yes. Circulating a list of undesirable wholesalers is an antitrust violation if done to obstruct trade and unduly suppress competition. The Sherman Act prohibits agreements in restraint of trade. It is rare that overt proof of such an agreement will be found. Rather, such an agreement may be inferred if such restraint is a natural consequence of an industry practice. Here, the Association (D) mounted what essentially was a boycott of wholesalers who chose to compete with its members. That this was done via a blacklist rather than by an official agreement is irrelevant for Sherman Act purposes. The conspiracy to impair the trade of blacklisted wholesalers may be inferred. Affirmed.

▶ ANALYSIS

Boycotts are not necessarily violations of the Sherman Act. What matters is the ultimate goal and effect of the boycott. A boycott undertaken for political or social reasons, rather than for business reasons, will probably pass Sherman Act scrutiny.

Quicknotes

BOYCOTT A concerted effort to refrain from doing business with a particular person or entity.

CONSPIRACY Concerted action by two or more persons to accomplish some unlawful purpose.

RESTRAINT OF TRADE Agreement between entities, for the purpose of impeding free trade, that results in a monopoly, suppression of competition, or affecting prices.

SHERMAN ACT Makes every contract or conspiracy in unreasonable restraint of commerce illegal.

Klor's, Inc. v. Broadway-Hale Stores, Inc.

Appliance store (P) v. Department store (D)

359 U.S. 207 (1959).

NATURE OF CASE: Antitrust action for treble damages.

FACT SUMMARY: Klor's, Inc. (P) alleged that Broadway-Hale Stores, Inc. (D) used its large volume purchasing power to influence manufacturers not to deal with Klor's (P).

🏛 RULE OF LAW
The use of a retailer's large volume buying power to restrict manufacturer's power to deal with others is violative of the Sherman Act.

FACTS: Klor's, Inc. (P) operated an appliance store next to one of Broadway-Hale Stores, Inc.'s (Broadway-Hale) (D) stores. Klor's (P) was unable to obtain merchandise from many manufacturers and received poor terms from others. It alleged that this was the result of coercive pressures from Broadway-Hale (D) which was using its large volume purchasing power to freeze Klor (P) out of business. Broadway-Hale (D) did not deny the charge. It merely alleged that there were numerous other appliance stores in the area and the public was not being injured by its actions. Since the public was not being injured, there was no violation of the Sherman Act. Both the district court and the court of appeals found for Broadway-Hale (D) on this basis.

ISSUE: Where the freedom of manufacturers and sellers is inhibited by the actions of a single retailer has the Sherman Act been violated?

HOLDING AND DECISION: (Black, J.) Yes. Broadway-Hale's (D) actions resulted in a group boycott of Klor's (P). Such actions violate the Sherman Act. It results in Klor's (P) being excluded from competitive markets; manufacturers being denied certain customers; and the advancement of monopolistic tendencies. These are impermissible trade practices which inhibit free competition. The spirit of the Sherman Act may be violated where retailers are denied free access to manufactured goods. Based on the admissions by Broadway-Hale (D), its practices are a clear violation of the Sherman Act. Reversed and remanded.

▍ *ANALYSIS*

Restraints on dealing may be allowed for the purpose of imposing disciplinary sanctions. In *Molinas v. National Basketball Assn.*, 190 F. Supp. 241 (S.D.N.Y. 1961), the court held that a player might be suspended indefinitely for severe infractions of league rules. No antitrust violation is present even though no other club could hire him until the suspension was lifted.

Quicknotes

BOYCOTT A concerted effort to refrain from doing business with a particular person or entity.

SHERMAN ACT Makes every contract or conspiracy in unreasonable restraint of commerce illegal.

NYNEX Corporation v. Discon, Inc.

Telephone company (D) v. Telephone company (P)

525 U.S. 128 (1998).

NATURE OF CASE: Antitrust suit.

FACT SUMMARY: Discon, Inc. (P) alleged that NYNEX Corporation (D) engaged in unfair, improper, and anticompetitive activities in order to hurt Discon and benefit its competitor AT&T.

RULE OF LAW
The antitrust rule that group boycotts are illegal per se does not apply to a buyer's decision to buy from one seller rather than another when that decision cannot be justified in terms of ordinary competitive objectives.

FACTS: Discon, Inc. (P) sold removal services to NYNEX Corporation (D) and its subsidiaries (D). Discon (P) alleged that NYNEX (D) engaged in unfair, improper, and anticompetitive activities in order to hurt Discon and benefit its competitor AT&T. The district court dismissed the complaint for failure to state a claim. The court of appeals affirmed the dismissal with an exception for Discon's (P) claim that Materiel Enterprises switched its purchases from Discon (P) to AT&T as part of an attempt to defraud local telephone service customers.

ISSUE: Does the antitrust rule that group boycotts are illegal per se apply to a buyer's decision to buy from one seller rather than another when that decision cannot be justified in terms of ordinary competitive objectives?

HOLDING AND DECISION: (Breyer, J.) No. The antitrust rule that group boycotts are illegal per se does not apply to a buyer's decision to buy from one seller rather than another when that decision cannot be justified in terms of ordinary competitive objectives. The present case deals with only a vertical agreement and restraint that takes the form of depriving a supplier of a potential customer. To apply the per se rule here would convert business transactions that are improper for other reasons into treble-damages antitrust cases and would discourage firms from changing suppliers, even where no harm is posed to the competitive process. Vacated and remanded.

ANALYSIS

As the Court held in *Klor's, Inc. v. Broadway-Hale Stores, Inc.*, 359 U.S. 207 (1959), in order for the per se rule to apply in the boycott context, there must be a horizontal agreement. A vertical restraint cannot be illegal per se unless it includes some agreement on price or price levels.

Quicknotes

BOYCOTT A concerted effort to refrain from doing business with a particular person or entity.

PER SE RULE Rule that business transactions which in themselves constitute restraints on trade obviate the need to demonstrate an injury to competition in making out an antitrust case.

RESTRAINT OF TRADE Agreement between entities, for the purpose of impeding free trade, that results in a monopoly, suppression of competition, or affecting prices.

TREBLE DAMAGES An award of damages triple of the amount awarded by the jury and provided for by statute for violation of certain offenses.

Paramount Famous Lasky Corp. v. United States

Film producer/distributor (D) v. Federal government (P)

282 U.S. 30 (1930).

NATURE OF CASE: Antitrust action.

FACT SUMMARY: A standard film exhibition contract used in the film industry required film exhibitors to submit disputes to arbitration.

> 🏛 **RULE OF LAW**
> An industrywide practice of forcing retailers to submit disputes to arbitration may violate the Sherman Act.

FACTS: An agreement existed among ten motion picture distributors (D), who collectively controlled over 60 percent of all films seen in the United States, to impose a standard exhibition agreement upon film exhibitors. One clause in the standard agreement required the exhibitors to submit all disputes to arbitration. If the exhibitor refused, it was forced to pay an additional fee in order to exhibit one of the distributor's (D) films. Furthermore, the ten distributors (D) refused to contract with any exhibitor who failed to observe the agreement. The Government (P) challenged this as an antitrust violation. A district court agreed, and the U.S. Supreme Court granted review.

ISSUE: May an industrywide practice of forcing retailers to submit disputes to arbitration violate the Sherman Act?

HOLDING AND DECISION: (McReynolds, J.) Yes. An industrywide practice of forcing retailers to submit disputes to arbitration may violate the Sherman Act. When such a practice involves, as it does here, concerted action by manufacturers and/or distributors to restrict the retailers' liberty of action, the kind of anticompetitive, coercive activity prohibited by the Sherman Act is present. Such action constitutes a limitation on freedom of trade. Although arbitration may be appropriate for this industry, it may not be used as a guise to enter into an unusual agreement to suppress normal competition. Affirmed.

▶ *ANALYSIS*

At the time of this opinion, arbitration was not a favored remedy. The Federal Arbitration Act has since reversed this judicial attitude. Even so, the present case certainly remains vital, as it deals with the boycott aspect of the distributors' (D) agreement.

■≡■

Quicknotes

ARBITRATION An agreement to have a dispute heard and decided by a neutral third party, rather than through legal proceedings.

COERCION The overcoming of a person's free will as a result of threats, promises, or undue influence.

SHERMAN ACT Makes every contract or conspiracy in unreasonable restraint of commerce illegal.

■≡■

Northwest Wholesale Stationers, Inc. v. Pacific Stationery & Printing Co.

Purchasing cooperative (D) v. Wholesale/retailer (P)

472 U.S. 284 (1985).

NATURE OF CASE: Appeal from decision finding per se antitrust violation.

FACT SUMMARY: Northwest Wholesale Stationers, Inc. (D) appealed from a decision of the court of appeals that its expulsion of Pacific Stationery & Printing Co. (Pacific) (P) without procedural safeguards was a group boycott limiting Pacific's (P) ability to compete and was, therefore, a per se violation of § 1 of the Sherman Act.

🏛 RULE OF LAW
Not all concerted refusals to deal should be characterized as group boycotts limiting the ability to compete and therefore per se violative of § 1 of the Sherman Act, 15 U.S.C. 1.

FACTS: Northwest Wholesale Stationers, Inc. (Northwest) (D) was a purchasing cooperative, consisting of approximately 100 office supply retailers, acting as a wholesaler and a warehousing concern for the retailers. Pacific Stationery & Printing Co. (Pacific) (P) was a wholesaler and retailer of office supplies and had been a member of Northwest since 1958. Northwest (D) had a provision in its bylaws prohibiting its members from operating on both the wholesale and retail levels, but Pacific's (P) rights were preserved by a grandfather clause. When the controlling ownership of Pacific (P) changed, this change was not officially brought to the attention of Northwest's (D) directors, apparently in violation of its bylaws. In 1978 the membership of Northwest (D) voted to expel Pacific (P). The parties disputed the reasons for the expulsion, Pacific (P) contending that it was expelled because it maintained a wholesale operation. There was no evidence of any competitive injury as a result of the expulsion. Pacific (P) brought suit in 1980, alleging that its expulsion from Northwest (D) without procedural safeguards was therefore a per se violation of § 1 of the Sherman Act. The district court disagreed and, applying the rule of reason, found no anticompetitive effect and granted summary judgment for Northwest (D). The court of appeals reversed, finding a per se violation of § 1 of the Sherman Act, and from this decision, Northwest (D) appealed.

ISSUE: Should all concerted refusals to deal be characterized as group boycotts limiting the ability to compete and therefore per se violative of § 1 of the Sherman Act?

HOLDING AND DECISION: (Brennan, J.) No. Not all concerted refusals to deal should be characterized as group boycotts limiting the ability to compete and therefore per se violative of § 1 of the Sherman Act. While the court of appeals found the type of expulsion shielded by a mandate in the Robinson-Patman Act, it also felt the rule of reason should apply, and in the absence of procedural safeguards, the Robinson-Patman immunity did not shield the expulsion. But the focus of that inquiry is misdirected: the crucial question is whether the decision to expel falls within a category that is conclusively presumed to be anticompetitive. Cases relied on by the court of appeals evidence a broad mandate for self-regulation, but the mandate laid out in Robinson-Patman cannot be construed as such. No narrowing of the Sherman Act is necessary in order to accomplish the congressional policy of discretionary self-policing. Lack of procedural violations does not convert challenged actions into per se violations of the Sherman Act. The existence of a purchasing cooperative increases economic efficiency and tends to promote, rather than inhibit, competition. Expulsion does not necessarily imply anticompetitive animus. Unless the cooperative (D) possesses market power or exclusive access to an element essential to effective competition, the conclusion that expulsion is always anticompetitive is not warranted. The district court appears to have followed the correct path of analysis and in light of the absence of a showing of anticompetitive effect, properly entered judgment. Reversed and remanded.

▶ ANALYSIS

The Court's opinion in the present case seems to evidence the intent to limit per se violations to currently existing categories of anticompetitive practices. Strict adherence to this view will prevent the recognition of new per se categories perhaps at the expense of administrative efficiency in the handling of antitrust claims.

■=■

Quicknotes

BOYCOTT A concerted effort to refrain from doing business with a particular person or entity.

PER SE RULE Rule that business transactions which in themselves constitute restraints on trade obviate the need to demonstrate an injury to competition in making out an antitrust case.

ROBINSON-PATMAN ACT Makes price discrimination unlawful if the intent is to harm competition.

RULE OF REASON The standard for determining whether there has been a violation of § 1 of the Sherman Antitrust Act, requiring a determination of whether the activity

Continued on next page.

unreasonably restrains competition as demonstrated by actual harm.

SUMMARY JUDGMENT Judgment rendered by a court in response to a motion by one of the parties, claiming that the lack of a question of material fact in respect to an issue warrants disposition of the issue without consideration by the jury.

■━━■

FTC v. Indiana Federation of Dentists

Federal agency (P) v. Professional organization (D)

476 U.S. 447 (1986).

NATURE OF CASE: Appeal from an antitrust violation.

FACT SUMMARY: The Federal Trade Commission (FTC) (P) contended that the Indiana Federation of Dentists (D) pursued an unfair method of competition by encouraging member dentists to refuse to submit X-rays with insurance claim forms.

🏛 RULE OF LAW
A horizontal conspiracy to deprive consumers of a service by a professional organization violates antitrust laws.

FACTS: The Indiana Federation of Dentists (D) encouraged its member dentists to refuse to send patient X-rays to insurance companies, frustrating the latter's ability to evaluate the necessity of proposed treatment. The Federal Trade Commission (FTC) (P) concluded this eliminated competition among dentists willing to provide X-rays and those unwilling to do so, and thus violated antitrust laws. The court of appeals reversed, and the U.S. Supreme Court granted certiorari.

ISSUE: Does a horizontal conspiracy to deprive consumers of a service by a professional organization violate antitrust laws?

HOLDING AND DECISION: (White, J.) Yes. A horizontal conspiracy to deprive consumers of a service by a professional organization violates antitrust laws. In this case, if no conspiracy existed, some dentists would refuse to send X-rays, and patients would be forced to go elsewhere or lose insurance benefits. Thus, an element of competition existed on this point. The conspiracy eliminated this competition and violated the antitrust laws. This conspiracy is analogous to a group boycott and is thus improper. Reversed.

▶ ANALYSIS

Even though the issue in this case did not specifically involve the provision of dental services, the type of anticompetitive action was viewed as sufficiently material to constitute a violation. The collection of insurance benefits is a major part of modern health care, and the stated purpose of the concerted action in this case was the maintenance of the dentists' economic viability. A decrease in compensation could result if the insurer insisted upon a less expensive yet effective alternative treatment. The absence of insurance benefits renders the dentist less favorable to the consumer, and thus the issue in this case was material.

Quicknotes

BOYCOTT A concerted effort to refrain from doing business with a particular person or entity.

CERTIORARI A discretionary writ issued by a superior court to an inferior court in order to review the lower court's decisions; the Supreme Court's writ ordering such review.

HORIZONTAL CONSPIRACY Agreement entered into by entities at the same level of production for the purpose of restraining trade.

Associated Press v. United States

Publishers' cooperative (D) v. Federal government (P)

326 U.S. 1 (1945).

NATURE OF CASE: Antitrust action under the Sherman Act.

FACT SUMMARY: The bylaws of the Associated Press (AP) (D) restricted the ability of members to sell AP news to nonmembers and granted members the right to block the admission of new members.

🏛 RULE OF LAW
When competitors band together, to deny their joint product to others, the practice violates the Sherman Act.

FACTS: The Associated Press (AP) (D) was the largest news gathering agency in the United States. Its members pooled their individual news gathering facilities for the common benefit of all members. AP's (D) bylaws prohibited the sale of AP news to any nonmember. Members are also given the power to block membership applications of nonmembers. The Government (P) brought an antitrust action against AP (D) alleging that its bylaws violated the Sherman Act since they constituted an unreasonable restraint of competition. AP (D) alleged that it did not occupy a monopoly position in the market; other comparable alternative services were available; individuals should be allowed to determine with whom they wish to associate and to whom they wish to sell their product; and the public suffered no injury since it could read AP (D) news in any member newspaper. The district court found that the bylaws constituted a prima facie violation of the Sherman Act regardless of any actions pursuant to them.

ISSUE: May, competitors band together to deny their product to third parties?

HOLDING AND DECISION: (Black, J.) No. A business may deal with whomever it chooses. However, this freedom does not extend to combinations formed to restrict access of their joint product to third parties; where many entities combine to restrict their competitive market the practice violates the Sherman Act. A monopoly is not required. The Sherman Act does not require that the government wait until the monopoly has been accomplished. Thus, the fact that alternatives to AP (D) exist is immaterial. Through its members, AP (D) controls a large share of the news gathering and reporting market. AP's (D) bylaws not only foreclose access to such news to nonmembers, but it also allows members to block membership in AP (D). Both of these practices constitute unreasonable and impermissible restraints on competition on their face, regardless of their actual effect. These restraints also have the effect of blocking potential entrants into the field by creating roadblocks to such entry. The fact that the public can obtain AP (D) news is also immaterial. The public's choice of newspapers has been unreasonably restricted. It is the combination which is unlawful with its potential for injury to competition. Independent businesses may not associate to stifle competition. The bylaws are unlawful, and an injunction against them, adherence to them by members or similar bylaws is issued. Affirmed.

▷ ANALYSIS

In *Dalmo Sales Co. v. Tysons Corner Regional Shopping Center*, 308 F. Supp. 988 (D.D.C. 1970), the court refused to issue an injunction against a shopping center which refused to allow discount stores space. Three department store tenants and the center agreed that discount stores would be excluded. The court held that this was not a combination in restraint of trade.

■=■

Quicknotes

COMBINATION (ANTITRUST DEFINITION) Alliance of entities, for the purpose of impeding free trade, that results in a monopoly, suppression of competition, or affecting prices.

MONOPOLY A privilege or right conferred upon an individual or entity granting it the exclusive power to manufacture, sell and distribute a particular service or commodity; a market condition in which one or a few companies control the sale of a product or service thereby restraining competition in respect to that article or service.

PRIMA FACIE An action in which the plaintiff introduces sufficient evidence to submit an issue to the judge or jury for determination.

RESTRAINT OF COMPETITION Agreement between entities, for the purpose of impeding free trade, that result in a monopoly, the suppression of competition, or affecting prices.

SHERMAN ACT Makes every contract or conspiracy in unreasonable restraint of commerce illegal.

■=■

Missouri v. National Organization for Women

State (P) v. Women's organization (D)

620 F.2d 1301 (8th Cir. 1980), *cert. denied*, 449 U.S. 842 (1980).

NATURE OF CASE: Appeal from dismissal of action for damages under the Sherman Act.

FACT SUMMARY: The National Organization for Women (D) urged organizations not to hold their conventions in Missouri until Missouri (P) ratified the Equal Rights Amendment.

🏛 RULE OF LAW
Using a boycott in a noncompetitive political arena for the purpose of influencing legislation is not proscribed by the Sherman Act.

FACTS: In response to Missouri's failure to ratify the Equal Rights Amendment, the National Organization for Women (NOW) (D) organized a convention boycott of Missouri (P) products and facilities. The State of Missouri (P) filed an action, contending that the boycott violated § 1 of the Sherman Act. The district court held no violation to have occurred and dismissed the case. Missouri (P) appealed.

ISSUE: Is a boycott, politically motivated to achieve a legislative goal, proscribed by the Sherman Act?

HOLDING AND DECISION: (Stephenson, J.) No. Using a boycott in a noncompetitive political arena for the purpose of influencing legislation is not proscribed by the Sherman Act. The focus of the Sherman Act is upon commercial activity. When the goal of economic activity is political rather than commercial, application of the Sherman Act would not further the purpose behind the law. Further, to apply the Act to politically motivated activities would raise serious First Amendment concerns. Had Congress intended to enter such a constitutionally sensitive area, it would have explicitly done so. In this case, NOW's (D) efforts to influence the legislature's action on the Equal Rights Amendment are beyond the scope and intent of the Sherman Act. NOW's (D) boycott activities are privileged based on the First Amendment right to petition and the U.S. Supreme Court's recognition of that important right when it collides with the commercial effects of trade restraints. Affirmed.

▶ ANALYSIS

The Supreme Court arrived at a similar conclusion in a subsequent case, *NAACP v. Claiborne Hardware Co.*, 458 U.S. 886 (1982). The Court found that a civil rights boycott by the NAACP against local store owners was entitled to First Amendment protection, insofar as assembly, petition, and speech were used to further the boycott's aims. The purpose of the NAACP was not to destroy the legitimate competition, but to influence governmental action to further social and racial justice.

■■■

Quicknotes

BOYCOTT A concerted effort to refrain from doing business with a particular person or entity.

EQUAL RIGHTS AMENDMENT Its passage would have mandated a stricter review of classifications based on sex, but it failed to gain the support of thirty-eight states necessary for adoption.

FIRST AMENDMENT Prohibits Congress from enacting any law respecting an establishment of religion, prohibiting the free exercise of religion, abridging freedom of speech or the press, the right of peaceful assembly and the right to petition for a redress of grievances.

RESTRAINT OF TRADE Agreement between entities, for the purpose of impeding free trade, that results in a monopoly, suppression of competition, or affecting prices.

SHERMAN ACT Makes every contract or conspiracy in unreasonable restraint of commerce illegal.

■■■

Vertical Restrictions

Quick Reference Rules of Law

Leegin Creative Leather Products, Inc. v. PSKS, Inc., dba Kay's Kloset...Kay's Shoes

Manufacturer (D) v. Retailer (P)

551 U.S. 877 (2007).

NATURE OF CASE: Appeal from judgment finding a per se violation of § 1 of the Sherman Act.

FACT SUMMARY: Leegin Creative Leather Products, Inc. (Leegin) (D) stopped selling to PSKS, Inc.'s (PSKS's) (P) Kay's Kloset store when Leegin (D) discovered that Kay's Kloset had been marking down Leegin's (D) goods, and PSKS (P) sued for violation of § 1 of the Sherman Act. Leegin (D) contended that the U.S. Supreme Court's longstanding rule of per se illegality for vertical price restrains should be overruled and replaced with a rule of reason.

🏛 **RULE OF LAW**
Vertical price restraints are to be judged by the rule of reason and are not per se illegal.

FACTS: Given its policy of refusing to sell to retailers that discounted its goods, including its Brighton line of fashion accessories, below suggested prices, Leegin Creative Leather Products, Inc. (Leegin) (D) stopped selling to PSKS, Inc.'s (PSKS's) (P) Kay's Kloset store when Leegin (D) discovered that Kay's Kloset had been marking down the entire Brighton line. PSKS (P) filed suit, alleging, inter alia, that Leegin (D) violated the antitrust laws by entering into vertical agreements with its retailers to set minimum resale prices. The U.S. Supreme Court granted certiorari in the case, and Leegin (D) contended that the Court's longstanding rule of per se illegality for vertical price restrains should be overruled and replaced with a rule of reason. [The procedural posture of the case is not indicated in the casebook extract.]

ISSUE: Are vertical price restraints to be judged by the rule of reason and are not per se illegal?

HOLDING AND DECISION: (Kennedy, J.) Yes. Vertical price restraints are to be judged by the rule of reason and are not per se illegal. This case raises the issue of whether the rule of per se illegality for vertical price restraints, first handed down in *Dr. Miles Medical Co. v. John D. Park & Sons Co.*, 220 U.S. 373 (1911), should be replaced with a rule of reason. The accepted standard for testing whether a practice restrains trade in violation of § 1 is the rule of reason, which requires the fact finder to weigh "all of the circumstances," including "specific information about the relevant business" and "the restraint's history, nature, and effect." Resort to per se rules is confined to restraints "that would always or almost always tend to restrict competition and decrease output." Thus, a per se rule is appropriate only after courts have had considerable experience with the type of restraint at issue, and only if they

can predict with confidence that the restraint would be invalidated in all or almost all instances under the rule of reason. Accordingly, any departure from the rule-of-reason standard must be based on demonstrable economic effects rather than on formalistic line drawing. The reasons upon which *Dr. Miles* relied, including a treatise published in 1628, do not justify a per se rule governing the American economy today, given that those reasons did not consider economic effects or procompetitive effects, of vertical price restraints. Therefore, it is necessary to examine, in the first instance, the economic effects of vertical agreements to fix minimum resale prices and to determine whether the per se rule is nonetheless appropriate. Economics literature is replete with procompetitive justifications for a manufacturer's use of resale price maintenance, and the few recent studies on the subject also cast doubt on the conclusion that the practice meets the criteria for a per se rule. The justifications for vertical price restraints are similar to those for other vertical restraints. Minimum resale price maintenance can stimulate interbrand competition among manufacturers selling different brands of the same type of product by reducing intrabrand competition among retailers selling the same brand. This is important because the antitrust laws' primary purpose is to protect interbrand competition. A single manufacturer's use of vertical price restraints tends to eliminate intrabrand price competition; this in turn encourages retailers to invest in services or promotional efforts that aid the manufacturer's position as against rival manufacturers. Resale price maintenance may also give consumers more options to choose among low-price, low-service brands; high-price, high-service brands; and brands falling in between. Absent vertical price restraints, retail services that enhance interbrand competition might be underprovided because discounting retailers can free ride on retailers who furnish services and then capture some of the demand those services generate. Retail price maintenance can also increase interbrand competition by facilitating market entry for new firms and brands and by encouraging retailer services that would not be provided even absent free riding. Setting minimum resale prices may also have anticompetitive effects; and unlawful price fixing, designed solely to obtain monopoly profits, is an ever-present temptation. Resale price maintenance may, for example, facilitate a manufacturer cartel or be used to organize retail cartels. It can also be abused by a powerful manufacturer or retailer. Thus, the potential anticompetitive consequences of vertical price restraints must not be ignored or underestimated.

Continued on next page.

Notwithstanding the risks of unlawful conduct, it cannot be stated with any degree of confidence that retail price maintenance "always or almost always tend[s] to restrict competition and decrease output." Vertical retail-price agreements have either procompetitive or anticompetitive effects, depending on the circumstances in which they were formed; and the limited empirical evidence available does not suggest efficient uses of the agreements are infrequent or hypothetical. A per se rule should not be adopted for administrative convenience alone. Such rules can be counterproductive, increasing the antitrust system's total cost by prohibiting procompetitive conduct the antitrust laws should encourage. And a per se rule cannot be justified by the possibility of higher prices absent a further showing of anticompetitive conduct. The antitrust laws primarily are designed to protect interbrand competition from which lower prices can later result. The argument for a per se rule overlooks that, in general, the interests of manufacturers and consumers are aligned with respect to retailer profit margins. Resale price maintenance has economic dangers. If the rule of reason were to apply, courts would have to be diligent in eliminating their anticompetitive uses from the market. Factors relevant to the inquiry are the number of manufacturers using the practice, the restraint's source, and a manufacturer's market power. The rule of reason is designed and used to ascertain whether transactions are anticompetitive or procompetitive. This standard principle applies to vertical price restraints. As courts gain experience with these restraints by applying the rule of reason over the course of decisions, they can establish the litigation structure to ensure the rule operates to eliminate anticompetitive restraints from the market and to provide more guidance to businesses. Moreover, stare decisis does not compel continued adherence to the per se rule here. Because the Sherman Act is treated as a common-law statute, its prohibition on restraints of trade evolves to meet the dynamics of present economic conditions. The rule of reason's case-by-case adjudication implements this common-law approach. Here, respected economics authorities suggest that the per se rule is inappropriate. Also, both the Department of Justice and the Federal Trade Commission—the antitrust enforcement agencies with the ability to assess the long-term impacts of resale price maintenance agreements—recommend replacing the per se rule with the rule of reason. In addition, this Court has "overruled [its] precedents when subsequent cases have undermined their doctrinal underpinnings." It is not surprising that the Court has distanced itself from *Dr. Miles*' rationales, because the case was decided not long after the Sherman Act was enacted, when the Court had little experience with antitrust analysis. Only eight years after *Dr. Miles*, the Court reined in the decision, holding that a manufacturer can suggest resale prices and refuse to deal with distributors who do not follow them. More recently, the Court has tempered, limited, or overruled once strict nonprice vertical restraint prohibitions. The *Dr. Miles* rule is also inconsistent with a principled framework for it makes little economic sense when analyzed with the Court's other vertical restraint cases. Deciding that procompetitive effects of resale price maintenance are insufficient to overrule *Dr. Miles* would call into question cases those other cases. Finally, PSKS's (P) arguments for reaffirming *Dr. Miles* based on stare decisis do not require a different result, as there is little economic justification for the current differential treatment of vertical price and nonprice restraints. In sum, the per se rule for vertical price restraints is a flawed antitrust doctrine that does not serve the interests of consumers. Accordingly, *Dr. Miles* is overruled, and vertical price restraints are to be judged according to the rule of reason. [Reversed.]

DISSENT: (Breyer, J.) The economic arguments the majority uses to justify disregarding principles of stare decisis have been know for over half a century, yet Congress has repeatedly found in these argument insufficient grounds for overturning the per se rule. The problem with these economics-based arguments is that sometimes they point to beneficial aspects of vertical price restraints and sometimes they point to anticompetitive consequences. For example agreements setting minimum resale prices may have serious anticompetitive effects by diminishing or eliminating price competition among dealers of single or multiple brands. Such agreements can also help reinforce competition-inhibiting behaviors of companies in concentrated industries. Empirical studies have shown that in most cases resale price maintenance tends to produce higher consumer prices than would otherwise be the case. On the other hand, there are procompetitive consumer benefits that may arise from such agreements, including the facilitation of new entry and elimination of free riding. Moreover, where a producer and not a group of dealers, seeks a resale price maintenance agreement, there can be procompetitive benefits because, other things being equal, producers should want to encourage price competition among their dealers. By doing so they will often increase profits by selling more of their product. However, because law, unlike economics, is an administrative system based on rules and precedents, before concluding that courts should apply a rule of reason, the frequency of benefits vs. harms should be determined. Because it is not easy for courts to identify instances in which the benefits are unlikely to outweigh potential harms, *Dr. Miles*'s bright-line, century-old rule should be retained. Without such a rule, it might be impractical for enforcement officials to bring criminal proceedings, and since enforcement resources are limited, that loss may tempt some producers or dealers to enter into agreements that are, on balance, anticompetitive. Additionally, the ordinary criteria for overruling an earlier case have not been met here. First, this is a statutory case, rather than a constitutional case, and the Court applies stare decisis more rigidly to statutory cases. Second, the case being overruled, and all the cases that have affirmed it, is 100 years old; *Dr. Miles* is not a new decision that may have been wrongly decided. Third, the per se rule has not created an

Continued on next page.

unworkable legal regime. To the contrary, the administration of the per se rule has been practical. Fourth, the per se rule is well-settled. Fifth, because contract rights and possibly property rights are at issue militates against overruling, as does longstanding reliance on the rule by Congress and entire sectors of the economy. The majority wrongly minimizes the importance of this reliance and its impact on consumers. Sixth, the fact that a rule of law has become "embedded" in our "national culture" argues strongly against overruling. The only stare decisis justification the majority provides for overturning *Dr. Miles* is that the Court has treated the Sherman Act as a common-law statute. However, the common law tradition would not have permitted overruling *Dr. Miles,* as common-law courts rarely overruled well-established earlier rules outright. Modifying the per se rule to make an exception, for example, for new entry, would be consistent with the common law tradition, but not the approach adopted by the majority. In sum, every state decisis concern the Court has hitherto mentioned counsels against overruling here.

▶ *ANALYSIS*

The effect of the per se rule on antitrust cases is that proof of market power or anticompetitive effects is not necessary. Thus, under the per se rule, evidence of procompetitive effects is excluded, and here, the district court excluded such evidence and the court of appeals affirmed. Under a rule of reason, such evidence would be admitted. Accordingly, the case was remanded for the court's weighing of this and other evidence as to market power and anticompetitive or procompetitive effects.

■■■

Quicknotes

RULE OF REASON The standard for determining whether there has been a violation of § 1 of the Sherman Antitrust Act, requiring a determination of whether the activity unreasonably restrains competition as demonstrated by actual harm.

STARE DECISIS Doctrine whereby courts follow legal precedent unless there is good cause for departure.

VERTICAL AGREEMENTS Agreements entered into by entities at different levels of production for the purpose of restraining trade.

■■■

United States v. Colgate & Co.

Federal government (P) v. Manufacturer (D)

250 U.S. 300 (1919).

NATURE OF CASE: Antitrust action for price controls.

FACT SUMMARY: Colgate & Co. (D) informed retailers that it would refuse to sell to them if they failed to follow Colgate's price list.

🏛 RULE OF LAW
So long as no monopoly is present, a manufacturer is free to impose conditions on retailers as a condition precedent to further sales.

FACTS: Colgate & Co. (Colgate) (D) refused to sell its products to retailers who refused to abide by Colgate's price list. The Government (P) charged that such practices violated the Sherman Act as a restraint on trade and competition. The trial court found that Colgate (D) had no monopolistic control of the market. It had the power and right to deal with anyone it chose. While the retailers could sell to anyone they chose, Colgate (D) was also free to not deal with retailers not conforming to price schedules.

ISSUE: May, a manufacturer make the adherence to price schedules a condition precedent to further orders?

HOLDING AND DECISION: (McReynolds, J.) Yes. Colgate (D) does not control the market. The public may buy numerous "like-kind" products. Colgate (D) is free to sell to anyone it wishes. If it wishes to impose price schedules on retailers carrying its products, it may do so if no formal agreement exists which requires or restricts the retailer's freedom. The coercive practice of refusing to deal with retailers not following price schedules is within Colgate's (D) power to deal as it chooses with its products. This practice does not violate antitrust law. Affirmed.

▶ ANALYSIS

Colgate hinges on the fact that the retailer is not obligated to follow price lists. However, if a retailer wishes to continue carrying Colgate's (D) products, it must accede to the price schedule. Price-fixing agreements violate antitrust law and are unenforceable. It is difficult to see the difference between the two forms of price-fixing. Both are equally anticompetitive and the sanction for the violation of either form is a withholding of future orders. The Court is engaged in an argument over semantics.

■══■

Quicknotes

CONDITION PRECEDENT The happening of an uncertain occurrence, which is necessary before a particular right or interest may be obtained or an action performed.

MONOPOLY A privilege or right conferred upon an individual or entity granting it the exclusive power to manufacture, sell and distribute a particular service or commodity; a market condition in which one or a few companies control the sale of a product or service thereby restraining competition in respect to that article or service.

PRICE-FIXING An illegal combination in violation of the Sherman Antitrust Act entered into for the purpose of setting prices below the natural market rate.

RESTRAINT OF TRADE Agreement between entities, for the purpose of impeding free trade, that results in a monopoly, suppression of competition, or affecting prices.

SHERMAN ACT Makes every contract or conspiracy in unreasonable restraint of commerce illegal.

■══■

State Oil Company v. Khan

Lessor (D) v. Lessee (P)

522 U.S. 3 (1997).

NATURE OF CASE: Action alleging violation of § 1 of the Sherman Act.

FACT SUMMARY: Khan (P) claimed that State Oil Company (D) violated § 1 of the Sherman Act by preventing Khan (P) from raising or lowering gas prices.

🏛 RULE OF LAW
Vertical maximum price fixing is not a per se violation of § 1 of the Sherman Act.

FACTS: Khan (P) entered into an agreement with State Oil Company (D) to lease and operate a gas station and convenience store. The agreement provided that Khan (P) would obtain the station's gasoline supply from State Oil (D) at a price equal to the suggested retail price set by State Oil (D), less a margin of 3.25 cents a gallon. Khan (P) fell behind in lease payments and State Oil (D) brought eviction proceedings. Khan (P) brought suit alleging State Oil (D) had engaged in price fixing in violation of § 1 of the Sherman Act by preventing Khan (P) from raising or lowering gas retail prices. The district court entered summary judgment for State Oil (D) on the basis that Khan (P) failed to state a per se Sherman Act violation or antitrust injury or harm to competition. The court of appeals reversed and the U.S. Supreme Court granted certiorari.

ISSUE: Is vertical maximum price fixing a per se violation of § 1 of the Sherman Act?

HOLDING AND DECISION: (O'Connor, J.) No. Vertical maximum price fixing is not a per se violation of § 1 of the Sherman Act. The Court in *Albrecht v. Herald Co.*, 390 U.S. 145 (1968), held that vertical maximum price fixing is a per se violation of that statute. In reconsidering this decision, the Court has recognized that low prices benefit consumers regardless of how those prices are set, so long as they are above predatory levels and do not threaten competition. Thus it is difficult to maintain that vertically imposed maximum prices could harm consumers or competition to the extent necessary to justify their per se invalidation, but rather could exacerbate problems related to the unrestrained exercise of market power by monopolist-dealers. Therefore, vertical maximum price fixing should be evaluated under the rule of reason.

▶ ANALYSIS

Section 1 violations are typically analyzed under a rule-of-reason approach, requiring the fact finder to decide whether the practice in issue poses an unreasonable restraint on trade, taking into account certain factors. Per se treatment is only appropriate once the court's experience with a particular type of restraint allows it to predict with confidence that the rule of reason will forbid it. Courts are reluctant to adopt per se rules.

Quicknotes

CERTIORARI A discretionary writ issued by a superior court to an inferior court in order to review the lower court's decisions; the Supreme Court's writ ordering such review.

PER SE RULE Rule that business transactions which in themselves constitute restraints on trade obviate the need to demonstrate an injury to competition in making out an antitrust case.

PRICE-FIXING An illegal combination in violation of the Sherman Antitrust Act entered into for the purpose of setting prices below the natural market rate.

RULE OF REASON The standard for determining whether there has been a violation of § 1 of the Sherman Antitrust Act, requiring a determination of whether the activity unreasonably restrains competition as demonstrated by actual harm.

SUMMARY JUDGMENT Judgment rendered by a court in response to a motion by one of the parties, claiming that the lack of a question of material fact in respect to an issue warrants disposition of the issue without consideration by the jury.

Monsanto Co. v. Spray-Rite Service Corp.

Manufacturer (D) v. Distributor (P)

465 U.S. 752 (1984).

NATURE OF CASE: Appeal from award held that Spray-Rite Service Corp. (P) survived a directed verdict by showing Monsanto Co. (D) terminated its price-cutting distributorship in response to complaints from other distributors.

FACT SUMMARY: Monsanto Co. (D) contended that, for it to be shown that it had engaged in price-fixing with its distributors, evidence that they were acting in concert with each other was required.

🏛 RULE OF LAW
To state a cause of action for price-fixing a plaintiff distributor must prove that the manufacturer and other distributors were acting in concert to illegally fix prices.

FACTS: Spray-Rite Service Corp. (Spray-Rite) (P) was a distributor of herbicides, some of which were manufactured by Monsanto Co. (D). Monsanto (D) canceled Spray-Rite's (P) distributorship, and Spray-Rite (P) sued, contending the cancellation was induced by complaints from other Monsanto (D) distributors concerning the low price at which Spray-Rite (P) sold the products. It contended this showed a price-fixing scheme in violation of the Sherman Act. Monsanto (D) moved for a directed verdict on the basis that Spray-Rite (P) had failed to meet its burden of proving a price-fixing scheme. The jury found for Spray-Rite (P), and the court of appeals affirmed the denial of the directed verdict motion. The U.S. Supreme Court granted certiorari.

ISSUE: Can a cause of action for price-fixing be stated merely by showing a distributorship was canceled due to price-cutting complaints from other distributors to the manufacturer?

HOLDING AND DECISION: (Powell, J.) No. To state a cause of action for price-fixing, a plaintiff distributor must prove that the manufacturer and the other distributors were acting in concert to illegally fix prices. The evidentiary standard adopted by the appellate court ignores the danger of failing to distinguish between independent action of the manufacturer and illegal price-fixing. Illegal price-fixing requires more than a showing of cancellation due to distributor complaints. It requires a showing of concerted action. Thus, the standard adopted by the court of appeals was inadequate. However, evidence was presented to show Monsanto (D) had in fact threatened price-cutting distributors with cancellation. Such distributors then agreed to sell at Monsanto's (D) price. This clearly established the requisite concerted action. Affirmed.

CONCURRENCE: (Brennan, J.) The Court correctly upholds long-standing precedent in reaffirming the rule upon which it relied today.

▶ ANALYSIS

It must be borne in mind that not all activities jointly undertaken by manufacturers and distributors are illegal. Nonprice restrictions may be improved by the manufacturer and agreed to by distributors without running afoul of the antitrust laws. These restrictions may of course cross the line of prohibition and are, therefore, judged by the "Rule of Reason." Concerted actions relating to price are per se illegal.

━━━

Quicknotes

CERTIORARI A discretionary writ issued by a superior court to an inferior court in order to review the lower court's decisions; the Supreme Court's writ ordering such review.

DIRECTED VERDICT A verdict ordered by the court in a jury trial.

PRICE-FIXING An illegal combination in violation of the Sherman Act entered into for the purpose of setting prices below the natural market rate.

RULE OF REASON The standard for determining whether there has been a violation of § 1 of the Sherman Antitrust Act, requiring a determination of whether the activity unreasonably restrains competition as demonstrated by actual harm.

━━━

Continental T.V., Inc. v. GTE Sylvania, Inc.

Franchisee (D) v. Franchisor (P)

433 U.S. 36 (1977).

NATURE OF CASE: Appeal from reversal of an award for damages in an action based on restraint of trade.

FACT SUMMARY: GTE Sylvania, Inc. (P), a manufacturer, argued that its prohibition against the sale of its products other than from specified locations should be analyzed under the rule of reason, while Continental T.V., Inc. (D), its franchisee, recommended a per se approach.

> **RULE OF LAW**
> A nonprice vertical restraint should be judged under the rule of reason.

FACTS: To increase its declining market share in national television sales, GTE Sylvania, Inc. (Sylvania) (P) adopted a franchise plan, limiting the number of franchises for any given area and requiring each franchisee to sell his Sylvania (P) products only from the location or locations at which he was franchised. One of Sylvania's (P) franchisees, Continental T.V., Inc. (Continental) (D), protested Sylvania's (P) decision to grant a new franchise only a mile from Continental's (D) San Francisco location. Sylvania (P) later denied Continental's (D) application for a franchise in Sacramento. As relations between the two deteriorated, Sylvania (P) reduced Continental's (D) credit line, after which Continental (D) withheld all payments owed. Sylvania (P) terminated Continental's (D) franchises and filed a diversity action to recover the moneys owed and the secured merchandise held by Continental (D). Continental (D) filed a cross-claim, alleging restraint of trade in violation of the Sherman Act. The jury was instructed that, if it found territorial restrictions on Sylvania's (P) part, it must conclude that a per se violation of the Sherman Act had occurred. The jury did so find and awarded damages to Continental (D). The court of appeals reversed, having concluded that a rule of reason applied. Continental (D) appealed.

ISSUE: Should a nonprice vertical restraint be judged under the rule of reason?

HOLDING AND DECISION: (Powell, J.) Yes. A nonprice vertical restraint should be judged under the rule of reason. The district court's jury instruction in this case was based on the rationale of *United States v. Arnold, Schwinn & Co.*, 388 U.S. 365 (1967). However, per se rules of illegality like the one stated in *Schwinn* are appropriate only when they relate to conduct that is manifestly anticompetitive. Vertical restrictions like Sylvania's (P) location clause promote interbrand competition by allowing the manufacturer to achieve certain efficiencies in the distribution of his products. These "redeeming virtues" are implicit in every decision sustaining vertical restrictions under the rule of reason. Because there is no persuasive support for expanding the per se rule of *Schwinn*, it must be overruled. Thus, the

rule of reason governs the vertical restriction at issue here, and the decision of the court of appeals is affirmed.

CONCURRENCE: (White, J.) While the location clause at issue here is not a per se violation of the Sherman Act and should be judged under the rule of reason, this result does not require overruling *Schwinn*. This case is distinguishable from *Schwinn* because Sylvania's (P) conduct carried with it less potential for restraint of intrabrand competition and more potential for stimulating interbrand competition.

ANALYSIS

Section 1 of the Sherman Act prohibits every contract, combination, or conspiracy in restraint of trade or commerce. Since the early years of this century, a judicial gloss on the statutory language of § 1 of the Sherman Act has established the "rule of reason" as the prevailing standard of analysis. The Court noted that the great weight of scholarly opinion had been critical of the *Schwinn* decision, and a number of the federal courts confronted with analogous vertical restrictions had sought to limit its reach.

Quicknotes

COMBINATION (ANTITRUST DEFINITION) Alliance of entities, for the purpose of impeding free trade, that results in a monopoly, suppression of competition, or affecting prices.

CONSPIRACY Concerted action by two or more persons to accomplish some unlawful purpose.

DIVERSITY ACTION An action commenced by a citizen of one state against a citizen of another state or against an alien, involving an amount in controversy of $10,000 or more, over which the federal court has jurisdiction.

PRICE-FIXING An illegal combination in violation of the Sherman Act entered into for the purpose of setting prices below the natural market rate.

RESTRAINT OF TRADE Agreement between entities, for the purpose of impeding free trade, that results in a monopoly, suppression of competition, or affecting prices.

RULE OF REASON The standard for determining whether there has been a violation of § 1 of the Sherman Antitrust Act, requiring a determination of whether the activity unreasonably restrains competition as demonstrated by actual harm.

SHERMAN ACT Makes every contract or conspiracy in unreasonable restraint of commerce illegal.

Tampa Electric Co. v. Nashville Coal Co.

Public utility (D) v. Coal company (P)

365 U.S. 320 (1961).

NATURE OF CASE: Defense under § 3 of the Clayton Act to a breach of contract action.

FACT SUMMARY: Tampa Electric Co. (D) entered into a 20-year coal requirements contract with Nashville Coal Co. (P).

RULE OF LAW
Where the buyer and seller are in the same state, the relevant market may still be found to be regional or even national.

FACTS: Tampa Electric Co. (Tampa) (D) entered into a 20-year contract with Nashville Coal Co. (P) to purchase all of its coal requirements to operate its generators. Tampa (D) subsequently refused to honor its contract and commitments. Nashville Coal (P) sued, and Tampa (D) alleged as a defense that the contract violated § 3 of the Clayton Act. Tampa (D) alleged that its obligation foreclosed a substantial share of the Florida coal market to competitors. The court found that the relevant market was Florida and the contract involved 18 percent of the total coal sold there. Summary judgment was rendered in favor of Tampa (D) on this basis. Nashville Coal (P) appealed alleging that the relevant market was composed of a number of Southern states and the contract only constituted a small share of this market.

ISSUE: Where the buyer and seller are from the same state, should the state rather than the natural multistate market be deemed the relevant market for antitrust purposes?

HOLDING AND DECISION: (Clark, J.) No. In determining the appropriate market it is necessary to consider the area in which the seller and its competitors do business. An artificial market based on the seller and purchaser cannot be created. Here, Nashville Coal (P) does business in an area composed from several states. Its contract with Tampa (D) constitutes less than one percent of this larger market. It is immaterial that the contract, over the 20-year period, will be worth $128 million. The total sales in the relevant market exceed $1 billion per year. Moreover, utilities must be able to obtain adequate power sources to operate their generators. The public's need for power must be protected. Requirements contracts are not per se unlawful and will only be violative of § 3 where they foreclose a substantial share of the market. The contract herein has no such anticompetitive effect. Reversed.

ANALYSIS

Tampa Electric differs from most exclusive dealings cases in that Tampa (D) sought the long-term contract. It then sought to escape from its liabilities by alleging that antitrust law had been violated. It would seem that where a buyer requests a long-term contract, antitrust policy should not be violated. Tampa (D) was not attempting any anticompetitive practice. It appears that the court focused on the activities of the wrong party in deciding this case.

Quicknotes

BREACH OF CONTRACT Unlawful failure by a party to perform its obligations pursuant to contract.

CLAYTON ACT Legislation passed by the U.S. Congress in 1914 as an amendment to clarify and supplement the Sherman Antitrust Act of 1890. The act prohibited various anti-competitive business practices and gave labor certain rights in disputes with management. It declared that "the labor of a human being is not a commodity or article of commerce."

REQUIREMENTS CONTRACT An agreement pursuant to which one party agrees to purchase all his required goods or services from the other party exclusively for a specified time period.

SUMMARY JUDGMENT Judgment rendered by a court in response to a motion by one of the parties, claiming that the lack of a question of material fact in respect to an issue warrants disposition of the issue without consideration by the jury.

Times-Picayune Publishing Co. v. United States

Publishing company (D) v. Federal government (P)

345 U.S. 594 (1953).

NATURE OF CASE: Action to enjoin an advertising tying arrangement.

FACT SUMMARY: In order to place an ad in the *Times-Picayune*, the only morning paper in New Orleans, an ad had to be placed in an affiliated afternoon paper.

🏛 RULE OF LAW
A tying arrangement is only illegal under the Sherman Act where a monopolistic position is held and a substantial volume of commerce in the "tied" product is restrained.

FACTS: The Times-Picayune Publishing Co. (Times-Picayune) (D) published the only morning paper in New Orleans. The city had two afternoon papers, the *States* (affiliated with the *Times-Picayune*) and the *Item*. In order to secure more advertising for the *States*, Times-Picayune (D) required that all advertising placed in the *Times-Picayune* also be placed in the *States*. The Government (P) brought suit under § 1 of the Sherman Act, alleging that this was an impermissible restraint on commerce and competition. The district court granted an injunction, finding that many advertisers could not afford to place ads in both afternoon papers and were forced to use the *States* if they wished to advertise in the *Times-Picayune* (D). Times-Picayune (D) argued that it was not a monopoly and therefore the tying arrangement did not violate the Sherman Act.

ISSUE: Where no monopoly is present, does a tying arrangement which restrains trade violate the Sherman Act?

HOLDING AND DECISION: (Clark, J.) No. To violate § 1 of the Sherman Act, both a monopolistic position must be held and free commerce in the "tied" product must be restrained. To establish a monopolistic condition only the *Times-Picayune's* dominance may be considered. The *Times-Picayune* controlled only about 40 percent of the advertising dollars spent on newspaper ads. This was not a dominant position in the market since if split in thirds, its share would be 33 percent. This small increment over average did not give the *Times-Picayune* the type of dominance over the market which the Sherman Act's prohibitions are directed at. It had no copyright or patent on the news and advertisers were free to reject the "package deal" and to advertise in the Item. If the Government (P) had brought its action under § 3 of the Clayton Act it would only have had to prove monopolistic dominance or a significant restraint, not both as is required under the Sherman Act. Here, legitimate business aims caused the tying arrangement. The mere refusal to sell one's product or service is not a per se violation. Reversed.

▶ ANALYSIS

Market dominance is presumed where a patented or copyrighted article is involved. The position in the *Times-Picayune* case of economic dominance has been gradually eroded by such cases as *Northern Pacific Railway Co. v. U.S.*, 356 U.S. 1 (1958) and *U.S. v. Loew's, Inc.*, 371 U.S. 38, 45-47 (1962). These cases held that sufficient economic power with respect to the tying product was sufficient. This is an amorphous standard involving the buyer's freedom of choice.

■══■

Quicknotes

RESTRAINT OF TRADE Agreement between entities, for the purpose of impeding free trade, that results in a monopoly, suppression of competition, or affecting prices.

SHERMAN ACT Makes every contract or conspiracy in unreasonable restraint of commerce illegal.

TYING CONTRACT An agreement that a seller will only sell a specified product to a buyer if the buyer also agrees to purchase another product.

■══■

Northern Pacific Railway v. United States

Railroad (D) v. Federal government (P)

356 U.S. 1 (1958).

NATURE OF CASE: Action to enjoin tying agreements in leases and deeds to real property.

FACT SUMMARY: Northern Pacific Railway (D) sold a vast amount of land containing preferential shipping agreements to various purchasers.

RULE OF LAW
Where a seller exercises economic dominance over a market so that the purchaser's free exercise of judgment is curtailed, no tying arrangements are permissible.

FACTS: As an inducement to build a railroad, Northern Pacific Railway (Railway) (D) was given vast amounts of land by the Government (P) and a number of states. It later sold or leased a large portion of this land. As a condition of lease or sale it was agreed that any shipping to be done would be given to the railroad if it met the price of competitors and gave equal service. The Government (P) argued that this type of tying arrangement violated the Sherman Act, and that the vast amount of land owned by the Railway (D) gave it a position of economic dominance so that buyers had no choice but to accept the arrangement. The Railway (D) argued that it was not a monopoly within the meaning of *Times-Picayune*, 345 U.S. 594 (1953), and the restriction was not unreasonable per se. It further argued that it had agreed to meet the price and service of its competition.

ISSUE: Where a seller occupies a position of economic dominance in a market, is a tying arrangement restraining competition illegal per se?

HOLDING AND DECISION: (Black, J.) Yes. Tying arrangements are unreasonable whenever a party has sufficient economic power with respect to the tying product to appreciably restrain free competition in the market for the tied product, and a "not insubstantial" amount of interstate commerce is affected. The preferential shipping clause restrained trade and free competition. By virtue of its land sales, its competitors were denied a substantial amount of business. As an interstate railroad, a substantial amount of interstate commerce was affected. The vast land holdings with many preferential locations gave the Railway (D) a position of economic dominance that it used to restrain competition. Dominance is merely sufficient economic power to restrain free competition in the tied product. Having been established here, the arrangement is illegal per se, and reasonableness will not be considered. Affirmed.

ANALYSIS

Tying arrangements may be legal if (1) the purchaser is free to use or not use the tied product; (2) there are reasonable alternatives; and (3) the seller does not occupy a monopolistic position in the market. In any situation such as this, it is important to show that the tying agreement was reasonable. C.f. *F.T.C. v. Sinclair Refining Co.*, 261 U.S. 463 (1923).

Quicknotes

MONOPOLY A privilege or right conferred upon an individual or entity granting it the exclusive power to manufacture, sell and distribute a particular service or commodity; a market condition in which one or a few companies control the sale of a product or service thereby restraining competition in respect to that article or service.

SHERMAN ACT Makes every contract or conspiracy in unreasonable restraint of commerce illegal.

TYING AGREEMENT An agreement that a seller will only sell a specified product to a buyer if the buyer also agrees to purchase another product.

Jefferson Parish Hospital District No. 2 v. Hyde

Hospital (D) v. Physician (P)

466 U.S. 2 (1984).

NATURE OF CASE: Appeal from denial of damages for violation of antitrust regulations.

FACT SUMMARY: The court of appeals held that Jefferson Parish Hospital District No. 2's (D) contract with a group of anesthesiologists was illegal per se under the antitrust laws.

🏛 RULE OF LAW
Tie-in agreements are illegal only if the market power of the owner of the tying product allows him to unilaterally affect prices.

FACTS: Jefferson Parish Hospital District No. 2 (Jefferson) (D) executed a contract agreeing to require all consumers of their hospital operating rooms to use anesthesiologists employed by Roux and Associates. Hyde (P) sued after being denied hospital privileges based on the contract, contending the contract illegally tied the purchase of operating room use with a fixed source of anesthesiological services, in violation of antitrust laws. Jefferson (D) argued that since only 30 percent of the market for operating rooms belonged to other hospitals, it had an insufficient market share to manipulate consumers into using unwanted anesthesiologists. The district court dismissed the complaint, and the court of appeals reversed, holding the contract illegal per se. The U.S. Supreme Court granted certiorari.

ISSUE: Are tie-in agreements illegal per se regardless of the market power of the seller of the tying product?

HOLDING AND DECISION: (Stevens, J.) No. Tie-in agreements are illegal only if the market power of the owner of the operating rooms at Jefferson (D) went to other hospitals. Thus, Jefferson (D) did not have a sufficient market share to force patients to buy the tied product—the anesthesiologists affiliated with Roux. As a result, the agreement did not illegally fix prices. Reversed and remanded.

CONCURRENCE: (Brennan, J.) This agreement was not illegal per se.

CONCURRENCE: (O'Connor, J.) This agreement was not per se illegal. However, rather than analyzing it under the per se test, it should have been analyzed under the "Rule of Reason." Yet, even under this standard, it was not illegal. Tying arrangements have been subject to per se analysis only where there is proof that there is market power and anticompetitive effect. This requires an elaborate inquiry into the economic effects of the tying arrangement. Thus, applying a per se test in tying cases involves the costs of the rule of reason approach without achieving its benefits. Applying the per se test in tying cases has also led to a great deal of confusion. Therefore, the per se label applied to tying arrangements should be abandoned in favor of an inquiry on adverse economic effects, as well as potential economic benefits. Under the rule of reason, tying arrangements should be disapproved only where the tie-ins have a demonstrable exclusionary impact in the tied product market, or where the tie-ins facilitate the harmful exercise of market power that the seller possesses in the tying product market. To find economically harmful tying, power in the market for the tying product must be used to create additional market power in the market for the tied product, and the two markets and the two tied products must satisfy three threshold criteria. First, the seller must have power in the tying product market. Second, there must be a substantial threat that the tying seller will acquire market power in the tied-product market. Third, there must be a coherent economic basis for treating the tying and the tied products as distinct. However, under the rule of reason analysis, even where all three of these threshold requirements are met, a tying arrangement may be lawful where it entails economic benefits as well as harms and those benefits outweigh the harms. Here, applying these criteria, Jefferson (D) has market power, and it also poses a threat of acquiring market power over the provision of anesthesiological services by tying the sale of anesthesia to the sale of other hospital services. Nonetheless, the third threshold criteria, is not satisfied here: there is no sound economic reason for treating surgery and anesthesia services as separate services. Patients are interested in purchasing anesthesia only in connection with other hospital services, so Jefferson (D) cannot acquire additional market power by selling the two services together. Even if these services are distinct, here, tying does not violate § 1 of the Sherman Act because tying will not increase the seller's already absolute power over the volume of production of the tied product. On the other hand, such tying will confer significant benefits on Jefferson (D) and the patients it serves by improving patient care and efficient hospital operation. Finally, the contract here does not constitute exclusive dealing. There is no evidence that Jefferson (D) will block the availability of anesthesiologists that might deprive other hospitals of access to needed services, or that Roux associates will unreasonably narrow the range of choices available to other anesthesiologists in search of a hospital or patients. Therefore, the arrangement must be sustained under the rule of reason.

▶ ANALYSIS

In this case the Court points out tying arrangements carry pernicious qualities which must be closely scrutinized in

Continued on next page.

light of the Sherman Act. However, they should only be condemned if they restrain competition by forcing purchases which would otherwise not be made.

■═■

Quicknotes

CERTIORARI A discretionary writ issued by a superior court to an inferior court in order to review the lower court's decisions; the Supreme Court's writ ordering such review.

PER SE RULE Rule that business transactions which in themselves constitute restraints on trade obviate the need to demonstrate an injury to competition in making out an antitrust case.

RULE OF REASON The standard for determining whether there has been a violation of § 1 of the Sherman Antitrust Act, requiring a determination of whether the activity unreasonably restrains competition as demonstrated by actual harm.

TYING AGREEMENT An agreement that a seller will only sell a specified product to a buyer if the buyer also agrees to purchase another product.

■═■

Eastman Kodak Co. v. Image Technical Services, Inc.

Photo equipment manufacturer (D) v. Independent servicers (P)

504 U.S. 451 (1992).

NATURE OF CASE: Appeal from reversal of summary judgment dismissal of an antitrust action.

FACT SUMMARY: Eastman Kodak Co. (D), accused of antitrust violations with respect to repair of its units, contended that its lack of market power in the original equipment market necessarily precluded market power in repair of these units.

🏛 RULE OF LAW
Lack of market power as to primary equipment does not preclude market power in derivative aftermarkets.

FACTS: Eastman Kodak Co. (Kodak) (D), a manufacturer of photocopy equipment, held a significant segment of the market for this equipment, although the market remained competitive. Kodak (D) also provided repair and servicing of its equipment. In the early 1980s, small businesses began to appear offering independent servicing of Kodak (D) equipment. Kodak (D) responded by limiting replacement parts to buyers who agreed to use Kodak's (D) aftermarket services. The independent servicers, unable to obtain spare parts, largely were driven out of the market. In 1987, a class-action suit was brought by various independent servicing concerns. Kodak (D) successfully moved for summary judgment in the district court. The Ninth Circuit reversed, and the U.S. Supreme Court granted review.

ISSUE: Does lack of market power as to primary equipment preclude market power in derivative aftermarkets?

HOLDING AND DECISION: (Blackmun, J.) No. Lack of market power as to primary equipment does not preclude market power in derivative aftermarkets. Section 1 of the Sherman Act prohibits "tying," that is, an agreement to sell one product only on the condition that the buyer also purchase a tied product, provided that the seller has "appreciable economic power" in the tying market and the arrangement affects a substantial volume of commerce in the tied market. The tying market here is parts, the tied market is service. Kodak (D) urges adoption of a general rule, with which the district court agreed, that lack of monopoly power in the primary equipment market necessarily precludes market power in the aftermarkets. This is based on the contention that elasticity in the primary market necessitates elasticity in the aftermarket as a buyer who finds the aftermarket unappealing may go to a different primary market. This may be true in some cases but is not so necessarily true as to be capable of statement as a rule of law. Lack of consumer product information can undercut this analysis. Also, high initial investment cost may lead a consumer to remain in a noncompetitive

aftermarket. Instead, Kodak (D) has raised an issue to be passed upon by the trier of fact. For this reason, the court of appeals properly reversed the summary judgment as to § 1 of the Sherman Act. [The Court also agreed that Kodak (D) had engaged in predatory behavior, in violation of § 2 of the Sherman Act.] Affirmed.

DISSENT: (Scalia, J.) This Court has never before embraced the majority's thesis that a seller's inherent control over the unique parts for its own brand amounts to the sort of "market power" sufficient to apply the per se rule against tying arrangements. Since Kodak (D) lacked such market power, it also lacked the monopoly power to warrant heightened scrutiny of its exclusionary behavior.

▶ ANALYSIS

It would seem that a manufacturer could evade the scope of the Court's decision. The requirement of "appreciable economic power" in the tying market would not be met if the manufacturer could create a level of consumer demand for "original equipment" replacement parts (the tying product) for the original product that would turn consumers away from competitor-manufactured parts. The original manufacturer could do this by including an attractive warranty valid only when the product is serviced and repaired by authorized dealers using original replacement parts.

■■■

Quicknotes

CLASS ACTION A suit commenced by a representative on behalf of an ascertainable group that is too large to appear in court, who shares a commonality of interests and who will benefit from a successful result.

SUMMARY JUDGMENT Judgment rendered by a court in response to a motion by one of the parties, claiming that the lack of a question of material fact in respect to an issue warrants disposition of the issue without consideration by the jury.

TYING Selling a specified product to a buyer only if the buyer also agrees to purchase another product.

■■■

United States v. Microsoft Corp.

Federal government (P) v. Software corporation (D)

147 F.3d 935 (D.C. Cir. 1998).

NATURE OF CASE: Antitrust suit for violation of consent decree barring tying of separate products.

FACT SUMMARY: A consent decree prohibited Microsoft Corp. (D) from tying "other products," other than integrated products, to the sales of its personal computers. The Government (P) brought suit alleging that Microsoft's (D) bundling of its Internet browser with Windows 95 violated the consent decree.

> ## 🏛 RULE OF LAW
> A product is integrated where it combines the functionalities of two separate products to produce benefits that only the unified combination can achieve.

FACTS: A consent decree entered into in 1995 prohibited Microsoft Corp. (D) from tying "other products," other than integrated products, to the sales of its personal computers. Microsoft (D) was barred from entering into any license agreement that was conditioned upon the licensing of any separate product. The Government (P), fearing that Microsoft (D) was using its Internet browser (the tied product) to gain an unfair advantage on Netscape, its main rival as an Internet service provider, brought suit alleging that Microsoft's (D) bundling of its Internet browser with Windows 95 violated the consent decree. The district court ordered a preliminary injunction pending discovery. The court of appeals granted review.

ISSUE: Is a product integrated where it combines the functionalities of two separate products to produce benefits that only the unified combination can achieve?

HOLDING AND DECISION: (Williams, J.) Yes. A product is integrated where it combines the functionalities of two separate products to produce benefits that only the unified combination can achieve. First, integration requires a degree of unity, so that a product that can be created simply by combining two separate, independent products is not an integrated product. With regard to computer software and hardware, this means that where an end user can buy separate products and combine them to form a single product, the single product, if offered by a manufacturer, is not an "integrated" product. Here, Windows 95 unites the functionality of a browser, Internet Explorer (IE), with the functionality of an operating system in a way that purchasers could not. Also, the combination offered by the manufacture must be better in some respect than offering the two functionalities separately. This understanding is consistent with tying law, but does not mean that a court must find that an integrated product is superior to its stand-alone rivals; the combination must merely bring some advantage. On the facts of this case, Microsoft (D) has met its burden of providing plausible benefits that accrued from its integrated design as compared to an operating system combined with a stand-alone browser, such as Netscape's Navigator. Finally, there must be not only some benefits to the combination, but there must also be some reason that the manufacturer, and not the OEM or end user is doing the combining. Based on the available record, the Windows 95/IE package is a genuine integration, and, therefore, Microsoft (D) is not barred from offering it as one product under the consent decree. Reversed.

▶ ANALYSIS

In a more recent case involving Microsoft's (D) operating system and Internet browser, the district court found that Microsoft's (D) combination of Windows 98 and Internet Explorer (IE) constituted an illegal tying arrangement because the products were separate and consumers were forced to pay for the tied product even if the price of the product was zero. The court of appeals reversed again, this time finding that the tying arrangements must be considered under a rule of reason, and not per se, analysis. Although it gave weight to the separate products test, it added that the analysis did not stop there; also to be considered was whether the bundling of the two products could result in efficiencies, *United States v. Microsoft*, 87 F. Supp. 2d 30 (D.D.C. 2000), *rev'd* 253 F.3d 34 (D.C. Cir. 2001).

■=■

Quicknotes

CONSENT DECREE A decree issued by a court of equity ratifying an agreement between the parties to a lawsuit; an agreement by a defendant to cease illegal activity.

PRELIMINARY INJUNCTION A judicial mandate issued to require or restrain a party from certain conduct; used to preserve a trial's subject matter or to prevent threatened injury.

RULE OF REASON The standard for determining whether there has been a violation of § 1 of the Sherman Antitrust Act, requiring a determination of whether the activity unreasonably restrains competition as demonstrated by actual harm.

■=■

United States v. Microsoft Corp.

Federal government (P) v. Software company (D)

253 F.3d 34 (D.C. Cir.), *cert. denied*, 534 U.S. 952 (2001).

NATURE OF CASE: Appeal from judgment finding defendant engaged in illegal tying.

FACT SUMMARY: The Government (P) alleged that Microsoft Corp. (D) had created an illegal tying arrangement by bundling the Internet Explorer web browser with its Windows operating system (OS).

🏛 **RULE OF LAW**
The rule of reason, rather than per se analysis, governs the legality of tying arrangements involving platform software products.

FACTS: The Government (P) alleged (among other things) that Microsoft Corp. (D) had created an illegal tying arrangement by bundling the Internet Explorer (IE) web browser with its Windows operating system (OS). The facts underlying the tying allegation were that Microsoft (D): (1) required Windows licensees to license IE at a single price; (2) refused to allow OEMs to uninstall or remove IE from the Windows desktop; (3) designed Windows so users could not remove IE; and (4) designed Windows to override users' choice of default Web browser. The district court concluded that Microsoft's (D) contractual and technological bundling of the IE web browser (the "tied" product) with its Windows OS (the "tying" product) resulted in a tying arrangement that was per se unlawful. Microsoft (D) argued that the OS and IE were not separate products. The court of appeals granted review.

ISSUE: Does the rule of reason, rather than per se analysis, govern the legality of tying arrangements involving platform software products?

HOLDING AND DECISION: (Per curiam) Yes. The rule of reason, rather than per se analysis, governs the legality of tying arrangements involving platform software products. The district court concluded that Microsoft's (D) contractual and technological bundling of IE with the Windows OS resulted in a tying arrangement that was per se unlawful. Under the separate-products test, as announced in *Jefferson Parish Hospital District No. 2 v. Hyde*, 466 U.S. 2 (1984), whether one or two products are involved does not turn on the functional relation between them, so even if one product is completely useless without the other, that does not make them a single product for tying law. Also, there must be sufficient consumer demand for the purchase of the tied product separate from the tying product to identify a separate, distinct market in which it is efficient to offer the tied product on its own. The core concern is that tying prevents goods from competing directly for consumer choice on their merits. However, not all ties are bad. For example, bundling can save distribution and consumer transaction costs, and can capitalize on economies of

scope. This separate-products test, however, is not a direct inquiry into the efficiencies of a bundle. Instead, the test chooses proxies that balance cost savings against reducing consumer choice. In fact, there is merit to Microsoft's (D) argument that the entire consumer demand test would chill innovation to the detriment of consumers by preventing firms from integrating into their products new functionality previously provided by stand-alone products. In other words, the separate-products element of the per se rule may not give newly integrated products a fair shake. As the U.S. Supreme Court has warned, it is only after considerable experience with certain business relationships that courts classify them as per se violations. Here, Microsoft (D) argues that IE and Windows is an integrated physical product and that the bundling of IE APIs with Windows makes the latter a better applications platform for third-party software. But it is unclear how the benefits from IE APIs could be achieved by quality standards for different browser manufacturers. That is why a per se test that conclusively presumes the illegality of novel purported efficiencies from a software firm's decision to sell multiple functionalities as a single package, without elaborate inquiry as to the precise harm caused by such bundling, is troubling. The failure of the separate-products test to screen out certain cases of productive integration is particularly troubling in platform software markets. Not only is integration common in such markets, but it is common among firms without market power. In this case, there is not enough empirical evidence regarding the effect of Microsoft's (D) practice on the amount of consumer surplus created or consumer choice foreclosed by the integration of added functionality into platform software to exercise sensible judgment regarding that entire class of behavior. There is a need to know more than we do about the actual impact of these arrangements on competition to decide whether they should be classified as per se violations of the Sherman Act. Until then, the tying arrangements at issue in this case must be remanded for evaluation under the rule of reason. On remand, the Government (P) will have to show that Microsoft's (D) conduct unreasonably restrained competition, by making an inquiry into the actual effect of Microsoft's (D) conduct on competition in the tied good market (the putative market for browsers). Vacated and remanded.

▶ **ANALYSIS**

Because the Government (P) had lost on the question of market power as it related to the Government's (P) claim that Microsoft (D) had attempted to monopolize the browser

Continued on next page.

market, the court prohibited the Government (P) from relying on any theory on remand that would require the definition of a browser market or a showing of high entry barriers to such a market. This became moot because on remand, the Government (P) settled the case with Microsoft (D) and, as part of that settlement, dropped its tying claim.

■═■

Quicknotes

RULE OF REASON The standard for determining whether there has been a violation of § 1 of the Sherman Antitrust Act, requiring a determination of whether the activity unreasonably restrains competition as demonstrated by actual harm.

TYING Selling a specified product to a buyer only if the buyer also agrees to purchase another product.

■═■

Illinois Tool Works, Inc. v. Independent Ink, Inc.

Patent holder (D) v. Manufacturer (P)

547 U.S. 28 (2006).

NATURE OF CASE: Appeal from reversal of summary judgment for defendant in action for, inter alia, violation of § 1 of the Sherman Act.

FACT SUMMARY: Independent Ink, Inc. (P), an ink manufacturer, contended that Trident, Inc. and its parent company, Illinois Tool Works, Inc. (D), which held a patent on a printhead system and tied its unpatented ink to the printhead system, necessarily had market power in the market for the tying product as a matter of law solely by virtue of the patent on its printhead system, thereby rendering the tying arrangements per se violations of § 1 of the Sherman Act.

> ## RULE OF LAW
> The mere fact that a tying product is patented does not support the presumption of market power in the patented product.

FACTS: Trident, Inc. and its parent company, Illinois Tool Works, Inc. (collectively "Trident") (D) manufactured and marketed printing systems that included a patented printhead and ink container and unpatented ink, which they sold to original equipment manufacturers (OEMs) who agreed that they would purchase ink exclusively from Trident (D) and that neither they nor their customers would refill the patented containers with ink of any kind. Independent Ink, Inc. (Independent) (P) developed ink with the same chemical composition as Trident's (D) ink. Trident (D) brought a patent infringement action against Independent (P), but after that action was dismissed, Independent (P) filed suit seeking a judgment of noninfringement and invalidity of Trident's (D) patents on the ground that Trident (D) was engaged in illegal "tying" and monopolization in violation of §§ 1 and 2 of the Sherman Act. Granting summary judgment for Trident (D), the district court rejected Independent's (P) argument that Trident (D) necessarily had market power as a matter of law by virtue of the patent on the printhead system, thereby rendering the tying arrangements per se violations of the antitrust laws. The court of appeals reversed as to the § 1 claim, concluding that it had to follow the U.S. Supreme Court's precedents. The Supreme Court granted certiorari.

ISSUE: Does the mere fact that a tying product is patented support the presumption of market power in the patented product?

HOLDING AND DECISION: (Stevens, J.) No. The mere fact that a tying product is patented does not support the presumption of market power in the patented product. Courts encountered tying arrangements in the course of patent infringement litigation, but over the years, the Court's strong disapproval of tying arrangements has substantially diminished, as the Court has moved from relying on assumptions to requiring a showing of market power in the tying product. The assumption in earlier decisions that such "arrangements serve hardly any purpose beyond the suppression of competition," was rejected in cases involving unpatented tying products, and nothing in the subsequent cases suggested a rebuttable presumption of market power applicable to tying arrangements involving a patent on the tying good. The presumption that a patent confers market power initially arose outside the antitrust context as part of the patent misuse doctrine, and subsequently migrated to antitrust law through the Court's precedent. When Congress codified the patent laws for the first time, it initiated the untwining of the patent misuse doctrine and antitrust jurisprudence. While the Court's antitrust jurisprudence continued to rely on the assumption that tying arrangements generally serve no legitimate business purpose, Congress began chipping away at that assumption in the patent misuse context. Congress eventually amended the Patent Code to eliminate the presumption in the patent misuse context. While that amendment does not expressly refer to the antitrust laws, it invites reappraisal of the Court's per se rule. Based on the congressional judgment reflected in the amendment to the Patent Code, tying arrangements involving patented products should not be evaluated under a per se rule. Instead, any conclusion that an arrangement is unlawful must be supported by proof of power in the relevant market rather than by a mere presumption thereof. Moreover, Independent's (P) alternatives to retention of the per se rule—that the Court endorse a rebuttable presumption that patentees possess market power when they condition the purchase of the patented product on an agreement to buy unpatented goods exclusively from the patentee, or differentiate between tying arrangements involving requirements ties and other types of tying arrangements—are rejected as there is no support for them—either in case law or in the vast majority of academic literature, which recognizes that a patent does not necessarily confer market power. However, because Independent (P) reasonably relied on the Court's prior opinions in moving for summary judgment without offering evidence of the relevant market or proving Trident's (D) power within that market, Independent (P) should be given a fair opportunity to develop and introduce evidence on that issue, as well as other relevant issues, when the case returns to the district court. Vacated and remanded.

▶ ANALYSIS

Some commentators have expressed apprehension that after this decision, big businesses, arguably those more

Continued on next page.

likely to have market power, will be able to tie patented products in the marketplace with no concern for consumer welfare and virtually no fear of negative consequences since the burden of proof will be on those presumably small businesses that claim to have been injured. Others, however, believe that this is not the case, since plaintiffs who have been injured by anticompetitive effects may still prove market power and recover damages, just as in all other tying cases.

■═■

Quicknotes

ASSUMPTION Act of acceptance or presumption of truth without proof of demonstration.

PRESUMPTION A rule of law requiring the court to presume certain facts to be true based on the existence of other facts, thereby shifting the burden of proof to the party against whom the presumption is asserted to rebut.

TYING CONTRACT An agreement that a seller will only sell a specified product to a buyer if the buyer also agrees to purchase another product.

■═■

United States v. Jerrold Electronics Corp.

Federal government (P) v. Electronics Co. (D)

187 F. Supp. 545 (E.D. Pa.), *aff'd per curiam*, 365 U.S. 567 (1961).

NATURE OF CASE: Action based on antitrust violations.

FACT SUMMARY: Because Jerrold Electronics Corp. (Jerrold) (D) would only sell its television antenna systems as a single package, the Government (P) argued that Jerrold's (D) policy was a disguised tie-in.

🏛 RULE OF LAW
A full system sales unit may be reasonable where there are legitimate reasons for selling normally separate items in a combined form and economic conditions justify a policy of compulsory service.

FACTS: Jerrold Electronics Corp. (Jerrold) (D) sold its television antenna systems only as full systems, rather than as separate components, and only in conjunction with a compulsory service policy. Jerrold (D) considered this policy necessary to maintain the integrity of its equipment, which was considered the best available. Others in the field did not sell their systems exclusively as a single package. The number of pieces in each system varied considerably so that hardly any two versions of the alleged product were the same. Although Jerrold (D) sold its system as a single package, it priced each item of equipment individually. Moreover, Jerrold (D) required that only the electronic equipment in the system be purchased from Jerrold (D). Antennas and cable could be purchased elsewhere. The Government (P) brought this action, alleging that Jerrold's (D) policy constituted a tying arrangement in violation of federal antitrust law. Jerrold (D) contended this was not a case of tying the sale of one product to another, but merely the sale of a single product.

ISSUE: May, a full system sales unit be reasonable where there are legitimate reasons for selling normally separate items in a combined form and economic conditions justify a policy of compulsory service?

HOLDING AND DECISION: (Van Dusen, J.) Yes. A full system sales unit may be reasonable where there are legitimate reasons for selling normally separate items in a combined form and economic conditions justify a policy of compulsory service. Initially, Jerrold (D) could not have rendered the service it promised if the customer had been permitted to purchase any kind of equipment he desired. The limited knowledge and instability of equipment made specifications an impractical, if not impossible, alternative. However, as circumstances changed and the need for compulsory service contracts disappeared, the economic reasons for exclusively selling complete systems have been eliminated. Jerrold (D) has not established a need for the continued existence of its policy. Thus, its policy of selling full systems only was lawful at its inception but constituted a violation of § 1 of the Sherman Act and § 3 of the Clayton Act during part of the time it was in effect.

▶ ANALYSIS

The full system contract described above is usually challenged as applying to dealers, rather than to consumers. The downside of such contracts is that they may prevent dealers from purchasing competing lines of products and parts. On the other hand, full system contracts allow for economies of scale in production and distribution, resulting in lower prices.

■■■

Quicknotes

CLAYTON ACT Legislation passed by the U.S. Congress in 1914 as an amendment to clarify and supplement the Sherman Antitrust Act of 1890. The act prohibited various anti-competitive business practices and gave labor certain rights in disputes with management. It declared that "the labor of a human being is not a commodity or article of commerce."

SHERMAN ACT Makes every contract or conspiracy in unreasonable restraint of commerce illegal.

TYING AGREEMENT An agreement that a seller will only sell a specified product to a buyer if the buyer also agrees to purchase another product.

■■■

Monopoly Structure, Power and Conduct

Quick Reference Rules of Law

United States v. American Can Co.

Federal government (P) v. Can combine (D)

230 F. 859 (D. Md. 1916), *appeal dismissed*, 256 U.S. 706 (1921).

NATURE OF CASE: An action to dissolve a company for antitrust violations.

FACT SUMMARY: After a small number of men formed a "combination" that drove almost all other can makers out of the business, the Government (P) sought to dissolve American Can Co. (D) for antitrust violations.

> **RULE OF LAW**
> The right to dissolve a company shall be reserved until such time as the company's dominance and control over an industry make dissolution expedient.

FACTS: Norton (D), the Moores (D), and a few others developed a scheme to form a can combine, which eventually resulted in American Can Co. (D). They induced other can makers to sell out by convincing them that their only choices were to go out voluntarily or be driven out. What was most feared was that a can maker who did not go into the combine would have difficulty in getting tin plate, the raw material of his business. In every case, the option prices offered by American Can (D) were much more than the companies were worth. Almost all the options contained a covenant not to compete in can making for fifteen years. In addition, for six years American Can (D) cut off its competitors from the companies making the best can-making machinery. The Government (P) filed suit, seeking to dissolve American Can (D) for violations of the Anti-Trust Act of 1890.

ISSUE: Shall the right to dissolve the company be reserved until such time as the company's dominance and control over the industry make dissolution expedient?

HOLDING AND DECISION: (Rose, J.) Yes. When a company becomes large and powerful through unlawful acts, but uses that power without injury to the public, the right to dissolve the company shall be reserved until such time as the company's dominance and control over the industry make dissolution expedient. At trial, a great many consumers of cans testified that the price has tended downward. The cans have been more uniformly well made, the manufacturing cost is now less, each employee now receives more wages, and can users are protected against serious delays in delivery. Before the need to use the power reserved arises, Congress will hopefully find some method other than dissolution to deal with the problems that arise when a single corporation absorbs a large part of the productive capacity in any one line.

competition and by potential competition. Those in the trade were satisfied with American Can (D) and did not want it dissolved. The court noted that one who sells only one-half of the cans that are sold does not possess a monopoly in the same sense as he would if he sold all or nearly all of them.

━━■

Quicknotes

COMBINATION (ANTITRUST DEFINITION) Alliance of entities, for the purpose of impeding free trade, that results in a monopoly, suppression of competition, or affecting prices.

DISSOLUTION Annulment or termination of a formal or legal bond, tie or contract.

MONOPOLY A privilege or right conferred upon an individual or entity granting it the exclusive power to manufacture, sell and distribute a particular service or commodity; a market condition in which one or a few companies control the sale of a product or service thereby restraining competition in respect to that article or service.

━━■

ANALYSIS

The record showed that while American Can's (D) power was great, it was limited by a large volume of actual

United States v. Aluminum Co. of America

Federal government (P) v. Aluminum producer (D)

148 F.2d 416 (2d Cir. 1945).

NATURE OF CASE: Appeal from a judgment for the defendant in a suit to dissolve a company for violation of federal antitrust law.

FACT SUMMARY: Arguing that Aluminum Co. of America (Alcoa) (D) was the nation's only producer of aluminum for almost thirty years, the Government (P) sought dissolution of Alcoa (D) for monopolistic behavior.

🏛 RULE OF LAW
An unlawful monopoly exists where a company has sufficient market power to dominate an industry and where it acquired that power by engaging in anticompetitive, or monopolistic, acts.

FACTS: Aluminum Co. of America (Alcoa) (D), a producer of virgin aluminum ingot, entered into four successive "cartels" with foreign manufacturers of aluminum. Alcoa (D) secured covenants from the foreign producers either not to import ingots into the United States (P) at all or to do so under restrictions, which in some cases involved the fixing of prices. As a result of these and other practices, the Government (P) filed suit against Alcoa (D) in 1912, in which a consent decree was entered, declaring several of these covenants unlawful and enjoining their performance. In 1937, the Government (P) again filed suit, seeking additional relief, including dissolution of Alcoa (D) for violating federal antitrust law against monopolistic behavior. The trial court ruled in Alcoa's (D) favor, finding that Alcoa (D) had only 33 percent of the market share. In arriving at that figure, the court included both the virgin ingot and the secondary (scrap) aluminum markets. The Government (P) appealed.

ISSUE: Does an unlawful monopoly exist where a company has sufficient market power to dominate an industry and where it acquired that power by engaging in anticompetitive, or monopolistic, acts?

HOLDING AND DECISION: (Hand, J.) Yes. An unlawful monopoly exists where a company has sufficient market power to dominate an industry and where it acquired that power by engaging in anticompetitive, or monopolistic, acts. However, a company is an "innocent" monopolist where that dominance has been thrust upon it by its own skill or efficiency. Alcoa's (D) size has never been anything other than a monopoly, and it utilized that size for abuse. Given Alcoa's (D) position in 1940, it was not an "innocent" monopolist. The district court incorrectly included the secondary market in its calculation of Alcoa's (D) market share. Alcoa's (D) market share of the virgin ingot market was over 90 percent. Thus, its monopoly of ingot was of the kind covered by § 2 of the Sherman Act, and that part of the judgment which held that it was not, must be reversed.

▶ ANALYSIS

Because of Alcoa's (D) increased efficiency, it was able to sell its ingots at higher prices to independent firms manufacturing aluminum "sheets" while pricing its own sheets lower, thereby effectuating a "price squeeze." Although Judge Hand's court did not find that the price squeeze was part of Alcoa's (D) attempt to monopolize the market, he did articulate a price squeeze test, making it unlawful for a monopolist to charge more than a "fair price" for a primary product while at the same time charging so little for a secondary product that its second-level competitors cannot make a "living profit." However, it is possible that prices that squeeze a "second level" may actually benefit consumers whenever the "second-level" firm is itself a monopolist.

Quicknotes

CARTEL An agreement between manufacturers or producers of the same product so as to form a monopoly.

COVENANT A written promise to do, or to refrain from doing, a particular activity.

MONOPOLY A privilege or right conferred upon an individual or entity granting it the exclusive power to manufacture, sell and distribute a particular service or commodity; a market condition in which one or a few companies control the sale of a product or service thereby restraining competition in respect to that article or service.

PRICE-FIXING An illegal combination in violation of the Sherman Act entered into for the purpose of setting prices below the natural market rate.

SHERMAN ACT Makes every contract or conspiracy in unreasonable restraint of commerce illegal.

United States v. United Shoe Machinery Corp.

Federal government (P) v. Shoe machine manufacturer (D)

110 F. Supp. 295 (D. Mass. 1953), *aff'd per curiam*, 347 U.S. 521 (1954).

NATURE OF CASE: Antitrust action against a monopoly.

FACT SUMMARY: Through patents, service, technological advances and long-term leases of its equipment, United Shoe Machinery Corp. (D) occupied a dominant position in the shoe machinery field.

> 🏛 **RULE OF LAW**
> Where market control and industry dominance is not solely due to the elimination of competition through the unfettered effect of the free enterprise system, an unlawful monopoly may be found.

FACTS: United Shoe Machinery Corp. (United Shoe) (D) controlled approximately 85 percent of the domestic shoe machinery business in the United States. It had achieved this position of dominance through patents, excellent machinery, prompt free repair service, and close working ties with shoe manufacturers. Each year United Shoe (D) spent millions on research seeking to improve its machines. It produced a full line of all machines necessary to handle the many steps necessary to producing shoes. Its major machines were leased rather than sold. Typical leases were for ten years with favorable terms and deposit returns if the machines were kept for the full period or replaced by United Shoe (D) equipment. Equipment actually sold was based on a sliding rate. If United Shoe (D) had competition in the market, it operated on a small profit margin. If no competition existed, it charged a higher price. The Government (P) brought an antitrust action against United Shoe (D). It alleged (1) that United Shoe (D) had secured its monopoly position through unlawful methods in restraint of trade in violation of §§ 1 and 2 of the Sherman Act (*U.S. v. Aluminum Co. of America*, 148 F.2d 416 (2d Cir. 1945)); (2) that United Shoe (D) had the power to exclude competition and had exercised it (*U.S. v. Griffith*, 334 U.S. 100 (1948)); and (3) that United Shoe (D) had violated a broader approach suggested in *Griffith* by acquiring market dominance through the use of methods which were not solely the result of unfettered free competition. The Government (P) argued that the long-term leases, price differentials based on the existence of competition and free service had, as its primary purpose and effect, the establishment and perpetuation of United Shoe's (D) monopoly position. These practices placed entry barriers on the market and were secured by United Shoe's (D) market dominance.

ISSUE: May a manufacturer who has secured its position of dominance through lawful means still be guilty of unlawful monopolistic practices?

HOLDING AND DECISION: (Wyzanski, J.) Yes. United Shoe (D) has not engaged in any unlawful practices;

therefore, the Government's (P) first position cannot prevail under the rationale stated in *Aluminum Company*. A business should not be penalized for obtaining control of the market because it puts out a better product, works harder, etc. Where dominance has been achieved solely through lawful means and within the context of the free enterprise system, no violation of antitrust law has occurred. However, where its practices, even though lawful, are designed to tie customers to it and make entry into the market more difficult, a violation may occur. Whenever such practices are not required by market demands, a violation occurs. Here, United Shoe (D) could have sold its machinery outright. Even though leasing was an industry practice, United Shoe (D) could have been competitive through outright sales. Secondly, its use of a sliding price scale depending on the existence of competition allowed it to take advantage of its size and dominant position. Finally, free service made entry more difficult. Since there were no independent service dealers, a new entrant had to hire and train its personnel in order to compete. Together, these practices show that United Shoe (D) attempted to tie its customers to it by long-term leases, favorable rates and free service. These practices were not strictly the result of free competition and made entry more difficult and expensive. Under the two theories enumerated in *Griffith*, United Shoe's (D) actions violate § 2 of the Sherman Act. Monopolistic motive or intent is immaterial. It is the power or potential to exercise its dominant position which must be curbed. The remedy should attempt to rectify the effect of the monopolistic practices complained of by the Government (P). However, the remedy must be realistically possible. Since United Shoe (D) did most of its business out of one main plant, it was not feasible to break it up. It was also not possible to forbid all leasing. This would drive many manufacturers out of business if they were unable to pay for the equipment. This court cannot regulate United Shoe's (D) pricing structure. There are too many factors which enter into this area. Further, some price regulation must be expected from large manufacturers. The court agrees with the Government (P) that the leases should be purged of all restrictive covenants, all equipment should be offered for sale, and sales terms should be monitored for fairness. Since United Shoe (D) has placed itself in a monopoly position, it cannot complain of different treatment from the rest of the industry. The sale of machinery should eventually create a secondary used machinery market which will curb United's (D) monopoly power. The purging of lease restrictions will remove several entry barriers. Judgment for the Government (P).

Continued on next page.

▶ *ANALYSIS*

It is difficult to imagine how any business controlling a dominant share of a market would not violate one of the three tests enumerated here. No business is conducted to make free competition easy. The strictures of a competitive market make it both desirable and necessary to operate in a method calculated to keep old customers and to acquire new ones. United Shoe (D), as compared to most monopolists prosecuted by the Government (P), was "pure as the driven snow." The key to this decision is the leasing practice. This was calculated to secure for United Shoe (D) a greater share of and control over the market than it would have had through outright sales.

■═■

Quicknotes

MONOPOLY A privilege or right conferred upon an individual or entity granting it the exclusive power to manufacture, sell and distribute a particular service or commodity; a market condition in which one or a few companies control the sale of a product or service thereby restraining competition in respect to that article or service.

RESTRAINT OF TRADE Agreement between entities, for the purpose of impeding free trade, that results in a monopoly, suppression of competition, or affecting prices.

SHERMAN ACT § 2 Makes it a felony to monopolize or attempt to monopolize, or combine or conspire with any other person(s) to monopolize, any part of the trade or commerce among the states or with a foreign country.

TYING AGREEMENT An agreement that a seller will only sell a specified product to a buyer if the buyer also agrees to purchase another product.

■═■

United States v. E.I. du Pont de Nemours & Co.

Federal government (P) v. Manufacturer (D)

351 U.S. 377 (1956).

NATURE OF CASE: Action to enjoin a monopoly.

FACT SUMMARY: E.I. du Pont de Nemours & Co. (D) claimed that its position in the entire flexible packaging materials industry must be considered to determine whether its control of cellophane constituted a monopoly.

🏛 RULE OF LAW
Where competitive substitutes are available, dominance over a single process does not constitute monopolistic control over the market.

FACTS: E.I. du Pont de Nemours & Co. (du Pont) (D) controlled 75 percent of the cellophane market. The Government (P) argued that du Pont (D) was an unlawful monopoly under § 2 of the Sherman Act. The district court found that cellophane was merely one segment of the flexible packaging material market. There were sufficient competitive alternatives available to prevent du Pont (D) from being able to control or affect prices. Du Pont (D) argued that the fact that its patents and know-how prevented competition in the cellophane industry did not constitute a monopoly due to the existence of other competitive substitutes.

ISSUE: Can a monopoly be shown where there are competitive alternatives available to the monopolized process?

HOLDING AND DECISION: (Reed, J.) No. In order to determine the existence of a monopoly, the entire market must be considered. The market is determined by considering all reasonably interchangeable alternatives based on price, use and quality. If other products may be used instead of the alleged monopolistic product and their cost and quality is comparable, no monopoly exists. The district court found that cellophane only constituted 7 percent of the flexible packaging material sold. Several other processes were available for any use to which cellophane could be put. Du Pont (D) could not arbitrarily set the price for cellophane without an adverse effect on demand. Finally, du Pont (D) could not exclude competitors from the market, even as to cellophane (though this is immaterial). Since du Pont (D) cannot set price or restrict competition in the flexible packaging material market, it is not a monopoly within the meaning of § 2 of the Sherman Act. Affirmed.

▶ ANALYSIS

In some cases, the control of a distinct submarket is sufficient to find a monopoly. In *International Boxing Club v. United States*, 358 U.S. 242 (1959), the Court held that control of championship fights was a monopoly even though it was only a minor segment of the boxing industry. The market was deemed to be championship fights rather than the industry as a whole.

∎≡∎

Quicknotes

MONOPOLY A privilege or right conferred upon an individual or entity granting it the exclusive power to manufacture, sell and distribute a particular service or commodity; a market condition in which one or a few companies control the sale of a product or service thereby restraining competition in respect to that article or service.

SHERMAN ACT Makes every contract or conspiracy in unreasonable restraint of commerce illegal.

∎≡∎

Telex Corp. v. IBM Corp.

Marketer (P) v. Computer manufacturer (D)

510 F.2d 894 (10th Cir.), *cert. dismissed*, 423 U.S. 802 (1975).

NATURE OF CASE: Appeal from a judgment defining the relevant market for a product in an action based on federal antitrust law.

FACT SUMMARY: Telex Corp. (P), which marketed peripheral devices compatible with central processing units (CPUs) in IBM Corp.'s (D) computers, charged IBM (D) with monopolization in the manufacture, distribution, sale, and leasing of plug compatible peripheral products attached to its CPUs.

🏛 RULE OF LAW
In determining whether the power exists to control prices or to exclude competition, the relevant market of a product must include all products reasonably interchangeable with that product.

FACTS: Telex Corp. (P) marketed peripheral devices that were plug-compatible with IBM Corp.'s (D) CPUs in its computers. Those devices included magnetic tape drives, magnetic disk drives, magnetic drums, magnetic strip files, printers, and memory units. Telex (P) filed a complaint, charging IBM (D) with monopolization in the manufacture, distribution, sale, and leasing of plug compatible peripheral products attached to its CPUs. The court concluded that while IBM (D) did not have monopoly power in the industry as a whole, the products market was practically restricted. IBM (D) contended, however, that the court's determination of the relevant market for peripheral products was incorrect because it was limited mainly to peripheral products plug compatible with IBM's (D) equipment. Thus it failed to include other peripheral equipment marketed by Telex (P). IBM (D) appealed.

ISSUE: Must the relevant market of a product include all products reasonably interchangeable with that product in determining whether there existed the power to control prices or to exclude competition?

HOLDING AND DECISION: (Per curiam) Yes. In determining whether the power exists to control prices or to exclude competition, the relevant market of a product must include all products reasonably interchangeable with that product. Peripherals manufactured for one CPU can easily be adapted for use by other systems through the use of an interface. Manufacturers of peripherals that were plug-compatible with IBM's (D) CPUs were free to adapt their products through interface changes to plug into non-IBM systems. IBM (D) has thus proven reasonable interchangeability. Hence, the market should include all peripheral products. Cross-elasticity exists because these products, although not fungible, are fully interchangeable and may be interchanged with minimal financial outlay. The lower court's very restrictive definition of the product market was plain error. Reversed.

▶ ANALYSIS

While the trial court recognized the presence of interchangeability of use and the presence of cross-elasticity, it thought that these factors were not sufficiently immediate. Cross-elasticity of demand requires that the market include close substitutes as part of the product category. Cross-elasticity of supply is also considered in making a determination of market power.

■=■

Quicknotes

MONOPOLY A privilege or right conferred upon an individual or entity granting it the exclusive power to manufacture, sell and distribute a particular service or commodity; a market condition in which one or a few companies control the sale of a product or service thereby restraining competition in respect to that article or service.

■=■

United States v. Grinnell Corp.

Federal government (P) v. Alarm manufacturer (D)

384 U.S. 563 (1966).

NATURE OF CASE: Action seeking an injunction under § 2 of the Sherman Act.

FACT SUMMARY: Grinnell Corp. (D) controlled 87 percent of the automatic central alarm system market.

🏛 RULE OF LAW
A distinctive type of service within a larger market may be deemed a monopoly where no comparable alternative service exists.

FACTS: Grinnell Corp. (D) controlled 87 percent of the automatic central alarm system market. In certain areas serviced by Grinnell (D), competitors were present. Alternatives such as guards, dogs, etc. were also available to those who did not wish to use Grinnell (D). Most insurance companies gave preferential rates to businesses using automatic alarm systems such as was supplied by Grinnell Corp. (D). Because of the existence of other competitors and services, Grinnell (D) could not arbitrarily set prices. The Government (P) brought an antitrust action under §§ 1 and 2 of the Sherman Act to enjoin price-fixing activities, activities in restraint of trade, and to dissolve the monopoly. The court found that the central automatic alarm system was a distinct submarket in the security field. It found that no reasonable alternative existed and that 87 percent control of the submarket constituted a monopoly. It found that certain offices were operated at a loss to injure competition and that these factors constituted violations of §§ 1 and 2 of the Sherman Act.

ISSUE: Is control of a significant portion of a submarket for which no reasonable alternative exists sufficient to constitute a monopoly?

HOLDING AND DECISION: (Douglas, J.) Yes. A distinctive type of service within a larger market may be deemed a monopoly where no comparable alternative service exists. The existence of the larger market does not foreclose a finding that the submarket is the appropriate level of inquiry to determine if a monopoly is present. Here, the automatic central alarm system provides a unique and superior method of property protection. It allows property owners to obtain favorable rates and does not require the presence of obtrusive guards and/or dogs. Eighty-seven percent control of the market is sufficient control to constitute a monopoly. Grinnell's (D) market dominance must be deemed established when it can afford to operate certain offices at a loss to prevent competition. Where one occupying a position of market dominance uses its power to drive out competition or to restrict entry into the market, such practices constitute a violation of §§ 1 and 2 of the Sherman Act. Grinnell (D) is ordered to divest itself of control of its stock in these companies.

DISSENT: (Fortas, J.) The majority has failed to consider the relevant market and product lines carefully enough. The Government (P) has defined the market as "insurance accredited central station protection services." This narrows the market too severely. The market is deemed to be nationwide, yet the nature of the services is local, i.e., fixed locations, nonmovable equipment and premises, etc. The correct geographical market herein is local and the line of commerce is the entire security products market.

▶ ANALYSIS

Grinnell (D) was also guilty of price discrimination under § 2 of the Clayton Act. When prices are lowered in a given area to below that of one's competitors for the purpose of driving them out of business it is an unlawful method of competition which may be enjoined. However, to invoke the Clayton Act's prohibitions it would be necessary to show that Grinnell (D) was dealing in a product since the Act is not directed to services. Since a central alarm system involves both a product and a service, the Government (P) probably proceeded under the Sherman Act to prevent this problem from being raised before the court.

■==■

Quicknotes

CLAYTON ACT Legislation passed by the U.S. Congress in 1914 as an amendment to clarify and supplement the Sherman Antitrust Act of 1890. The act prohibited various anti-competitive business practices and gave labor certain rights in disputes with management. It declared that "the labor of a human being is not a commodity or article of commerce."

MONOPOLY A privilege or right conferred upon an individual or entity granting it the exclusive power to manufacture, sell and distribute a particular service or commodity; a market condition in which one or a few companies control the sale of a product or service thereby restraining competition in respect to that article or service.

PRICE-FIXING An illegal combination in violation of the Sherman Act entered into for the purpose of setting prices below the natural market rate.

RESTRAINT OF TRADE Agreement between entities, for the purpose of impeding free trade, that results in a monopoly, suppression of competition, or affecting prices.

SHERMAN ACT § 1 Prohibits price-fixing.

SHERMAN ACT § 2 Makes it a felony to monopolize or attempt to monopolize, or combine or conspire with any other person(s) to monopolize, any part of the trade or commerce among the states or with a foreign country.

■==■

Berkey Photo, Inc. v. Eastman Kodak Co.

Photofinisher (P) v. Photo equipment manufacturer (D)

603 F.2d 263 (2d Cir. 1979), *cert. denied*, 444 U.S. 1093 (1980).

NATURE OF CASE: Appeal from a jury award of damages in an antitrust action.

FACT SUMMARY: Berkey Photo, Inc. (P), a photofinisher and a competitor of Eastman Kodak Co. (Kodak) (D), brought suit, alleging that Kodak's (D) introduction of its 110 camera system, tied to introduction of its Kodacolor II film, constituted a violation of § 2 of the Sherman Act.

🏛 RULE OF LAW
Any firm, even a monopolist, may keep its innovations secret from its rivals as long as it wishes.

FACTS: Berkey Photo, Inc. (Berkey) (P) competed with Eastman Kodak Co. (Kodak) (D) in providing photo-finishing services and had formerly manufactured and sold cameras as well. Berkey (P) did not manufacture film but purchased Kodak (D) film for resale to its customers and also bought photofinishing equipment and supplies from Kodak (D). Berkey (P) filed suit, alleging that every aspect of its association with Kodak (D) had been infected by Kodak's (D) monopoly power, willfully acquired, maintained, and exercised in violation of § 2 of the Sherman Act. Berkey (P) specifically alleged that Kodak's (D) policy of tying the introduction of its 110 photographic system to introduction of its Kodacolor II film constituted both an attempt to monopolize and actual monopolization of the camera market. Further, Berkey (P) argued that Kodak (D) had a duty to disclose limited types of information to certain competitors under specific circumstances. The jury awarded damages to Berkey (P). Kodak (D) appealed.

ISSUE: May any firm, even a monopolist, keep its innovations secret from its rivals as long as it wishes?

HOLDING AND DECISION: (Kaufman, J.) Yes. Any firm, even a monopolist, may keep its innovations secret from its rivals as long as it wishes forcing them to catch up on the strength of their own efforts after a new product is introduced. A monopolist is encouraged by § 2 to compete aggressively, and any success that it achieves through innovation, is clearly tolerated by the antitrust laws. Kodak's (D) introduction of a new format was not rendered an unlawful act of monopolization in the camera market because the firm also manufactured film to fit the camera. Moreover, no court has ever imposed the duty to disclose that Berkey (P) seeks to create here. Finally, although the restriction of Kodacolor II to the 110 format may have been unjustified, there was no evidence that Berkey (P) was injured by this course of action. Thus, the facts of this case do not justify an award of damages to Berkey (P). Reversed.

▶ ANALYSIS

The existence of monopoly power is tolerated insofar as is necessary to preserve competitive incentives and to be fair to the firm that has attained its position innocently. An integrated business like Kodak (D) does not offend the Sherman Act whenever one of its departments benefits from association with a division possessing a monopoly in its own market. So long as a firm competes in several fields, it is to be expected that it will seek the competitive advantages of its broad-based activity.

Quicknotes

MONOPOLY A privilege or right conferred upon an individual or entity granting it the exclusive power to manufacture, sell and distribute a particular service or commodity; a market condition in which one or a few companies control the sale of a product or service thereby restraining competition in respect to that article or service.

SHERMAN ACT § 2 Makes it a felony to monopolize or attempt to monopolize, or combine or conspire with any other person(s) to monopolize, any part of the trade or commerce among the states or with a foreign country.

TYING Selling a specified product to a buyer only if the buyer also agrees to purchase another product.

California Computer Products v. IBM Corp.

Manufacturer of computer products (P) v. Computer manufacturer (D)

613 F.2d 727 (9th Cir. 1979).

NATURE OF CASE: Appeal from a judgment for the defendant in an action for violation of federal antitrust law.

FACT SUMMARY: After IBM Corp. (D) developed a new line of computers that integrated disk drive and memory functions into the CPU itself, California Computer Products (P), a manufacturer of peripheral products such as disk drives and memory units compatible with IBM's (D) mainframe computers and central processing units (CPUs), filed suit, alleging illegal monopolistic behavior in violation of the Sherman Act.

🏛 RULE OF LAW
Even where a company is a monopolist, it has the right to redesign its products to make them more attractive to buyers, whether by reason of lower manufacturing cost and price or improved performance.

FACTS: California Computer Products (CalComp) (P) manufactured peripheral products such as disk drives and memory units, which were compatible with IBM Corp. (D) mainframe computers and CPUs. When new technology allowed IBM (D) to introduce a new line of computers, integrating disk drive and memory functions into the CPU itself, CalComp (P) filed suit, alleging that IBM's (D) new design was illegal monopolization in violation of § 2 of the Sherman Act. CalComp (P) characterized IBM's (D) design changes as "technological manipulation" that did nothing to improve performance, and complained that the newly integrated functions were priced below their nonintegrated counterparts. The trial court found for IBM (D). CalComp (P) appealed.

ISSUE: Even where a company is a monopolist, does it have the right to redesign its products to make them more attractive to buyers, whether by reason of lower manufacturing cost and price or improved performance?

HOLDING AND DECISION: (Choy, J.) Yes. Even where a company is a monopolist, it has the right to redesign its products to make them more attractive to buyers, whether by reason of lower manufacturing cost and price or improved performance. Price and performance are inseparable parts of any competitive offering, and equivalent performance at lower cost represents a superior product from the buyer's point of view. At trial, one of CalComp's (P) own witnesses stated that, in general, the manufacturer will try and minimize his costs, and where he integrates the control unit the assumption must be that he is achieving a lower cost solution. CalComp's (P) chairman also stated that, as a result of integration, the customer used less floor space, which tends to be relatively expensive in a computer room. IBM (D) was under no duty to help CalComp (P) or other peripheral equipment manufacturers survive or expand. Affirmed.

▶ ANALYSIS

CalComp (P) developed its peripheral products by "reverse engineering," i.e., copying IBM's (D) peripheral products. In this case then, CalComp (P) could be considered a free rider. The express purpose of patent laws is to give innovative companies, such as IBM (D), monopoly profits to reward them for their innovations. Such rewards provide a continued incentive to innovate.

■=■

Quicknotes

MONOPOLY A privilege or right conferred upon an individual or entity granting it the exclusive power to manufacture, sell and distribute a particular service or commodity; a market condition in which one or a few companies control the sale of a product or service thereby restraining competition in respect to that article or service.

SHERMAN ACT Makes every contract or conspiracy in unreasonable restraint of commerce illegal.

■=■

United States v. Microsoft Corp.

Federal government (P) v. Software company (D)

253 F.3d 34 (D.C. Cir.), *cert. denied*, 534 U.S. 952 (2001).

NATURE OF CASE: Appeal from judgment finding defendant in violation of the Sherman Act and ordering various remedies.

FACT SUMMARY: The Government (P) and several States (P) alleged that Microsoft Corp. (D), the nation's largest manufacturer of Intel-compatible PC operating systems (OS), had committed several violations of §§ 1 and 2 of the Sherman Act.

🏛 **RULE OF LAW**

(1) Monopoly power of a company may be inferred where the company has a 95 percent share of the relevant market, where there are significant barriers to entry in that market, and the company owns a monopoly product in that market.

(2) The conduct of a monopolist that has exclusionary anticompetitive effect, and for which there is no procompetitive justification, supports a claim of monopolization under § 2 of the Sherman Act.

(3) To prevail, a plaintiff seeking liability under § 2 of the Sherman Act does not have to present direct proof that a defendant's continued monopoly power is precisely attributable to its anticompetitive conduct.

(4) A court's remedies decree must be vacated where the court fails to hold a remedies-specific evidentiary hearing when there are disputed facts; the court fails to provide adequate reasons for its decreed remedies; and the scope of liability has been altered by a higher court.

FACTS: In 1998, the Government (P) and several States (P) alleged that Microsoft Corp. (D), the nation's largest manufacturer of Intel-compatible PC operating systems (OS), had violated §§ 1 and 2 of the Sherman Act. The plaintiffs charged four distinct violations of the Sherman Act: (1) unlawful exclusive dealing arrangements in violation of § 1; (2) unlawful tying of Internet Explorer (IE) to Windows 95 and Windows 98 in violation of § 1; (3) unlawful maintenance of a monopoly in the PC operating system market in violation of § 2; and (4) unlawful attempted monopolization of the Internet browser market in violation of § 2. The States (P) also brought pendent claims charging Microsoft (D) with violations of various State antitrust laws. The district court adopted an expedited trial schedule and received evidence through summary witnesses, and found that Microsoft (D) had committed antitrust violations by (a) maintaining a monopoly in the market for Intel-compatible PC operating systems in violation of § 2; (b) attempting to gain a monopoly in the market for Internet browsers (especially Netscape's Navigator) in violation

of § 2; and (c) illegally tying two purportedly separate products, Windows and IE, in violation of § 1. Accordingly, the district court issued a Final Judgment that required Microsoft (D) to submit a proposed plan of divestiture, with the company to be split into an operating systems business and an applications business. Microsoft (D) challenged the district court's legal conclusions as to its liability for all alleged antitrust violations. The court of appeals granted review.

ISSUES:

(1) Can monopoly power of a company be inferred where the company has a 95 percent share of the relevant market, where there are significant barriers to entry in that market, and the company owns a monopoly product in that market?

(2) Does the conduct of a monopolist that has exclusionary anticompetitive effect, and for which there is no procompetitive justification, support a claim of monopolization under § 2 of the Sherman Act?

(3) To prevail, must a plaintiff seeking liability under § 2 of the Sherman Act present direct proof that a defendant's continued monopoly power, is precisely attributable to its anticompetitive conduct?

(4) Must a court's remedies decree be vacated where the court fails to hold a remedies-specific evidentiary hearing when there are disputed facts; the court fails to provide adequate reasons for its decreed remedies; and the scope of liability has been altered by a higher court?

HOLDING AND DECISION: (Per curiam)

II. MONOPOLIZATION

A. Monopoly Power

(1) Yes. Monopoly power of a company may be inferred where the company has a 95 percent share of the relevant market, where there are significant barriers to entry in that market, and the company owns a monopoly product in that market. A necessary element of the offense of monopolization is the possession of monopoly power in the relevant market. The district court was correct in defining the relevant market as Intel-compatible PC operating systems, and in finding that Microsoft (D) had a 95 percent share of the market, and that its position was protected by a substantial entry barrier. Microsoft (D) argues that the district court improperly excluded three types of competing products: non-Intel compatible operating systems (e.g., Apple's Mac OS), operating systems for non-PC devices (e.g., handheld computers), and "middleware" products, which are software products that expose their own Application Programming Interfaces

Continued on next page.

(APIs). As to non-Intel compatible operating systems, such as Mac OS, Microsoft (D) failed to challenge the district court's factual finding, i.e., that consumers would not switch from Windows to Mac OS in response to a substantial price increase because of the costs of acquiring the new hardware needed to run Mac OS, and the great learning curve in switching systems. The same is true as to non-PC based competitors—Microsoft (D) did not challenge the district court's findings, in particular, that most consumers would use them only as a supplement, not as a substitute for, their PCs. Finally, as to middleware, every OS has different APIs. Ostensibly, if middleware were written for multiple operating systems, Microsoft (D) argues, middleware could usurp the operating system's platform function and might eventually take over other operating system functions. The district court found, however, that no middleware product could now, or in the near future, expose enough APIs to serve as a platform for popular applications, much less take over all operating system functions. Again, Microsoft (D) failed to challenge these findings. The district court also found a structural barrier to entry—the "applications barrier to entry"—which stems from two characteristics of the software market: (1) most consumers prefer operating systems for which a large number of applications have already been written; and (2) most developers prefer to write for operating systems that already have a substantial consumer base. This situation ensures that applications will continue to be written for the already dominant Windows, which in turn ensures that consumers will continue to prefer it over other operating systems. The success of middleware would eradicate that "chicken and egg" problem, but, as the district court found, that prospect is a long way off.

B. Anticompetitive Conduct

(2) Yes. The conduct of a monopolist that has exclusionary anticompetitive effect, and for which there is no procompetitive justification, supports a claim of monopolization under § 2 of the Sherman Act. To be condemned as exclusionary, a monopolist's conduct must have an anticompetitive effect, by harming the competitive process and thereby consumers. Under § 2 of the Sherman Act, if a prima facie case demonstrates anticompetitive effect, the monopolist may offer a procompetitive justification for its conduct, and if it does so, the burden shifts back to the plaintiff to rebut that claim. If the procompetitive justification is unrebutted, the plaintiff, to prevail, must show that any anticompetitive harm outweighs any procompetitive effect. The district court held Microsoft (D) liable for: (1) the way in which it integrated IE into Windows; (2) its various dealings with Original Equipment Manufacturers (OEMs), Internet Access Providers (IAPs), Internet Content Providers (ICPs), Independent Software Vendors (ISVs), and Apple Computer (Apple); (3) its efforts to contain and to subvert Java technologies; and (4) its course of conduct as a whole.

1. Licenses Issued to OEMs

As to licenses Microsoft (D) issued to OEMs, the district court found that restrictions in these licenses reduced usage

share of Netscape's browser and, thereby, protected Microsoft's (D) operating system monopoly by keeping rival browsers from gaining the critical mass of users necessary to attract developer attention away from Windows as the platform for software development. Thus, by gaining market share in the browser market, Microsoft (D) could protect threats to its monopoly in the OS market. In particular, Microsoft (D) prohibited OEM's from removing desktop icons, folders, and Start menu entries providing access to IE, which prevented the OEMs from installing a second browser out of increased support costs associated with servicing confused customers. There was evidence that the fear of such confusion deterred many OEMs from installing multiple browsers. Microsoft (D) also prohibited the OEMs from modifying the initial boot sequence, which prevented the OEMs from enabling users to choose from a list of IAPs (many of which used Netscape Navigator rather than IE in their Internet access software). Along with other similar restrictions that prevented OEMs from promoting rival browsers and IAPs, the case has been made that Microsoft (D) reduced rival browsers' usage share not by improving its own product, but, rather, by preventing OEMs from taking actions that could increase rivals' share of usage. Microsoft (D) attempts to justify the license restrictions by asserting that it is simply exercising its rights as the holder of valid copyrights. This argument borders on the frivolous, because Microsoft (D) is wrong in asserting that it has an unfettered right to use its intellectual property in any way it wishes. The only license restriction Microsoft (D) seriously defends as necessary to prevent a substantial alteration of its copyrighted work is the prohibition on OEMs from automatically launching a substitute user interface upon completion of the boot process. Insofar as this restriction prevented the Windows desktop from ever being seen by the user, it is upheld as non-exclusionary. Accordingly, with the exception of the one restriction prohibiting OEMs from automatically launching a substitute user interface upon completion of the boot process, all the other restrictions represent Microsoft's (D) use of its market power to protect its monopoly, and, therefore, they violate § 2 of the Sherman Act.

2. Integration of IE and Windows

Microsoft (D) bound IE more tightly to Windows as a technical matter, by having IE software as an irremovable component of Windows, which prevented OEMs from preinstalling other browsers and deterred consumers from using them. Any attempt to remove IE would cripple Windows. Although the courts are deferential to product innovation, this does not mean that a monopolist's product design changes are per se lawful. Again, this change reduced the usage share of rival browsers, not by making Microsoft's (D) own browser more attractive to consumers, but, rather, by discouraging OEMs from distributing rival

Continued on next page.

products. Therefore, this change had anticompetitive effects that protected Microsoft's (D) own operating system monopoly. This integration also discouraged consumers from using a browser other than IE by systematically overriding the users' preference of browser, if other than IE. Finally, Microsoft (D) commingled IE code with critical operating system files, so that any attempt to eliminate the browser code would cripple Windows. Such commingling also had anticompetitive, exclusionary effect. Thus, a prima facie case is made out on this issue. Microsoft (D) attempts to justify the integration of IE with Windows by claiming that, at least with respect to its override of the user's choice of default browser, there were valid technical reasons for such an override. These included that fact that certain Windows features were not supported by Navigator. Because the government (P) did not rebut this justification, Microsoft (D) cannot be held liable for this aspect of its product design.

3. Agreements with Internet Access Providers

The district court found that Microsoft's (D) agreements with various IAPs were exclusionary because Microsoft (D) offered IE free of charge to the IAPs, and then offered a bounty for each customer the IAP signed up for service using the IE browser. In effect, the court concluded that Microsoft (D) was acting to preserve its monopoly by offering IE to IAPs at an attractive price. Similarly, the district court held Microsoft (D) liable for developing the IE Access Kit (IEAK), a software package that allows an IAP to "create a distinctive identity for its service in as little as a few hours by customizing the [IE] title bar, icon, start and search pages," and offering the IEAK to IAPs free of charge, on the ground that those acts, too, helped Microsoft (D) preserve its monopoly. Finally, the district court found that Microsoft (D) agreed to provide easy access to IAPs' services from the Windows desktop in return for the IAPs' agreement to promote IE exclusively and to keep shipments of internet access software using Navigator under a specific percentage, typically 25 percent. Because the law does not condemn even a monopolist from offering its product at an attractive price, Microsoft (D) cannot be liable for offering either IE or the IEAK free of charge or even at negative prices. Therefore, Microsoft's (D) development of the IEAK does not violate the Sherman Act. With regard to Microsoft's (D) exclusive contracts with IAPs concerning desktop placement, the plaintiffs must prove that the probable effect of the exclusive deals would be to foreclose competition in a substantial share of the relevant market. Under § 1 of the Sherman Act, the district court found that because Microsoft (D) had not completely excluded Netscape from reaching any potential user by some means of distribution, no matter how ineffective, such agreements did not violate that section. However, the district court found that the agreements severely restricted Netscapes' access to those distribution channels leading most efficiently to the acquisition of browser usage share, and held, therefore, that the agreements violated § 2. Microsoft (D)

argued that a holding of no liability under § 1 should preclude a finding of liability under § 2. Although the prudential concerns of both sections are the same, a monopolist's use of exclusive contracts may give rise to a § 2 violation. Here, the plaintiffs have demonstrated that Microsoft (D) managed to preserve its monopoly by entering into exclusive contracts with IAPs, which constitute one of the two major channels by which browsers can be distributed. Therefore, the contracts with the IAPs were exclusionary devices that violated § 2.

4. Dealings with . . . Apple Computer

The district court held that Microsoft's (D) dealings with Apple violated the Sherman Act, by having Apple agree to switch from promoting Navigator to bundling the most current version of IE with Mac OS. This exclusive deal had a substantial impact on the distribution of rival browsers. If a browser developer ports its product to a second operating system, such as the Mac OS, it can continue to display a common set of APIs. Thus, usage share, not the underlying operating system, is the primary determinant of the platform challenge a browser may pose. Pre-installation of a browser is one of the two most important methods of browser distribution, and Apple had a not insignificant share of worldwide sales of operating systems. Accordingly, Microsoft's (D) deal with Apple must be regarded as anticompetitive. Because Microsoft (D) offers no procompetitive justifications for this exclusive deal with Apple, it is held violative of § 2.

5. Java

Java is a set of technologies developed by Sun Microsystems that enables software written to Java to run on almost any computer operating system. The district court found that Microsoft (D) took four steps to exclude Java from developing as a viable cross-platform threat: (a) designing a Java Virtual Machine (JVM) incompatible with the original one; (b) entering into contracts, the so-called "First Wave Agreements," requiring major ISVs to promote Microsoft's JVM exclusively; (c) deceiving Java developers about the Windows-specific nature of the tools it distributed to them; and (d) coercing Intel to stop participating in the improvement of Java technologies. First, the JVM Microsoft (D) developed runs faster in Windows, and per se does not have an anticompetitive effect. A monopolist does not violate the antitrust laws simply by developing a product that is incompatible with those of rivals. Therefore, the district court's finding of liability is reversed as to Microsoft's (D) development of its own JVM. Second, the First Wave Agreements, which conditioned receipt of Windows technical information on the ISVs agreement to promote Microsoft's (D) JVM exclusively, had an anticompetitive effect on the promotion of original JVM since, as a practical matter, developers were required to make Microsoft's (D) JVM the default in the software they developed. Because the cumulative effect of this deal was

Continued on next page.

anticompetitive—because it had the effect of seriously impeding the distribution of Sun's JVM and foreclosed a substantial portion of the field for JVM distribution—and because Microsoft (D) offered no procompetitive justification for it, it violates the Sherman Act. Third, Microsoft (D) intended to and did deceive developers into unwittingly writing Java applications that ran only on Windows by making the developers think that they were using Microsoft (D) tools for developing cross-platform applications, when in fact those tools could produce applications that could run only on Windows. This conduct served to protect Microsoft's (D) monopoly of the operating system in a way not attributable to the superiority of the OS or to the acumen of its makers, had no procompetitive justification, and violates § 2. Finally, Microsoft (D) prevented firms such as Intel from aiding in the creation of cross-platform interfaces. After coercive pressure from Microsoft (D), Intel abandoned such efforts. This had anticompetitive effect, as intended by Microsoft (D). Again, Microsoft (D) offers no procompetitive justifications for this conduct, which, therefore, is held to violate § 2.

C. Causation

(3) No. To prevail, a plaintiff seeking liability under § 2 of the Sherman Act does not have to present direct proof that a defendant's continued monopoly power is precisely attributable to its anticompetitive conduct. Microsoft (D) argues that there is no causal link between its anticompetitive conduct, in particular its foreclosure of Netscape's and Java's distribution channels, and the maintenance of its operating system monopoly. It argues, wrongly, that to prove such a link, the district court would have had to find that Navigator and Java would have developed into serious cross-platform threats to erode the applications barrier to entry. There is no precedent that, as to § 2 liability in an equitable enforcement action, plaintiffs must present direct proof that a defendant's continued monopoly power is precisely attributable to its anticompetitive conduct. Courts may infer causation when exclusionary conduct is aimed at producers of nascent technologies, even though it is impossible to recreate "a product's hypothetical technological development in a world absent the defendant's exclusionary conduct." Microsoft's (D) causation argument is more pertinent to the question of the appropriate remedy, i.e., whether the court should impose a structural remedy or merely enjoin the offensive conduct, than to the question of liability.

V. REMEDY

(4) Yes. A court's remedies decree must be vacated where the court fails to hold a remedies-specific evidentiary hearing when there are disputed facts; the court fails to provide adequate reasons for its decreed remedies; and the scope of liability has been altered by a higher court. The district court's remedies order must be vacated because: (1) the court failed to hold a remedies-specific evidentiary hearing when there were disputed facts; (2) the court failed to provide adequate reasons for its decreed remedies; and (3) this Court has

revised the scope of Microsoft's (D) liability and it is impossible to determine to what extent that should affect the remedies provisions. On remand, the district court must reconsider whether the use of the structural remedy of divestiture is appropriate with respect to Microsoft (D), which argues that it is a unitary company. The dissolution of unitary companies has not traditionally been ordered, in part because to do so entails great logistical difficulty and threatens to greatly reduce the company's efficiency, and because this remedy has been used primarily for antitrust violations whose heart is intercorporate combination and control. In devising an appropriate remedy, the district court, in addition to considering whether Microsoft (D) is a unitary company, also should consider whether plaintiffs have established a sufficient causal connection between Microsoft's (D) anticompetitive conduct and its dominant position in the OS market. Mere existence of an exclusionary act does not itself justify full feasible relief against the monopolist to create maximum competition. Rather, structural relief, which is designed to eliminate the monopoly altogether, requires a clearer indication of a significant causal connection between the conduct and creation or maintenance of the market power. Absent such causation, the antitrust defendant's unlawful behavior should be remedied by an injunction against continuation of that conduct.

▶ *ANALYSIS*

This case has been one of the most widely discussed antitrust cases in recent decades. The court in this case also reversed the district court's finding that Microsoft (D) unlawfully attempted to monopolize the browser market, on the grounds that the relevant browser market had not been properly defined and because entry barriers into this market were not shown to be high. More importantly, the court held that the rule of reason, rather than per se analysis, governs the legality of tying arrangements involving platform software products. This holding is seen as a significant contribution to tying doctrine. The U.S. Supreme Court denied certiorari in this case, letting stand the court of appeals' pronouncement on the applicability of the rule of reason to tying cases involving software platforms. Finally, as the court discusses in the opinion, this case raises a practical issue of how meaningful antitrust litigation is in an industry, such as the computer industry, where by the time a large and complex case is resolved, many of the products, firms, and marketplace are likely to have changed dramatically.

■=■

Quicknotes

CERTIORARI A discretionary writ issued by a superior court to an inferior court in order to review the lower court's decisions; the Supreme Court's writ ordering such review.

Continued on next page.

EVIDENTIARY HEARING   Hearing pertaining to the evidence of the case.

MONOPOLY   A privilege or right conferred upon an individual or entity granting it the exclusive power to manufacture, sell and distribute a particular service or commodity; a market condition in which one or a few companies control the sale of a product or service thereby restraining competition in respect to that article or service.

SHERMAN ACT   Makes every contract or conspiracy in unreasonable restraint of commerce illegal.

Independent Service Organizations Antitrust Litigation

Independent service organizations (P) v. Intellectual property owner/seller (D)

203 F.3d 1322 (Fed. Cir. 2000).

NATURE OF CASE: Appeal from dismissal of antitrust action on summary judgment.

FACT SUMMARY: Xerox (D), a manufacturer, seller, and servicer of copiers established a policy of not selling its patented copier parts or copyrighted software to independent service organizations (ISOs), including CSU (P), unless they were also end-users. CSU (P) brought suit alleging that Xerox's (D) refusal to sell or license its patented parts and copyrighted software violated the Sherman Act. Xerox (D) counterclaimed for patent and copyright infringement.

RULE OF LAW
If a patent or copyright is lawfully acquired, the patent or copyright holder's unilateral refusal to sell or license its patented invention or copyrighted expression, is not unlawful exclusionary conduct, where the exercise of the intellectual property right does not exceed the scope of the intellectual property right.

FACTS: Xerox (D) manufactures, sells, and services copiers. It established a policy of not selling parts unique to some of its copiers to independent service organizations (ISOs), including CSU (P), unless they were also end-users of the copiers. To maintain its existing business of servicing Xerox (D) equipment, CSU (P) used parts cannibalized from used Xerox (D) equipment, parts obtained from other ISOs, and parts purchased through a limited number of its customers. CSU (P) filed suit alleging that Xerox (D) violated the Sherman Act by setting the prices on its patented parts much higher for ISOs than for end-users to force ISOs to raise their prices. This would eliminate ISOs in general and CSU (P) in particular, as competitors in the relevant service markets for copiers and printers. Xerox (D) counterclaimed for patent and copyright infringement and contested CSU's (P) antitrust claims as relying on injury solely caused by Xerox (D)'s lawful refusal to sell or license patented parts and copyrighted software. The district court granted summary judgment to Xerox (D). The court of appeals granted review.

ISSUE: If a patent or copyright is lawfully acquired, is the patent or copyright holder's unilateral refusal to sell or license its patented invention or copyrighted expression unlawful exclusionary conduct where the exercise of the intellectual property right does not exceed the scope of the intellectual property right?

HOLDING AND DECISION: (Mayer, C.J.) No. If a patent or copyright is lawfully acquired, the patent or copyright holder's unilateral refusal to sell or license its patented invention or copyrighted expression, is not unlawful exclusionary conduct, where the exercise of the intellectual

property right does not exceed the scope of the intellectual property right. The applicable law respecting Xerox's (D) refusal to sell its patented parts is federal circuit law, which has exclusive jurisdiction over patent issues. The applicable law respecting Xerox's (D) refusal to sell or license its copyrighted manuals and software is the law of the regional circuit in which the district court sits (here, the Tenth Circuit). Determination of whether a patent holder meets the Sherman Act elements of monopolization or attempt to monopolize is governed by the rules of application of the antitrust laws to market participants, with due consideration to the exclusivity that inheres in the patent grant. Even where an intellectual property owner has market power, such market power does not impose on the owner an obligation to license the use of that property to others. Although no court has imposed antitrust liability for a unilateral refusal to sell or license a patent, the patent owner's right to exclude is not without limit. Where the patent owner brings an enforcement action that has an anticompetitive effect, the owner is exempt from the antitrust law unless the intellectual property to be licensed was fraudulently obtained, or the infringement claim is a sham to conceal an attempt to harm a competitor. Here, CSU (P) makes no claim that Xerox (D) obtained its patents through fraud. Also, to prove that a suit falls within the sham exception to immunity, an antitrust plaintiff must prove that the suit was both objectively baseless and subjectively motivated by a desire to impose collateral, anticompetitive injury rather than to obtain a justifiable legal remedy. Accordingly, if a suit is not objectively baseless, an antitrust defendant's subjective motivation is immaterial. CSU (P) has alleged that Xerox (D) misused its patents, but has not claimed that Xerox's (D) patent infringement counterclaims were shams. CSU (P) instead alleges that Xerox (D) illegally sought to leverage its dominance in the equipment and parts market into dominance in the service market. However, absent exceptional circumstances, a patent may confer the right to exclude competition altogether in more than one antitrust market. The rebuttable presumption, whereby it is presumed that a monopolist's exercise of the statutory right to exclude provides a valid business justification for consumer harm, requires, for an assessment of pretext, an evaluation of the patent holder's subjective motivation for exercising its intellectual property rights. This rebuttable presumption is inapposite in this jurisdiction, where precedent provides that if a patent suit is not objectively baseless, an antitrust defendant's subjective motivation, is immaterial. In the absence of any indication of illegal tying, fraud, or sham litigation, the patent holder may enforce the statutory right to exclude others from making, using, or selling the claimed

Continued on next page.

invention free from liability under the antitrust laws so long as any anticompetitive effect does not illegally extend beyond the statutory patent grant. It is the infringement defendant and not the patentee that bears the burden to show that one of these exceptional situations exists, and, in the absence of such proof, the patentee's motivations for asserting his statutory right to exclude will not be evaluated. Even in cases where the infringement defendant has met this burden, which CSU (P) has not, he must then also prove the elements of the Sherman Act violation. Here, Xerox's (D) refusal to sell its patented parts did not exceed the scope of the patent grant and, therefore, Xerox (D) is not liable in antitrust. The property right granted by copyright law cannot be used without limits to extend power in the marketplace beyond what Congress intended. Neither the Supreme Court nor the regional court of appeals has directly addressed the antitrust implications of a unilateral refusal to sell or license copyrighted expression. A different court of appeals rejected a claim of illegal tying that was supported only by evidence of a unilateral decision to license copyrighted material to some but not to others. Yet another court of appeals has approached this issue by creating a rebuttable presumption that an author's desire to exclude others from use of his copyrighted work is presumptively a business justification for any immediate harm to consumers—the burden to overcome this presumption is firmly on the antitrust plaintiff. Under this approach, the subjective motivation of the copyright owner is not examined absent any evidence that the copyrights were obtained unlawfully or were used to gain monopoly power beyond the statutory copyright granted by Congress. In the absence of such definitive rebuttal evidence, Xerox's (D) refusal to sell or license its copyrighted works was squarely within the rights granted by Congress to the copyright holder and did not constitute a violation of the antitrust laws. Affirmed.

▶ *ANALYSIS*

In this case, the court appears to conclude that any condition placed on a license is exempt from antitrust laws unless the intellectual property to be licensed was fraudulently obtained, an infringement claim by the property holder is a sham to conceal an attempt to harm a competitor, or the refusal is part of a tie-in sales strategy.

■■■■

Quicknotes

COPYRIGHT Refers to the exclusive rights granted to an artist pursuant to Article I, section 8, clause 8 of the United States Constitution over the reproduction, display, performance, distribution, and adaptation of his work for a period prescribed by statute.

INFRINGEMENT Conduct in violation of statue or that interferes with another's rights pursuant to law.

MONOPOLY A privilege or right conferred upon an individual or entity granting it the exclusive power to manufacture, sell and distribute a particular service or commodity; a market condition in which one or a few companies control the sale of a product or service thereby restraining competition in respect to that article or service.

PATENT A limited monopoly conferred on the invention or discovery of any new or useful machine or process that is novel and nonobvious.

SHERMAN ACT Makes every contract or conspiracy in unreasonable restraint of commerce illegal.

■■■■

Brooke Group Ltd. v. Brown & Williamson Tobacco Corp.

Tobacco company (P) v. Tobacco company (D)

509 U.S. 209 (1993).

NATURE OF CASE: Appeal from a judgment for the defendant as a matter of law after an award of treble damages to the plaintiff in an antitrust action.

FACT SUMMARY: After Brown & Williamson Tobacco Corp. (D) entered the generic cigarette market in competition with Brooke Group Ltd. (Liggett) (P), Liggett (P) filed suit, alleging predatory pricing which violated federal antitrust law.

🏛 RULE OF LAW
To establish competitive injury due to a rival's low prices, a plaintiff must prove that the prices are below its rival's costs and that the competitor has a reasonable prospect of recoupment.

FACTS: To increase its market share, Brooke Group Ltd. (Liggett) (P) introduced generic cigarettes. As the economy market expanded, other firms entered since the growth of generics came at the expense of their branded cigarettes. Brown & Williamson Tobacco Corp. (B & W) (D) produced its own generic brand, not only matching Liggett's (P) prices, but beating them. Liggett (P) and B & W (D) engaged in a price war at the wholesale level, with B & W (D) maintaining a real advantage. Liggett (P) then filed suit, alleging that B & W's (D) price discrimination had a reasonable possibility of injuring competition, that it was integral to a scheme of predatory pricing, and that B & W (D) had cut prices below its costs. The jury awarded damages to Liggett (P), which the district court trebled. However, after review, the court held that B & W (D) was entitled to judgment as a matter of law. The court of appeals affirmed. Liggett (P) appealed.

ISSUE: To establish competitive injury due to a rival's low prices, must a plaintiff prove that the prices are below its rival's costs and that the competitor has a reasonable prospect of recoupment?

HOLDING AND DECISION: (Kennedy, J.) Yes. To establish competitive injury due to a rival's low prices, a plaintiff must prove that the prices are below its rival's costs and that the competitor has a reasonable prospect of recoupment. Here, the record contains sufficient evidence from which a reasonable jury could conclude that B & W (D) envisioned or intended an anticompetitive course of events and that for about eighteen months the prices on its generic cigarettes were below its costs. A jury could further conclude that this below-cost pricing imposed losses on Liggett (P) that it was unwilling to sustain. However, Liggett (P) has failed to demonstrate competitive injury as a matter of law because the evidence is inadequate to show that B & W (D) had a reasonable prospect of recouping its losses from below-cost pricing through slowing the growth of generics. Affirmed.

DISSENT: (Stevens, J.) The Robinson-Patman Act was designed to reach price discriminations in their incipiency, before the harm to competition is effected. It is enough that they "may" have the proscribed effect. Thus, Liggett (P) need not show any actual harm to competition but only the reasonable possibility that such harm would flow from B & W's (D) conduct. When the facts are viewed in the light most favorable to Liggett (P), it is clear that there is sufficient evidence in the record that the "reasonable possibility" of competitive injury required by the statute actually existed.

▶ ANALYSIS

The Robinson-Patman Act, which amended § 2 of the original Clayton Act, offers no exclusion from coverage when primary-line injury occurs in an oligopoly setting. Unlike the provisions of the Sherman Act, which speak only of various forms of express agreement and monopoly, the Robinson-Patman Act is phrased in broader, disjunctive terms, prohibiting price discrimination "where the effect of such discrimination may be substantially to lessen competition or tend to create a monopoly." Liggett's (P) theory of competitive injury through oligopolistic price coordination depends upon a complex chain of cause and effect. Although the majority found Liggett's (P) theory of liability was within the reach of the Act as an abstract matter, relying on tacit coordination among oligopolists as a means of recouping losses from predatory pricing was "highly speculative."

Quicknotes

CLAYTON ACT Legislation passed by the U.S. Congress in 1914 as an amendment to clarify and supplement the Sherman Antitrust Act of 1890. The act prohibited various anti-competitive business practices and gave labor certain rights in disputes with management. It declared that "the labor of a human being is not a commodity or article of commerce."

OLIGOPOLISTIC A market condition in which the industry for a particular product is dominated by only a few companies.

PREDATORY PRICING Pricing below the cost of production of a product with the intent of driving competitors out of business.

ROBINSON-PATMAN ACT § 2 Makes price discrimination unlawful if the intent is to harm competition.

TREBLE DAMAGES An award of damages triple of the amount awarded by the jury and provided for by statute for violation of certain offenses.

Weyerhaeuser Co. v. Ross-Simmons Hardwood Lumber Co., Inc.

Timber company (D) v. Sawmill (P)

127 S. Ct. 1069 (2007).

NATURE OF CASE: Appeal from affirmance of judgment for plaintiff in predatory bidding action under § 2 of the Sherman Act.

FACT SUMMARY: Ross-Simmons Hardwood Lumber Co., Inc. (Ross-Simmons) (P), a sawmill, alleged that Weyerhaeuser Co. (D), a timber company, drove Ross-Simmons (P) out of business by bidding up the price of sawlogs to a level that prevented Ross-Simmons (P) from being profitable. Weyerhaeuser Co. (D) contended that the appropriate test for predatory bidding should be based on the test for predatory pricing formulated in the U.S. Supreme Court's *Brooke Group Ltd. v. Brown & Williamson Tobacco Corp.*, 509 U.S. 209 (1993).

🏛 **RULE OF LAW**
To prevail on a predatory-bidding claim, a plaintiff must show that that the alleged predator's bidding on the buy side caused the cost of the relevant output to rise above the revenues generated in the sale of those outputs and that the alleged predator has a dangerous probability of recouping the losses incurred in bidding up input prices through the exercise of monopsony power.

FACTS: Ross-Simmons Hardwood Lumber Co., Inc. (Ross-Simmons) (P), an alder hardwood sawmill, was the first to operate a sawmill in a certain geographic area, but eventually Weyerhaeuser Co. (D) had six mills in the same area. While Weyerhaeuser (D) made significant capital investments in its operations and increased efficiency, Ross-Simmons (P) made few such investments. Logs represent up to 75 percent of a sawmill's total costs, and from 1998 to 2001, the price of alder sawlogs increased while prices for finished hardwood lumber fell. These divergent trends in input and output prices cut into the mills' profit margins, and Ross-Simmons (P) suffered heavy losses during this time, leading to the closure of the mill in 2001. Ross-Simmons (P) filed suit under § 2 of the Sherman Act, alleging that Weyerhaeuser Co. (D) drove it out of business by bidding up the price of alder sawlogs to a level that prevented Ross-Simmons (P) from being profitable. Proceeding on this "predatory-bidding" theory, Ross-Simmons (P) argued that Weyerhaeuser (D) had overpaid for alder sawlogs to cause sawlog prices to rise to artificially high levels as part of a plan to drive Ross-Simmons (P) out of business. As proof that this practice had occurred, Ross-Simmons (P) pointed to Weyerhaeuser's (D) large share of the alder purchasing market, rising alder sawlog prices during the alleged predation period, and Weyerhaeuser's (D) declining profits during that same period. The district court, inter alia, rejected Weyerhaeuser's (D) proposed predatory-bidding jury instructions that incorporated elements of the test

applied to predatory-pricing claims in *Brooke Group Ltd. v. Brown & Williamson Tobacco Corp.*, 509 U.S. 209 (1993). The jury returned a verdict against Weyerhaeuser (D), and the court of appeals affirmed rejecting Weyerhaeuser's (D) argument that *Brooke Group*'s standard should apply to predatory-bidding claims. The U.S. Supreme Court granted certiorari.

ISSUE: To prevail on a predatory-bidding claim, must a plaintiff show that the alleged predator's bidding on the buy side caused the cost of the relevant output to rise above the revenues generated in the sale of those outputs and that the alleged predator has a dangerous probability of recouping the losses incurred in bidding up input prices through the exercise of monopsony power?

HOLDING AND DECISION: (Thomas, J.) Yes. To prevail on a predatory-bidding claim, a plaintiff must show that that the alleged predator's bidding on the buy side caused the cost of the relevant output to rise above the revenues generated in the sale of those outputs and that the alleged predator has a dangerous probability of recouping the losses incurred in bidding up input prices through the exercise of monopsony power. Predatory pricing is a scheme in which the predator reduces the sale price of its product hoping to drive competitors out of business and, once competition has been vanquished, raises prices to an above competitive level. *Brooke Group* established two prerequisites to recovery on a predatory-pricing claim: First, a plaintiff must show that the prices complained of are below cost, because allowing recovery for above-cost price cutting could chill conduct—price cutting—that directly benefits consumers. Second, a plaintiff must show that the alleged predator had "a dangerous probability of recouping its investment in below-cost pricing," because without such a probability, it is highly unlikely that a firm would engage in predatory pricing. The costs of erroneous findings of predatory pricing liability are quite high because the mechanism by which a firm engages in predatory pricing, i.e., lowering prices, is the same mechanism by which a firm stimulates competition, and, therefore, mistaken liability findings would chill the very conduct the antitrust laws are designed to protect. Predatory bidding involves the exercise of market power on the market's buy, or input, side. To engage in predatory bidding, a purchaser bids up the market price of an input so high that rival buyers cannot survive, thus acquiring monopsony power, which is market power on the buy side of the market. Once a predatory bidder causes competing buyers to exit the market, it will attempt to drive down input prices to reap above competitive profits that will at least offset the losses it suffered in bidding up input prices.

Continued on next page.

Predatory-pricing and predatory-bidding claims are thus analytically similar, and the close theoretical connection between monopoly and monopsony suggests that similar legal standards should apply to both sorts of claims. Both involve the deliberate use of unilateral pricing measures for anticompetitive purposes and both require firms to incur certain short-term losses on the chance that they might later make above competitive profits. More importantly, predatory bidding mirrors predatory pricing in respects deemed significant in *Brooke Group*. Because rational businesses will rarely suffer short-term losses in hopes of reaping supra competitive profits, *Brooke Group*'s conclusion that "predatory pricing schemes are rarely tried, and even more rarely successful," applies with equal force to predatory-bidding schemes. Actions taken in a predatory-bidding scheme, like those in a predatory-pricing scheme, are often at the heart of competition and may ultimately benefit the consumer if the scheme fails. In fact, there are numerous legitimate reasons for bidding up the cost of inputs. Predatory bidding also presents less of a direct threat of consumer harm than predatory pricing, which achieves ultimate success by charging higher prices to consumers, because a predatory bidder does not necessarily rely on raising prices in the output market to recoup its losses. Given these similarities, *Brooke Group*'s two-pronged test should apply to predatory-bidding claims. A predatory-bidding plaintiff must prove that the predator's bidding on the buy side caused the cost of the relevant output to rise above the revenues generated in the sale of those outputs. Because the risk of chilling procompetitive behavior with too lax a liability standard is as serious here as it was in *Brooke Group*, only higher bidding that leads to below-cost pricing in the relevant output market will suffice as a basis for predatory-bidding liability. A predatory-bidding plaintiff also must prove that the defendant has a dangerous probability of recouping the losses incurred in bidding up input prices through the exercise of monopsony power. Making such a showing will require a close analysis of both the scheme alleged by the plaintiff and the relevant market's structure and conditions. Because Ross-Simmons (P) has conceded that it has not satisfied the *Brooke Group* standard, its predatory-bidding theory of liability cannot support the jury's verdict. Affirmed.

▎ *ANALYSIS*

There are myriad legitimate reasons—ranging from benign to affirmatively procompetitive—why a buyer might bid up input prices. A firm might bid up inputs as a result of miscalculation of its input needs or as a response to increased consumer demand for its outputs. A more efficient firm (such as Weyerhaeuser (D) here) might bid up input prices to acquire more inputs as a part of a procompetitive strategy to gain market share in the output market. A firm that has adopted an input-intensive production process might bid up inputs to acquire the inputs necessary for its process. Or a firm might bid up input prices to acquire excess inputs as a hedge against the risk of future rises in input costs or future input

shortages. Thus, this sort of high bidding is essential to competition and innovation on the buy side of the market.

■■■

Quicknotes

PREDATORY PRICING Pricing below the cost of production of a product with the intent of driving competitors out of business.

■■■

Cascade Health Solutions v. PeaceHealth

Hospital operator (P) v. Hospital operator (D)

515 F.3d 883 (9th Cir. 2008).

NATURE OF CASE: Cross-appeals in action for, inter alia, monopolization, conspiracy to monopolize, exclusive dealing, attempted monopolization, and price discrimination.

FACT SUMMARY: McKenzie-Willamette Hospital (P), a hospital operator, claimed that PeaceHealth (D), also a hospital operator, committed various antitrust violations by offering insurers bundled discounts on certain types of services (tertiary) if the insurers made PeaceHealth (D) their sole preferred provider for all hospital services.

🏛 RULE OF LAW
To prove that a bundled discount is exclusionary or predatory under § 2 of the Sherman Act, a plaintiff must show that, after allocating the discount given by the defendant on the entire bundle of products to the competitive product or products, the defendant sold the competitive product or products below its average variable cost of producing them.

FACTS: McKenzie-Willamette Hospital (McKenzie) (P) operated a hospital in a certain geographical area, while PeaceHealth (D) operated three. McKenzie's (P) hospital provided only primary and secondary acute care, whereas PeaceHealth (D) also offered tertiary care (more complex medical services). PeaceHealth (D) had a 75 percent share of primary and secondary services. PeaceHealth (D) offered insurers its services at a discounted reimbursement rate. The reimbursement rate is the price paid by the insurer for the hospital's services. McKenzie (P) brought suit alleging that PeaceHealth (D) had committed various antitrust violations, including monopolization, conspiracy to monopolize, exclusive dealing, attempted monopolization, and price discrimination. On its monopolization and attempted monopolization claims, McKenzie (P) theorized that PeaceHealth's (D) conduct was anticompetitve when it offered insurers bundled discounts of 35–40 percent on certain tertiary services if the insurers made PeaceHealth (D) their sole preferred provider for all hospital services—primary, secondary and tertiary. Bundling is the practice of offering, for a single price, two or more goods or services that could be sold separately. A bundled discount occurs when a firm sells a bundle of goods or services for a lower price than the seller charges for the goods or services purchased individually. The jury returned a verdict for PeaceHealth (D) on the monopolization, conspiracy to monopolize, and exclusive dealing claims, but found in favor of McKenzie (P) on the attempted monopolization and price discrimination claims. The district court trebled the damages awarded by the jury, and the court of appeals granted review.

ISSUE: To prove that a bundled discount is exclusionary or predatory under § 2 of the Sherman Act, must a plaintiff show that, after allocating the discount given by the defendant on the entire bundle of products to the competitive product or products, the defendant sold the competitive product or products below its average variable cost of producing them?

HOLDING AND DECISION: (Gould, J.) Yes. To prove that a bundled discount is exclusionary or predatory under § 2 of the Sherman Act, a plaintiff must show that, after allocating the discount given by the defendant on the entire bundle of products to the competitive product or products, the defendant sold the competitive product or products below its average variable cost of producing them. Bundled discounts generally favor buyers and can result in savings for the seller. Therefore, the Supreme Court has indicated that such price cutting is a practice that the antitrust laws aim to promote, since it can benefit consumers. Nevertheless, it is theoretically possible for a seller to use a bundled discount to exclude an equally or more efficient competitor, thus reducing consumer welfare. One example is where a competitor sells only a single product in the bundle and produces that product at a lower cost than the seller, but cannot match profitably the price created by the multi-product discount. This is true even if the post-discount prices for both the entire bundle and each product in the bundle are above the seller's cost. Here, the district court applied a rule that did not require below-cost pricing for any bundled-discount pricing practice to be deemed exclusionary. The problem with this standard, however, as noted by the Antitrust Modernization Commission (AMC) is that it does not consider whether the bundled discounts constitution competition on the merits, but simply concludes that all bundled discounts offered by a monopolist are anticompetitive with respect to competitors that do not have an equally diverse product line. Thus, this standard can protect a less efficient competitor to the detriment of consumer welfare. Moreover, this standard does not offer a clear standard by which a seller can assess whether its bundled rebates are anticompetitive. Given the endemic nature of bundled discounts throughout all spheres of the economy, this standard is rejected in favor of a standard that provides that the exclusionary conduct element of a claim arising under § 2 of the Sherman Act cannot be satisfied by reference to bundled discounts unless the discounts result in prices that are below an appropriate measure of the defendant's costs. The next issue that must be resolved, therefore, is how to define the appropriate measure of the seller's costs and how to determine whether discounted prices have fallen below that

Continued on next page.

mark. PeaceHealth (D) urges adopting an "aggregate discount" measure, which would condemn bundled discounts as anticompetitive only if the discounted price of the entire bundle does not exceed the seller's incremental cost to produce the entire bundle. Such a rule, however, is not necessary in multi-product discounting cases, since alternative rules exist that are more likely to identify anticompetitive bundled discounting practices while simultaneously causing little harm to competition. One such rule deems a bundled discount exclusionary if the plaintiff can show that it was an equally efficient producer of the competitive product, but the defendant's bundled discount made it impossible for the plaintiff to continue to produce profitably the competitive product. Under this standard, a plaintiff must prove either that the monopolist has priced below its average variable cost or the plaintiff is at least as efficient a producer of the competitive product as the defendant, but that the defendant's pricing makes it unprofitable for the plaintiff to continue to produce. Thus, under this standard, above-cost prices are not per se legal. Instead, below-cost prices are simply one beacon for identifying discounts that create the risk of excluding firms that are as efficient as the defendant—the unique anticompetitive risk posed by bundled discounts. A downside of this standard, however, is that it does not provide guidance to sellers who wish to offer procompetitive bundled discounts because the standard looks to the actual plaintiff's costs, which the seller likely will not know, and might encourage more litigation than necessary. Yet another alternative cost-based rule, which is adopted here, is a "discount attribution" standard, whereby the full amount of the discounts given on the bundle are allocated to the competitive product or products. If the resulting price of the competitive product or products is below the defendant's incremental cost to produce them, the trier of fact may find that the bundled discount is exclusionary. This standard makes the defendant's bundled discounts legal unless the discounts have the potential to exclude a hypothetical equally efficient producer of the competitive product—rather than an actual plaintiff. This rule thus has the benefit of providing clear guidance to sellers as to whether their bundled discounts will run afoul of the antitrust laws, since the seller can ascertain its own prices and cost of production. Such an approach is also supported by leading antitrust commentators and judges. While liability under this rule has to the potential to sweep more broadly than under the other standards, it will permit courts to obtain the experience necessary for determining whether bundled discounts are anticompetitive. Finally, the appropriate measure of incremental cost is marginal cost—the increase to total cost that occurs as a result of producing one additional unit of output. However, because the incremental cost of making and selling the last unit cannot readily be inferred from conventional business accounts, which typically go no further than showing observed average variable cost, variable cost is a suitable surrogate for marginal cost. Accordingly, prices below average variable cost can indicate predation. Therefore, in the bundled discounts context, the appropriate measure of costs for the cost-based standard is average variable cost.

Because the district court's jury instruction was premised on the wrong legal standard, it contained an error of law. Reversed.

▶ ANALYSIS

The Antitrust Modernization Commission (AMC) has proposed that courts should adopt a three-part test to determine whether bundled discounts or rebates violate § 2 of the Sherman Act. To prove a violation of § 2, a plaintiff should be required to show each one of the following elements (as well as other elements of a § 2 claim): (1) after allocating all discounts and rebates attributable to the entire bundle of products to the competitive product, the defendant sold the competitive product below its incremental cost for the competitive product; (2) the defendant is likely to recoup these short-term losses; and (3) the bundled discount or rebate program has had or is likely to have an adverse effect on competition. The first element would subject bundled discounts to antitrust scrutiny only if they could exclude a hypothetical equally efficient competitor and provide sufficient clarity for businesses to determine whether their bundled discounting practices run afoul of § 2.

■=■

Quicknotes

SHERMAN ACT § 2 Makes it a felony to monopolize or attempt to monopolize, or combine or conspire with any other person(s) to monopolize, any part of the trade or commerce among the states or with a foreign country.

■=■

Aspen Skiing Co. v. Aspen Highlands Skiing Corp.

Ski mountain operator (P) v. Ski mountain operator (D)

472 U.S. 585 (1985).

NATURE OF CASE: Appeal from decision affirming finding of violation of antimonopoly laws.

FACT SUMMARY: Aspen Skiing Co. (D) appealed from a court of appeals decision affirming a judgment finding a violation of the antimonopoly laws, contending that the judgment could not stand as a matter of law because it rested with an assumption that a firm with monopoly power has a duty to cooperate with smaller rivals in a marketing arrangement in order to avoid the violation.

> ## RULE OF LAW
> If there is support in the record for a jury's conclusion that no valid business decision exists for the refusal of a firm with monopoly power to deal with smaller competitions, its judgment of a monopoly laws violation will be sustained.

FACTS: Aspen Highlands Skiing Corp. (Highlands) (P) operated a ski mountain facility in the Aspen area of Colorado. Three other mountain skiing facilities operated in the same area. These mountains were operated by Aspen Skiing Co. (Skiing) (D). Throughout the years, the operations in the area offered all-Aspen ticket programs of various designs, which allowed skiers in the area to utilize all the facilities in the area with a minimum of difficulties. Although there were some monitoring difficulties associated with the all-Aspen ticket, sales of the ticket were good, and the program was generally well received. During the 1970s, Skiing (D) became increasingly dissatisfied with the all-Aspen ticket and in 1977–78 refused to offer such a ticket unless Highlands (P) would accept a fixed share of the ticket revenues at a level lower than traditionally achieved by Highlands (P). For 1978–79 the fixed percentage offered by Skiing (D) was further reduced, and Skiing (D) refused to accept any counterproposals from Highlands (P). Highlands (P) attempted to market its own multi-area package, but Skiing (D) made it very difficult for it to do so. Skiing (D) refused to accept any vouchers from Highlands (P) and refused to sell Highlands (P) any ski lift tickets that they could package. Without the convenience of the previous tickets, Highlands' (P) program met with considerable resistance, and Highlands' (P) revenues began to drop off. Highlands (P) filed a complaint alleging violations of the Sherman Act's antimonopoly laws. The jury returned a $2.5 million verdict, and the district court awarded treble damages. The court of appeals affirmed, and from this decision, Skiing (D) appealed.

ISSUE: If there is support in the record for a jury's conclusion that no valid business reason exists for the refusal of a firm with monopoly power to deal with smaller competitors, will its judgment of a violation of the antimonopoly laws be sustained?

HOLDING AND DECISION: (Stevens, J.) Yes. If there is support in the record for a jury's conclusion that no valid business decision exists for the refusal of a firm with monopoly power to deal with smaller competitors, its judgments for violation of the antimonopoly laws will be sustained. Clearly, a business does not have the duty to cooperate with competitors, but the right is not unqualified. In the present case, Skiing (D) has elected to make an important change in the pattern of distribution that had existed in the skiing industry for many years and had served to further enhance that competitive market. Construing the record most favorably to Highlands (P), it is assumed that the jury followed the court's instructions. As such it must have concluded that no valid business reasons existed for Skiing's (D) refusal to cooperate in the marketing of the all-Aspen ticket. There is ample evidence in the record to support this conclusion. The superior quality of the all-Aspen ticket is attested to by its previous popularity, and it could be concluded that consumers were adversely affected by the elimination of the ticket. It is also readily apparent that Highlands' (P) share of the market declined as a result of the elimination of the all-Aspen ticket. Finally, Skiing (D) has offered no efficiency justification whatsoever for its pattern of conduct. Indeed, it appeared that Skiing (D) was willing to forgo substantial benefits associated with the ticket. Although not bold, relentless, and predatory, ample evidence exists for the conclusion that there was deliberate effort to discourage its customers from doing business with Highlands (P). Affirmed.

▶ ANALYSIS

This case is clearly an example of the Court's concern for the consumer. The Court in this particular case targeted the relative market as the purchaser of the all-area ticket. While Skiing's (D) activities clearly had an effect on Highlands (P), no particular consumer was prevented from skiing at either location. Had Skiing (D) not been so obvious in its effects but had merely allowed Highlands (P) to absorb the costs of the program, antitrust liability would not have been assessed.

Quicknotes

MONOPOLY A privilege or right conferred upon an individual or entity granting it the exclusive power to manufacture, sell and distribute a particular service or commodity; a

Continued on next page.

market condition in which one or a few companies control the sale of a product or service thereby restraining competition in respect to that article or service.

SHERMAN ACT Makes every contract or conspiracy in unreasonable restraint of commerce illegal.

TREBLE DAMAGES An award of damages triple of the amount awarded by the jury and provided for by statute for violation of certain offenses.

■≡■

Verizon Communications, Inc. v. Law Offices of Curtis V. Trinko, LLP

Incumbent local telephone company (D) v. Local telephone service customer (P)

540 U.S. 398 (2004).

NATURE OF CASE: Appeal from reversal of dismissal for failure to state a claim of action under § 2 of the Sherman Act.

FACT SUMMARY: Verizon Communications, Inc. (Verizon) (D), the incumbent local exchange carrier (LEC) serving New York State, contended that Law Offices of Curtis V. Trinko, LLP (P), a local telephone service customer of AT&T, failed to state a claim under § 2 of the Sherman Act when it alleged that Verizon (D) denied interconnection services to rivals in order to limit entry and had filled rivals' orders on a discriminatory basis as part of an anticompetitive scheme to discourage customers from becoming or remaining customers of competitive LECs.

🏛 RULE OF LAW
A complaint alleging breach of an incumbent local exchange carrier's duty under the Telecommunications Act of 1996 to share its network with competitors does not state a claim under § 2 of the Sherman Act.

FACTS: The Telecommunications Act of 1996 imposes upon an incumbent local exchange carrier (LEC) the obligation to share its telephone network with competitors, including the duty to provide access to individual network elements on an "unbundled" basis. New entrants, so-called competitive LECs, combine and resell these unbundled network elements (UNEs). Verizon Communications, Inc. (Verizon) (D) was the incumbent local exchange carrier (LEC) serving New York State. To foster increased competition, Verizon (D) had signed interconnection agreements with rivals such as AT&T, detailing the terms on which it would make its network elements available. Verizon (D) also entered the long-distance market. Competitive LECs complained that Verizon (D) was violating its obligation to provide access. A consent decree and orders issued from the state regulatory agency (PSC) and the Federal Communications Commission (FCC), which led to the imposition of financial penalties, remediation measures, and additional reporting requirements on Verizon (D). Law Offices of Curtis V. Trinko, LLP (P), a local telephone service customer of AT&T, then filed a class action alleging, inter alia, that Verizon (D) had filled rivals' orders on a discriminatory basis as part of an anticompetitive scheme to discourage customers from becoming or remaining customers of competitive LECs in violation of § 2 of the Sherman Act. The district court dismissed the complaint, concluding that the allegations of deficient assistance to rivals failed to satisfy § 2's requirements. The court of appeals reversed and reinstated the antitrust claim, and the U.S. Supreme Court granted certiorari.

ISSUE: Does a complaint alleging breach of an incumbent local exchange carrier's duty under the Telecommunications Act of 1996 to share its network with competitors state a claim under § 2 of the Sherman Act?

HOLDING AND DECISION: (Scalia, J.) No. A complaint alleging breach of an incumbent local exchange carrier's duty under the Telecommunications Act of 1996 to share its network with competitors does not state a claim under § 2 of the Sherman Act. The 1996 Act has no effect upon the application of traditional antitrust principles. Its saving clause, which provides that "nothing in this Act . . . shall be construed to modify, impair, or supersede the applicability of any of the antitrust laws," preserves claims that satisfy established antitrust standards, but does not create new claims that go beyond those standards. Established antitrust principles make clear that the mere possession of monopoly power, and the concomitant charging of monopoly prices, is not by itself unlawful, and, in fact, is part of the free-market system. Such power is only unlawful when it is accompanied by an element of anticompetitive conduct. Thus, the issue here is whether Verizon's (D) activities violate pre-existing antitrust standards or fits within existing exceptions. The leading case imposing § 2 liability for refusal to deal with competitors is *Aspen Skiing Co. v. Aspen Highlands Skiing Corp.*, 472 U.S. 585 (1985), in which the Court concluded that the defendant's termination of a voluntary agreement with the plaintiff suggested a willingness to forsake short-term profits to achieve an anticompetitive end. *Aspen* is at or near the outer boundary of § 2 liability, and the present case does not fit within the limited exception it recognized. Because the complaint does not allege that Verizon (D) ever engaged in a voluntary course of dealing with its rivals, its prior conduct sheds no light upon whether its lapses from the legally compelled dealing were anticompetitive. Moreover, the *Aspen* defendant turned down its competitor's proposal to sell at its own retail price, suggesting a calculation that its future monopoly retail price would be higher, whereas Verizon's (D) reluctance to interconnect at the cost-based rate of compensation available under the 1996 Ac, § 251(c)(3) is uninformative. More fundamentally, the *Aspen* defendant refused to provide its competitor with a product it already sold at retail, whereas here the unbundled elements offered pursuant to § 251 (c)(3) are not available to the public, but are provided to rivals under compulsion and at considerable expense. The Court's conclusion would not change even if it considered to be established law the "essential facilities" doctrine crafted by some lower courts and which was used by the court of appeals to conclude that the complaint might state a claim. The indispensable requirement for invoking that doctrine is

Continued on next page.

the unavailability of access to the "essential facilities"; where access exists, as it does here by virtue of the 1996 Act, the doctrine serves no purpose, and the argument based on it is rejected. Finally, traditional antitrust principles do not justify adding the present case to the few existing exceptions from the proposition that there is no duty to aid competitors. Antitrust analysis must always be attuned to the particular structure and circumstances of the industry at issue. When a regulatory structure designed to deter and remedy anticompetitive harm exists, the additional benefit to competition provided by antitrust enforcement will tend to be small, and it will be less plausible that the antitrust laws contemplate such additional scrutiny. Here, Verizon (D) was subject to oversight by the FCC and the PSC, both of which responded to certain deficiencies raised in the complaint by imposing fines and other burdens on Verizon (D). Thus, the regulatory regime was an effective steward of the antitrust function. Against the slight benefits of antitrust intervention here must be weighed a realistic assessment of its costs. Allegations of violations of § 251 (c)(3) duties are both technical and extremely numerous, and hence difficult for antitrust courts to evaluate. Applying § 2's requirements to this regime can readily result in "false positive" mistaken inferences that chill the very conduct the antitrust laws are designed to protect. Reversed and remanded.

CONCURRENCE: (Stevens, J.) The court of appeals' decision should have been reversed on standing grounds.]

▶ *ANALYSIS*

Part of the Court's concern is that allegations of violations of § 251(c)(3) duties are difficult for antitrust courts to evaluate, not only because they are highly technical, but also because they are likely to be extremely numerous, given the incessant, complex, and constantly changing interaction of competitive and incumbent LECs implementing the sharing and interconnection obligations. As the Court notes, such difficulty for the generalist courts could lead to "false positives." An example of one false-positive risk is that an incumbent LEC's failure to provide a service with sufficient alacrity might have nothing to do with exclusion. The Court is also concerned that even if the problem of false positives did not exist, conduct consisting of anticompetitive violations of § 251 could well be beyond the practical ability of a judicial tribunal to control, since effective remediation of violations of regulatory sharing requirements will ordinarily require continuing supervision of a highly detailed degree. In short, the Court finds that the matter is one to be handled by more expert regulatory agencies rather than generalist antitrust courts.

■≡■

United States v. Dentsply International, Inc.

Federal government (P) v. Manufacturer of artificial teeth (D)

399 F.3d 181 (3d Cir. 2005), *cert. denied,* 546 U.S. 1089 (2006).

NATURE OF CASE: Appeal from denial of injunctive relief and from judgment for defendant in action under, inter alia, § 2 of the Sherman Act.

FACT SUMMARY: The Government (P) contended that Dentsply International, Inc. (D), a manufacturer of artificial teeth, acted unlawfully to maintain its monopoly through its use of an exclusivity policy that discouraged or prevented its dealers from adding competitors' teeth to their lines of products.

🏛 **RULE OF LAW**

An exclusivity policy imposed by a monopolist manufacturer on its dealers violates § 2 of the Sherman Act where it forecloses competition and has no business justification.

FACTS: Dentsply International, Inc. (Dentsply) (D), a manufacturer of artificial teeth, dominated the market for prefabricated artificial teeth, enjoying a 75–80 percent market share on a revenue basis, and 67 percent on a unit basis. Dentsply (D) also manufactured other dental products, which were sold through a network of dealers. Dealers competed among themselves, as well as with manufacturers who sold directly to dental laboratories. For many years, Dentsply (D) operated under a policy that discouraged its dealers from adding competitors' teeth to their lines of products. Dentsply (D) eventually adopted "Dealer Criterion 6," which provides that to effectively promote Dentsply (D) products, authorized dealers "may not add further tooth lines to their product offering." This policy was enforced against dealers with the exception of those who had carried competing products before the policy went into effect. Although dissatisfied with the policy, none of the dealers gave up the popular Dentsply (D) teeth to sell competitors' products. Dentsply (D), which had considered selling directly, decided not to for fear that dealers would retaliate by refusing to buy its other products. Dentsply (D) effected aggressive price increases, and its profits from its artificial teeth business were the company's "cash cow." The Government (P) brought suit alleging various antitrust violations, including unlawful maintenance of a monopoly in violation of § 2 of the Sherman Act. Although the district court found that Dentsply's (D) business justification for Dealer Criterion 6 was pretextual and designed expressly to exclude its rivals from access to dealers, it concluded that other dealers were available and that direct sales to laboratories was a viable method of doing business. Additionally, the district court concluded that Dentsply (D) had not created a market with above competitive pricing; dealers were free to leave the network at any time; and Dentsply's (D) actions were not proven to have been successful in preventing new or potential competitors from gaining a foothold in the market.

The Government (P) appealed, contending that a monopolist that prevents rivals from distributing through established dealers has maintained its monopoly by acting with predatory intent and violates § 2. The court of appeals granted review.

ISSUE: Does an exclusivity policy imposed by a monopolist manufacturer on its dealers violate § 2 of the Sherman Act where it forecloses competition and has no business justification?

HOLDING AND DECISION: (Weis, J.) Yes. An exclusivity policy imposed by a monopolist manufacturer on its dealers violates § 2 of the Sherman Act where it forecloses competition and has no business justification. Exclusive dealing arrangements, while not per se illegal, may be improper if exercised by a monopolist to anticompetitive effect. Even if these elements are established, however, a monopolist still retains a business justification defense. Unlawful maintenance of a monopoly is demonstrated by proof that a defendant has engaged in anticompetitive conduct that reasonably appears to be a significant contribution to maintaining monopoly power. The first inquiry is thus whether Dentsply (D) had monopoly power. Here, the district court found that the relevant market was "the sale of prefabricated artificial teeth in the United States." The consumers in this market are dental laboratories, and manufacturers may provide product to this market directly, through dealers, or through a hybrid system. The relevant market thus can include sales both to the final consumer and a middleman. Therefore, the relevant market should be "the sale of artificial teeth in the United States both to laboratories and to the dental dealers." A prima facie case of monopoly power is made where the defendant has a 55 percent market share or greater, so here Dentsply's (D) share is more than adequate to establish a prima facie case of power. Maintenance of market share is a hallmark of monopoly power, and here, Dentsply (D) maintained its dominant share for more than ten years. The district court's conclusion that Dentsply (D) did not preclude competition from marketing to laboratories is flawed, since the reality is that over a period of years, because of Dentsply's (D) domination of dealers, direct sales were not a practical alternative for most manufacturers, whose access to key dealers was blocked. In other words, the apparent lack of aggressiveness by competitors was not a matter of apathy, but a reflection of the effectiveness of Dentsply's (D) exclusionary policy. Market realities, rather than theoretical possibilities of competition, must govern the determination of market power. As a reflection of market reality, Dentsply (D) managers testified that the purpose of Dealer Criterion 6 was to block competitive distribution

Continued on next page.

points and to deny laboratories a choice among competing products. Thus, the policy was clearly part of a plan to maintain monopolistic power. In addition to clear evidence of exclusion, there was evidence that Dentsply (D) controlled pricing—another indicator of monopoly power. Dentsply (D) did not reduce its prices when competitors elected not to follow its increases, and its profit margins kept growing over the years. The picture was of a manufacturer that set prices with little concern for its competitors, "something a firm without a monopoly would have been unable to do." Accordingly, the Government (P) established that Dentsply (D) possessed market power. The next inquiry, therefore, is whether Dentsply (D) used that power "to foreclose competition." While foreclosure need not be complete, it must be substantial. By keeping sales of competing teeth below the critical level necessary for any rival to seriously challenge Dentsply's (D) market position, Dealer Criterion 6 was "a solid pillar of harm to competition." One detrimental effect was that it locked in benefits provided by dealers to laboratories, including one-stop shopping, extensive credit services, discounts, and tooth returns (which accompany 30 percent of purchases). Manufacturers do not provide these benefits. Dealers also provide benefits to manufacturers, including efficiency of scale. Although a laboratory that buys directly from a manufacturer may be able to avoid the marginal costs associated with dealers, any savings must be weighed against the benefits, savings, and convenience offered by those dealers. Finally, dealers offer manufacturers more marketplace exposure and sales representative coverage than the manufacturers could generate on their own. Because of the benefits provided by dealers, the district court's conclusion that direct sales were a "viable" distribution method is flawed insofar as such viability is merely a theoretical possibility, rather than a practical or feasible option. Merely because an insignificant number of manufacturers engage in direct sales does not mean that such a distribution method is an effective means of competition. The proper inquiry is not whether direct sales enable a competitor to "survive" but rather whether direct selling "poses a real threat" to Dentsply's (D) monopoly; the answer is that it does not. Here, too, the economic realities of the market render the exclusive dealing arrangement, while technically at-will, as effective as those in written contracts. Another anticompetitive effect is that the laboratories' choice of products is effectively limited, since dealers are unable to fulfill a request for a competing product. Yet another anticompetitive effect is that competitors are effectively barred from entry into the marketplace, as there is no evidence that competitors could get dealers to switch to them from Dentsply (D), thanks to Dentsply's (D) longtime, vigorous and successful enforcement actions. The levels of sales that competitors could project in wooing dealers were miniscule compare to Dentsply's (D). Also, dealers were left with an all-or-nothing choice, and clearly acceded to the accompanying economic pressure. This effect was multiplied because the market for artificial teeth is not a dynamic one. Dentsply's (D) grip on its dealers effectively choked off the market for artificial teeth, leaving only a small sliver for competitors. For these reasons, the Government (P) established that Dentsply's (D) exclusionary policies and particularly Dealer Criterion 6 violated § 2. Dentsply (D) has offered no procompetitive business justification for its conduct or policies, and the district court was correct in concluding that any offered justifications, when compared to reality, were pretextual. Therefore, Dentsply's (D) exclusionary practices were not excused. This finding of liability supports a judgment against Dentsply (D). Reversed and remanded.

▶ *ANALYSIS*

In this case, the Government (P) also asserted claims for violations of § 3 of the Clayton Act (entering into illegal restrictive dealing agreements) and § 1 of the Sherman Act (use of unlawful agreements in restraint of interstate trade), which the district court rejected. The Government (P) did not appeal the rulings on these claims. While the district court had indicated that because it had found no liability under the stricter standards of § 3 of the Clayton Act, it followed that there was no violation of § 2 of the Sherman Act. The court of appeals rejected this reasoning, finding instead that a ruling in Dentsply's (D) favor on the § 1 and § 3 claims did not preclude the application of evidence of exclusive dealing to support the § 2 claim. As all of the evidence in the case also applied to the § 2 claim, liability under that section could support a judgment against Dentsply (D). Because different theories may be presented to establish a cause of action, a court's refusal to accept one theory rather than another neither undermines the claim as a whole, nor the judgment applying one of the theories. Thus, the Government (P) could obtain all the relief to which it was entitled under § 2 without reference to § 1 of the Sherman Act or § 3 of the Clayton Act.

■—■

Quicknotes

PRIMA FACIE EVIDENCE Evidence presented by a party, that is sufficient in the absence of contradictory evidence to support the fact or issue for which it is offered.

SHERMAN ACT § 2 Makes it a felony to monopolize or attempt to monopolize, or combine or conspire with any other person(s) to monopolize, any part of the trade or commerce among the states or with a foreign country.

■—■

Pacific Bell Telephone Co. dba AT&T California v. Linkline Communications, Inc.

Incumbent telephone company (D) v. Independent Internet service provider (P)

129 S. Ct. 1109 (2009).

NATURE OF CASE: Appeal from affirmance of judgment in action under § 2 of the Sherman Act.

FACT SUMMARY: AT&T (D), which owned infrastructure and facilities needed to provide digital subscriber line (DSL) service, contended that because it had no antitrust duty to deal with independent Internet service providers (ISPs) (P) who were using AT&T's (D) infrastructure and facilities to provide DSL service, the ISPs (P) did not state a claim for price-squeezing under § 2 of the Sherman Act when they asserted that AT&T (D) set a high price for the wholesale DSL transport service it sold and a low price for its own retail DSL service, thus squeezing the ISPs (P) and placing them at a competitive disadvantage.

RULE OF LAW

A price-squeeze claim may not be brought under § 2 of the Sherman Act when the defendant has no antitrust duty to deal with the plaintiff at wholesale.

FACTS: AT&T (D) owned infrastructure and facilities needed to provide digital subscriber line (DSL) service, a method of connecting to the Internet at high speeds over telephone lines. As a condition for a recent merger, the Federal Communications Commission (FCC) required AT&T (D) to provide wholesale DSL transport service to independent firms at a price no greater than the retail price of AT&T's DSL service. Independent Internet service providers (ISPs) (P) that competed with AT&T (D) in the retail DSL market in California did not own all the facilities needed to supply DSL service, and therefore had to lease wholesale DSL transport service from AT&T (D). The ISPs (P) filed suit under § 2 of the Sherman Act, asserting that AT&T (D) unlawfully "squeezed" their profit margins by setting a high price for the wholesale DSL transport service it sold and a low price for its own retail DSL service. This maneuver allegedly placed the ISPs (P) at a competitive disadvantage, allowing AT&T (D) to maintain monopoly power in the DSL market. AT&T (D) defended on the ground that the claims were foreclosed by *Verizon Communications Inc. v. Law Offices of Curtis V. Trinko, LLP,* 540 U.S. 39 (2004), in which the U.S. Supreme Court held that a firm with no antitrust duty to deal with its rivals has no obligation to provide those rivals with a "sufficient" level of service. The district court ruled that *Trinko* was not controlling because it did not address price-squeeze claims; the court of appeals concurred. The U.S. Supreme Court granted certiorari.

ISSUE: May a price-squeeze claim be brought under § 2 of the Sherman Act when the defendant has no antitrust duty to deal with the plaintiff at wholesale?

HOLDING AND DECISION: (Roberts, C.J.) No. A price-squeeze claim may not be brought under § 2 of the Sherman Act when the defendant has no antitrust duty to deal with the plaintiff at wholesale. Businesses are generally free to choose the parties with which they will deal, as well as the prices, terms, and conditions of that dealing. In rare circumstances, a dominant firm may incur antitrust liability for purely unilateral conduct, such as charging "predatory" prices. There are also limited circumstances in which a firm's unilateral refusal to deal with its rivals can give rise to antitrust liability. Here, the ISPs (P) do not allege predatory pricing, and the district court concluded that there was no antitrust duty to deal. Here, the challenge is to a different type of unilateral conduct in which a firm "squeezes" its competitors' profit margins. This requires the defendant to operate in both the wholesale ("upstream") and retail ("downstream") markets. By raising the wholesale price of inputs while cutting its own retail prices, the defendant can raise competitors' costs while putting downward pressure on their revenues. Price-squeeze plaintiffs assert that defendants must leave them a "fair" or "adequate" margin between wholesale and retail prices. The issue, therefore, is whether a price-squeeze claim can stand where the defendant has no obligation under the antitrust laws to deal with the plaintiff at wholesale. Any challenge to AT&T's wholesale prices is foreclosed by a straightforward application of *Trinko*, which made clear that a firm with no antitrust duty to deal in the wholesale market certainly has no obligation to deal under terms and conditions favorable to its competitors. Had AT&T (D) simply stopped providing DSL transport service to the ISPs (P), it would not have run afoul of the Sherman Act. Thus, it was not required to offer this service at the wholesale prices the ISPs (P) would have preferred. The other component of a price-squeeze claim is the assertion that the defendant's retail prices are "too low." Here too there is no support in existing antitrust doctrine for the ISPs' (P) claim. "[C]utting prices in order to increase business, often is, the very essence of competition." To avoid chilling aggressive price competition, the Court has carefully limited the circumstances under which plaintiffs can state a Sherman Act claim by alleging that the defendant's prices are too low. Specifically, to prevail on a predatory pricing claim, a plaintiff must demonstrate that: (1) "the prices complained of are below an appropriate measure of its rival's costs"; and (2) there is a "dangerous probability" that the defendant will be able to recoup its "investment" in below-cost prices. (*Brooke Group*). The complaint here has not alleged that AT&T's (D) conduct met either *Brooke*

Continued on next page.

Group requirement. Recognizing a price-squeeze claim where the defendant's retail price remains above cost would invite the precise harm the Court sought to avoid in *Brooke Group*. Firms might raise retail prices or refrain from aggressive price competition to avoid potential antitrust liability. Thus, the ISPs' (P) claim, looking to the relation between wholesale and retail prices, is thus nothing more than an amalgamation of meritless claims at each level. If there is no duty to deal at the wholesale level and no predatory pricing at the retail level, then a firm is certainly not required to price both of these services in a manner that preserves its rivals' profit margins. Institutional concerns also militate against recognizing such a price-squeezing claim. The Court has repeatedly emphasized the importance of clear rules in antitrust law, and recognizing price-squeeze claims would require courts simultaneously to police both the wholesale and retail prices to ensure that rival firms are not being squeezed. Courts would be aiming at a moving target, since it is the interaction between these two prices that may result in a squeeze. Moreover, firms seeking to avoid price-squeeze liability will have no safe harbor for their pricing practices. The most commonly articulated standard for price squeezes is that the defendant must leave its rivals a "fair" or "adequate" margin between wholesale and retail prices; this test is nearly impossible for courts to apply without conducting complex proceedings like rate-setting agencies. Some amici argue that a price squeeze should be presumed if the defendant's wholesale price exceeds its retail price. However, if both the wholesale price and the retail price are independently lawful, there is no basis for imposing antitrust liability simply because a vertically integrated firm's wholesale price is greater than or equal to its retail price. On remand, the district court should consider whether an amended complaint filed by the ISPs (P) states a claim upon which relief may be granted. Reversed and remanded.

▶ ANALYSIS

Those disagreeing with the Court's decision, including the Federal Trade Commission, emphasize that price squeezing has long been recognized in the lower courts and that price squeezing risks competitive harms by deterring competition at the wholesale level, where new entrants not only face the basic barriers to entry that have led to the monopoly in the first place, but also face the prospect that the price squeezing has driven away most potential customers. There is also potential harm at the retail level through the removal of competition that would put pressure on the monopolist to improve not only price, but quality of service. The Court addressed these concerns by saying that given developments in economic theory and antitrust jurisprudence, the Court's recent decisions in *Trinko* and *Brooke Group* are more pertinent to the issue.

Quicknotes

UNILATERAL One-sided; involving only one person.

Spectrum Sports, Inc. v. McQuillan

Distributor (D) v. Distributor (P)

506 U.S. 447 (1993).

NATURE OF CASE: Review of verdict awarding damages for antitrust violations.

FACT SUMMARY: The McQuillans (P) contended that Hamilton-Kent and Spectrum Sports, Inc. (D) had violated the Sherman Act, although they had no proof that they would monopolize the market or had intent to do so.

> ## 🏛 RULE OF LAW
> A violation of § 2 of the Sherman Act does not occur absent proof of an intent to monopolize and dangerous probability of such monopolization.

FACTS: Hamilton-Kent Manufacturing, through its parent corporation, owned the patent on Sorbothane, a type of polymer useful in various applications, including athletic and equestrian products. The McQuillans (P) purchased exclusive distribution rights to Sorbothane equestrian products. They later received the rights to distribute athletic equipment. Subsequently, Hamilton elected to terminate their position as athletic equipment distributors. When the McQuillans (P) balked at this, Hamilton terminated its entire contract with the McQuillans (P), awarding it to Spectrum Sports, Inc. (Spectrum) (D). The McQuillans (P) sued for antitrust violations. At trial, no evidence was presented of intent to monopolize any given market by Spectrum (D) or that a dangerous probability of such monopolization existed. The jury found a violation of § 2 of the Sherman Act. A verdict of nearly $2 million was rendered, which the court trebled. The Ninth Circuit affirmed, and the U.S. Supreme Court granted review.

ISSUE: Does a violation of § 2 of the Sherman Act occur absent proof of an intent to monopolize and dangerous probability of such monopolization?

HOLDING AND DECISION: (White, J.) No. A violation of § 2 of the Sherman Act does not occur absent proof of an intent to monopolize and dangerous probability of such monopolization. While § 1 of the Act forbids conspiracies in restraint of trade, § 2 of the Act deals with single firms that monopolize. Section 2 forbids monopolization or attempts to monopolize. The elements of monopolization are undefined in the statute. Unlike a price-fixing scheme, which is clearly monopolistic behavior, the line between legitimate hard work by a single firm and monopolistic behavior can be quite hard to draw. For that reason, all courts of appeal which have considered the issue, apart from the Ninth Circuit in this case, have held that elements of a § 2 violation are intent to monopolize and a dangerous probability of monopolization. This Court agrees with this approach. To hold otherwise would run the risk of punishing a business for being successful due to hard, aggressive work, which is not a result contemplated by § 2. Consequently, as these conditions precedent to liability were absent here, there can be no liability. Reversed.

▶ ANALYSIS

Section 1 of the Sherman Act deals with anticompetitive acts by two or more entities, and § 2 deals with such behavior by single firms. Since conspiracies in restraint of trade are perceived as more dangerous than acts by lone businesses, the sanctions under § 1 tend to be more draconian than those under § 2.

■▬■

Quicknotes

MONOPOLY A privilege or right conferred upon an individual or entity granting it the exclusive power to manufacture, sell and distribute a particular service or commodity; a market condition in which one or a few companies control the sale of a product or service thereby restraining competition in respect to that article or service.

SHERMAN ACT § 1 Prohibits price-fixing.

SHERMAN ACT § 2 Makes it a felony to monopolize or attempt to monopolize, or combine or conspire with any other person(s) to monopolize, any part of the trade or commerce among the states or with a foreign country.

TREBLE DAMAGES An award of damages triple of the amount awarded by the jury and provided for by statute for violation of certain offenses.

■▬■

Mergers and Acquisitions

Quick Reference Rules of Law

United States v. Columbia Steel Co.

Federal government (P) v. Steel company (D)

334 U.S. 495 (1948).

NATURE OF CASE: Appeal from the denial of an injunction against the acquisition of a company in an action under §§ 1 and 2 of the Sherman Act.

FACT SUMMARY: When United States Steel Corporation (D), a producer of rolled steel products used in fabrication, attempted to acquire Consolidated Steel, the largest independent steel fabricator on the west coast, the Government (P) sought to enjoin the acquisition, alleging restraint of competition in part through vertical integration.

🏛 RULE OF LAW
Exclusive dealings between companies, brought about by vertical integration or otherwise, are legal unless they unreasonably restrict the opportunities of competitors to market their product.

FACTS: United States Steel Corporation (D) produced rolled steel products, the major component used in the fabrication of finished steel products. United States Steel (D) and its subsidiaries [including Columbia Steel Co. (Columbia) (D)] planned to purchase Consolidated, the largest independent steel fabricator on the west coast. The Government (P) argued that the acquisition of Consolidated constituted an illegal restraint of interstate commerce, in part through vertical integration, because all manufacturers except United States Steel (D) would be excluded from supplying Consolidated's requirements for rolled steel products. United States Steel (D) argued that the market for rolled steel should be the national market, of which Consolidated's market share was less than one-half of one percent. The Government (P) argued that the relevant market was the 11-state area in which Consolidated sold its products. The district court ruled in United States Steel's (D) favor. The Government (P) appealed, and the U.S. Supreme Court granted review.

ISSUE: Are exclusive dealings between companies, brought about by vertical integration or otherwise, legal unless they unreasonably restrict the opportunities of competitors to market their product?

HOLDING AND DECISION: (Reed, J.) Yes. Exclusive dealings between companies, brought about by vertical integration or otherwise, are legal unless they unreasonably restrict the opportunities of competitors to market their product. In determining the legality of vertical integration, it is important to characterize the nature of the market to be served and the leverage on the market which the particular vertical integration creates or makes possible. The so-called vertical integration resulting from the acquisition of Consolidated does not unreasonably restrict the opportunities of the competitor producers of rolled steel to market their product. The relevant competitive market is the total demand for rolled steel products in the 11-state area. Over the past ten years, Consolidated has accounted for only three percent of that demand, and if expectations as to the development of the western steel industry are realized, Consolidated's proportion may be expected to be lower than that in the future. Affirmed.

▶ ANALYSIS

The Court applied the standards laid down in *United States v. Paramount Pictures*, 334 U.S. 131 (1948). In *Paramount*, the Court held that control by the major producers-distributors of nearly 75 percent of the first-run theaters in cities with a population over 100,000 was not in itself illegal. In addition to the nature of the market and leverage, a second test considered important in the *Paramount* case was the intent or purpose with which the combination was conceived.

■=■

Quicknotes

COMBINATION (ANTITRUST DEFINITION) Alliance of entities, for the purpose of impeding free trade, that results in a monopoly, suppression of competition, or affecting prices.

INJUNCTION A court order requiring a person to do or prohibiting that person from doing a specific act.

RESTRAINT OF COMPETITION Agreement between entities, for the purpose of impeding free trade, that results in a monopoly, the suppression of competition, or affecting prices.

VERTICAL INTEGRATION The ownership of the entire chain of production of a product from raw materials to the final merchandise.

■=■

United States v. E.I. du Pont de Nemours & Co.

Federal government (P) v. Multinational corporation (D)

353 U.S. 586 (1957).

NATURE OF CASE: Action under § 7 of the Clayton Act against a vertical merger.

FACT SUMMARY: E.I. du Pont de Nemours & Co. (D) purchased a 23 percent stock interest in General Motors, a firm with which it did a large business.

🏛 RULE OF LAW
Where a stock acquisition has the tendency to foreclose a substantial share of a market to competitors, § 7 of the Clayton Act may be used to compel divestiture of the shares.

FACTS: E.I. du Pont de Nemours & Co. (du Pont) (D) purchased 23 percent of General Motors' shares. Du Pont (D) sold General Motors most of its finishes and fabrics. The Government (P) brought an antitrust action against du Pont (D) alleging that its contracts with General Motors were not the result of pure competition. The Government (P) alleged that du Pont's (D) acquisition of General Motors' stock gave it the power to foreclose a substantial share of the automotive market in fabrics and finishes from competitors. This practice violated § 7's prohibition against mergers and acquisitions in restraint of commerce. Du Pont (D) maintained that § 7 did not apply to stock acquisitions of noncompetitors and that General Motors' purchases represented a small percentage of the fabric and finish markets.

ISSUE: Does § 7 apply to stock acquisitions of noncompetitors which have the potential to restrain a significant amount of competition in a given market?

HOLDING AND DECISION: (Brennan, J.) Yes. Section 7 applies to all stock acquisitions whether they involve competitors (horizontal) or potential customers (vertical). Where the stock acquisition gives the party the power to foreclose a substantial share of a market or tends to create a monopoly in a line of commerce, § 7 may be used to compel divestiture of the shares. Here, the relevant market is the automotive industry, not, as du Pont (D) maintains, the entire fabric and finish industry. Since General Motors sells between 40 percent and 50 percent of the automobiles in the United States, the power to affect its business involves a substantial share of the industry. Since du Pont (D) supplies General Motors with most of its fabrics and finishes, it has foreclosed a substantial share of the industry to competitors. Du Pont's (D) dominant stock holding was acquired for the purpose of obtaining General Motors' business. This is sufficient without more to find that du Pont's (D) contracts with General Motors did not result from pure competition. Such vertical acquisitions are prohibited under § 7.

DISSENT: (Burton, J.) The Court ignores a critical issue, the lawfulness or unlawfulness of the stock acquisition at the time it occurred, and focuses instead on the probable anticompetitive effects of the continued holding of the stock at the time of the suit, some thirty years later. The result subjects a good-faith stock acquisition, lawful when made, to the hazard that its continued holding may make the acquisition illegal through unforeseen developments. Furthermore, the Court's characterization of the relevant market is incorrect.

▶ ANALYSIS

It is not necessary under § 7 to show that the stock acquisition actually achieved monopoly. It is sufficient that it brought the defendant measurably closer to that end. *Transamerica Corp. v. Board of Governors*, 206 F. 2d 163 (1953). The dissent in *du Pont* fixed on the fact that du Pont (D) did most of its fabric and finish business outside the auto industry. They felt that General Motor's share of the entire industry was minimal and no antitrust problem existed under the circumstances. Courts have a great deal of latitude in defining the relevant market, and this often is a deciding factor in a given case.

■■■

Quicknotes

CLAYTON ACT Legislation passed by the U.S. Congress in 1914 as an amendment to clarify and supplement the Sherman Antitrust Act of 1890. The act prohibited various anti-competitive business practices and gave labor certain rights in disputes with management. It declared that "the labor of a human being is not a commodity or article of commerce."

DIVESTITURE The divestment of an interest in a corporation pursuant to court order.

MONOPOLY A privilege or right conferred upon an individual or entity granting it the exclusive power to manufacture, sell and distribute a particular service or commodity; a market condition in which one or a few companies control the sale of a product or service thereby restraining competition in respect to that article or service.

■■■

Brown Shoe Co. v. United States (I)

Shoe manufacturer (D) v. Federal government (P)

370 U.S. 294 (1962).

NATURE OF CASE: Action to prevent merger under § 7 of the Clayton Act.

FACT SUMMARY: Brown Shoe Co. (D) purchased Kinney Shoes (D), the largest retailer of shoes in the country.

🏛 RULE OF LAW
The relevant market in horizontal mergers is those areas in which the merged companies were competitors.

FACTS: Brown Shoe Co. (Brown) (D), the third-largest shoe manufacturer, purchased Kinney Shoes (D), the largest retail shoe outlet in the country. Brown (D) also sold its shoes in numerous outlets throughout the country. The acquisition of Kinney (D) allowed Brown (D) to capture a larger share of the market and to exert more style setting power in its manufacturing operation. The Government (P) brought an antitrust action alleging that the merger both horizontally and vertically violated § 7 of the Clayton Act. The Government (P) argued that the merger with Kinney (D), which also has a small manufacturing division, increased the oligopolistic tendency of the market (vertical merger effect). The Government (P) also alleged that the horizontal effect of the merger was to give Brown (D) a larger share of the retail market, control outlets which would otherwise be free to stock the shoes of other manufacturers, grant Brown (D) a larger share in setting styles, etc. The Government (P) alleged that consolidation of manufacturing and/or retail outlets placed entry barriers on the market and foreclosed a substantial share of the market to competitors and that the relevant market was the entire United States. The Government (P) alleged that the appropriate market was those areas in which Kinney (D) and Brown (D) had been competitors.

ISSUE: Is the appropriate market for testing the validity of horizontal and vertical mergers the area in which the merged companies had been actual competitors?

HOLDING AND DECISION: (Warren, C.J.) Yes. Basically stated, where competitors are merged, competition is diminished. The proper market to test the validity of the merger is those areas in which the merged companies had been actual competitors. These are the appropriate areas to test the effect of the acquisition in order to determine whether or not the merger had an anticompetitive effect. Here, the prevailing practice in the industry is for the large manufacturers to take over other manufacturers, creating an oligopolistic tendency in the market. This condition is further exacerbated by acquisition of retail outlets. This tends to foreclose merchandising outlets to many manufacturers.

This procedure places entry barriers on both the manufacturing and retail market since it eliminates potential customers for new manufacturers and limits the supply of shoes available to independent retailers. Section 7 of the Clayton Act does not require the United States (P) to wait until a monopoly or oligopoly exists. Section 7 may be employed to prevent such situations at their inception. Reductions in a competitive market not justified by business exigencies may be enjoined. If the procedure herein is not checked, competition will be significantly foreclosed. The acquisition of the largest retail chain by the third-largest manufacturer cannot be deemed a minimal effect on the market. The merger is enjoined.

▌ ANALYSIS

Several justifications are available for mergers. It may be shown that the merged business was failing or that it had inadequate resources to compete. It may also be argued that the combination was necessary to enter the market or to compete with other firms. Finally, if the two merged corporations only competed in a relatively small area of the country, that fact alone would not save the merger if competition was substantially affected in that area. However, it would affect the relief which might be granted in the case. *United States v. Jerrold Electronics Corp.*, 187 F. Supp. 545 (D.C.E.D. Pa. 1960)

■══■

Quicknotes

CLAYTON ACT Legislation passed by the U.S. Congress in 1914 as an amendment to clarify and supplement the Sherman Antitrust Act of 1890. The act prohibited various anti-competitive business practices and gave labor certain rights in disputes with management. It declared that "the labor of a human being is not a commodity or article of commerce."

COMBINATION (ANTITRUST DEFINITION) Alliance of entities, for the purpose of impeding free trade, that results in a monopoly, suppression of competition, or affecting prices.

MONOPOLY A privilege or right conferred upon an individual or entity granting it the exclusive power to manufacture, sell and distribute a particular service or commodity; a market condition in which one or a few companies control the sale of a product or service thereby restraining competition in respect to that article or service.

OLIGOPOLISTIC A market condition in which the industry for a particular product is dominated by only a few companies.

■══■

Northern Securities Co. v. United States

Holding company (D) v. Federal government (P)

193 U.S. 197 (1904).

NATURE OF CASE: Appeal from a judgment finding a violation of federal antitrust law.

FACT SUMMARY: Northern Securities Co. (D), a holding company, acquired two large, parallel railroads which were essentially in competition with each other.

🏛 RULE OF LAW
A combination which tends to restrain interstate or international trade or commerce or tends to create a monopoly in such trade or commerce and deprives the public of the advantages that flow from free competition violates federal antitrust law.

FACTS: Northern Securities Co. (D), a holding company, was formed to acquire two large, parallel railroads operating in the northern United States. The railroad lines were competitors for long and short hauls. The Government (P) filed suit, alleging that acquisition of the two railroads violated § 1 of the Sherman Act. The Government (P) alleged that the railroads ceased, under such a combination, to be in active competition for trade and commerce along their respective lines and became, practically, one powerful consolidated corporation. The lower court ruled in the Government's (P) favor. Northern Securities (D) appealed.

ISSUE: Does a combination which tends to restrain interstate or international trade or commerce or tends to create a monopoly in such trade or commerce and deprives the public of the advantages that flow from free competition violate federal antitrust law?

HOLDING AND DECISION: (Harlan, J.) Yes. A combination which tends to restrain interstate or international trade or commerce or tends to create a monopoly in such trade or commerce and deprives the public of the advantages that flow from free competition violates federal antitrust law. The combination at issue here is a combination in restraint of interstate and international commerce, and that is enough to bring it under the condemnation of the Sherman Act. If such combination is not destroyed, all the advantages that would naturally come to the public under the operation of the general laws of competition, as between the two railroads, will be lost, and the entire commerce of the immense territory in the northern part of the United States between the Great Lakes and the Pacific at Puget Sound will be at the mercy of a single holding corporation.

DISSENT: (Holmes, J.) Great cases, like hard cases, make bad law. The court below argued as if maintaining competition were the expressed object of the Act. The Act says nothing about competition. The exact words hit two classes of cases and only two—contracts in restraint of trade

and combinations or conspiracies in restraint of trade. Combinations in restraint of trade are regarded as contrary to public policy because they monopolize, or attempt to monopolize, commerce among the states. But every railroad monopolizes, in a popular sense, the trade of some area. Under the majority's ruling today, even a partnership would become a combination in restraint of trade.

▶ ANALYSIS

Justice Brewer, in a concurring opinion, contended that: "It must also be remembered that under present conditions a single railroad is, if not a legal, largely a practical, monopoly, and the arrangement by which the control of these two competing roads was merged in a single corporation broadens and extends such monopoly." The decade immediately following passage of the Sherman Act contained the greatest merger movement in the nation's history. One possible explanation for this phenomenon is that since the Sherman Act prohibited consolidations through contract among competing companies, they chose to merge instead, thus creating the economies of scale that made business consolidations efficient.

■=■

Quicknotes

COMBINATION (ANTITRUST DEFINITION) Alliance of entities, for the purpose of impeding free trade, that results in a monopoly, suppression of competition, or affecting prices.

MONOPOLY A privilege or right conferred upon an individual or entity granting it the exclusive power to manufacture, sell and distribute a particular service or commodity; a market condition in which one or a few companies control the sale of a product or service thereby restraining competition in respect to that article or service.

PUBLIC POLICY Policy administered by the state with respect to the health, safety and morals of its people in accordance with common notions of fairness and decency.

RESTRAINT OF TRADE Agreement between entities, for the purpose of impeding free trade, that results in a monopoly, suppression of competition, or affecting prices.

SHERMAN ACT § 1 Prohibits price-fixing.

■=■

United States v. Columbia Steel Co.

Federal government (P) v. Steel company (D)

334 U.S. 495 (1948).

NATURE OF CASE: Appeal from the denial of an injunction against the acquisition of a company in an action under §§ 1 and 2 of the Sherman Act.

FACT SUMMARY: When United States Steel Corporation (D), a producer of rolled steel products used in fabrication, attempted to acquire Consolidated Steel, the largest independent steel fabricator on the west coast, the Government (P) sought to enjoin the acquisition, alleging restraint of competition in part on the basis of horizontal integration that allegedly would eliminate direct competition between the two companies as to steel fabrication.

🏛 RULE OF LAW
Elimination of competition through horizontal integration is not an unlawful restraint of trade where the competition between the acquiring company and the acquired company occurs in a national market and consumers would not be injured by the elimination of the competition; the types of products sold by the respective companies are different and direct competition as to those products is insubstantial; and any preclusion of potential future competition is speculative.

FACTS: United States Steel Corporation (D) produced rolled steel products, the major component used in the fabrication of finished steel products. United States Steel (D) and its subsidiaries [including Columbia Steel Co. (Columbia) (D)] planned to purchase Consolidated, the largest independent steel fabricator on the west coast. The Government (P) argued that the acquisition of Consolidated constituted an illegal restraint of interstate commerce, in part through horizontal integration, because allegedly competition between Consolidated and United States Steel's subsidiaries would be eliminated. United States Steel (D) argued that the appropriate market for fabricated structural steel products should be the national market, in which Consolidated had 84,533 tons of bookings compared with 10,000,000 tons of bookings nationwide over six years. The Government (P) argued that the relevant market was the 11-state area in which Consolidated sold its products. In that "Consolidated market," for the same time period, United States Steel's (D) share was 17 percent and Consolidated's 5 percent. For a later, one-year period, United States Steel (D) had 13 percent market share and Consolidated and Bethlehem Steel each had 11 percent. The next largest structural fabricators had 9 percent, 6 percent, and 3 percent of the total, respectively. United States Steel (D) also argued that that the bookings for fabricated structural steel products were of little significance because Consolidated and United States Steel (D) made different types of structural steel products insofar as Consolidated did only light and medium fabrication, whereas United States

Steel (D) did heavy fabrication. Finally, United States Steel (D) argued that there was little direct competition between the companies since only a small proportion of Consolidated's business fell in the category of structural steel products (16 percent of Consolidated's business was in structural steel products and 70 percent in plate fabrication), and that as to plate fabrication and miscellaneous work there was no competition with United States Steel (D) whatsoever. The district court ruled in United States Steel's (D) favor. The Government (P) appealed, and the U.S. Supreme Court granted review.

ISSUE: Is elimination of competition through horizontal integration an unlawful restraint of trade where the competition between the acquiring company and the acquired company occurs in a national market and consumers would not be injured by the elimination of the competition; the types of products sold by the respective companies are different and direct competition as to those products is insubstantial; and any preclusion of potential future competition is speculative?

HOLDING AND DECISION: (Reed, J.) No. Elimination of competition through horizontal integration is not an unlawful restraint of trade where the competition between the acquiring company and the acquired company occurs in a national market and consumers would not be injured by the elimination of the competition; the types of products sold by the respective companies are different and direct competition as to those products is insubstantial; and any preclusion of potential future competition is speculative. As to the size of the geographical market, the figures on which the Government (P) relies demonstrate that competition in structural steel products has been conducted on a national scale, and even the structural fabricators with the largest sales in the Consolidated market perform their fabrication operations outside the area, including United States Steel (D) and Bethlehem Steel. Purchasers of fabricated structural products have been able to secure bids from fabricators throughout the country, and therefore statistics showing the share of United States Steel (D) and Consolidated in the total consumption of fabricated structural products in any given geographical area do not indicate the extent to which consumers of these products would be injured through elimination of competition between the two companies. Regarding the comparison of the products made by United States Steel (D) and Consolidated, where one company engages in light and medium fabrication while the other engages in heavy fabrication, a showing that the two companies submitted bids for the same project

Continued on next page.

in a very small number of cases by itself does indicate conclusively that there is lack of competition, since knowledge that one party has submitted a bid may discourage others from bidding. However, the Government (P) has failed to adduce evidence that the types of structural steel products made by the respective companies are in fact similar. Based on the statistics that were presented, however, it would seem that competition between the two companies in the manufacture and sale of fabricated structural steel products is not substantial. Finally, the Government's (P) argument that permitting the acquisition would restrain substantial potential competition in the production and sale of other steel products than fabricated structural steel and pipe rests on speculation. The Government's (P) premise, that United States Steel (D) will be a stronger competitor through its acquisition of Consolidated, is not in doubt, but there is no evidence in the record that it would engage in certain areas of production, or that if it did, it would do so to such an extent as to unduly restrain trade. In other words, the possibilities of interference with future competition are too attenuated to warrant a finding of unlawful restraint. Affirmed.

▶ ANALYSIS

The Court's decision was driven, in part, by evidence that the U.S. west coast steel industry was developing, and that east coast fabricators would find it difficult to meet competition from west coast fabricators in the western market, since cheaper western rolled steel and freight rates would be a handicap to eastern fabricators. In view of the number of west coast fabricators and the ability of out-of-the-area fabricators to compete because of the specialized character of structural steel production in regard to orders and designs, the Court concluded that the acquisition was permissible. However, the Court cautioned that its holding did not imply that additional acquisitions of fabricating facilities for structural steel would not become monopolistic.

■≡■

Quicknotes

COMBINATION (ANTITRUST DEFINITION) Alliance of entities, for the purpose of impeding free trade, that results in a monopoly, suppression of competition, or affecting prices.

INJUNCTION A court order requiring a person to do or prohibiting that person from doing a specific act.

RESTRAINT OF COMPETITION Agreement between entities, for the purpose of impeding free trade, that results in a monopoly, the suppression of competition, or affecting prices.

HORIZONTAL INTEGRATION A merger of direct competitors producing or selling similar goods or services in the same geographic area.

■≡■

Brown Shoe Co. v. United States (II)

Shoe manufacturer (D) v. Federal government (P)

370 U.S. 294 (1962).

NATURE OF CASE: Appeal from a judgment finding that a proposed merger would violate federal antitrust law.

FACT SUMMARY: When Brown Shoe Co. (D) and Kinney Shoe Co. (D) contemplated a merger, the United States (P) brought suit, alleging that the merger would substantially lessen competition in the shoe industry, thus violating § 7 of the Clayton Act.

🏛 RULE OF LAW
Where the effects of a merger may be to substantially lessen competition in any significant market or in any section of the country, the merger, at least to that extent, is proscribed.

FACTS: A merger was contemplated between Kinney Shoe Co. (D), the eighth-largest seller of shoes in the United States, and Brown Shoe Co. (Brown) (D), the third-largest seller. Both companies also manufactured shoes. Thus, the proposed merger was both vertical and horizontal. The Government (P) contended that such a merger could substantially lessen competition in the manufacture and sale of shoes in the national market. Brown (D) contended that the merger would be shown not to endanger competition if the lines of commerce and the sections of the country were properly determined. Brown (D) also contended that competition in the shoe industry would not be diminished by the proposed merger because Kinney (D) manufactured less than 0.5 percent and retailed less than 2 percent of the nation's shoes. The district court found that the merger of the retail outlets would tend to substantially lessen competition. Brown (D) appealed.

ISSUE: Where the effects of a merger may be substantially to lessen competition in any significant market or in any section of the country, is the merger, at least to that extent, proscribed?

HOLDING AND DECISION: (Warren, C.J.) Yes. Where the effects of a merger may be substantially to lessen competition in any significant market or in any section of the country, the merger, at least to that extent, is proscribed. The record fully supports the district court's definition of the relevant geographic markets. In this fragmented industry, even if the combination controls a small share of a particular market, the fact that this share is held by a large national chain can adversely affect competition. One factor lending support to the district court's conclusion that this merger may substantially lessen competition is the history of tendency toward concentration in the industry. Brown (D) presented no mitigating factors nor demonstrated a need for combination to enable it to compete better with those dominating the relevant markets. Thus, the Government (P) has sustained its burden of proof.

▶ ANALYSIS

As a result of this merger, Brown (D) moved into second place nationally in terms of retail stores directly owned, giving Brown (D) about 7.2 percent of the nation's retail shoe stores. Of course, some of the results of large integrated or chain operations are beneficial to consumers. But the Court recognized Congress's desire to promote competition through the protection of viable, small, locally owned businesses.

Quicknotes

CLAYTON ACT, § 7 Prohibits the acquirement of stock or assets if the effect of such acquisition is to substantially lessen competition or create a monopoly.

VERTICAL INTEGRATION The ownership of the entire chain of production of a product from raw materials to the final merchandise.

United States v. Philadelphia National Bank

Federal government (P) v. Bank (D)

374 U.S. 321 (1963).

NATURE OF CASE: Appeal from a judgment for the defendant in an antitrust action seeking to enjoin a merger as violative of federal antitrust law.

FACT SUMMARY: When a merger was proposed between Philadelphia National Bank (D) and Girard Trust Corn Exchange Bank (D), the Government (P) sought to enjoin the merger for violating § 7 of the Clayton and Sherman Acts.

🏛 RULE OF LAW
A merger which produces a firm controlling an undue percentage share of the relevant market, significantly increasing the concentration of firms in that market, is so inherently likely to lessen competition substantially that it must be enjoined.

FACTS: The Philadelphia National Bank (PNB) (D) and Girard Trust Corn Exchange Bank (Girard) (D) proposed a merger. They were, respectively, the second- and third-largest of forty-two commercial banks with head offices in the Philadelphia metropolitan area. The Government (P) sought to enjoin the merger, contending that concentration of commercial banking was inimical to the free play of competitive forces. The district court found that the products and services available at commercial banks composed a distinct line of commerce and that the area in which PNB (D) and Girard (D) had their offices was the relevant section of the country. The Government (P) appealed the court's ruling in favor of PNB (D).

ISSUE: Is a merger which produces a firm controlling an undue percentage share of the relevant market, significantly increasing the concentration of firms in that market, so inherently likely to lessen competition substantially that it must be enjoined?

HOLDING AND DECISION: (Brennan, J.) Yes. A merger which produces a firm controlling an undue percentage share of the relevant market, significantly increasing the concentration of firms in that market, is so inherently likely to lessen competition substantially that it must be enjoined. This will be true unless clear evidence shows that the merger is not likely to have such anticompetitive effects. The appropriate "section of the country"—i.e., the relevant geographical market in which the anticompetitive effects of merger should be appraised—is the four-county Philadelphia metropolitan area. Presently, PNB (D) and Girard (D) control between them approximately 44 percent of the area's commercial banking business. After the merger they will control 59 percent. This increase is significant, thus raising an inference that

the effect of the proposed merger may be substantially to lessen competition. It must, therefore, be enjoined.

▶ ANALYSIS

Congressional opposition to the holding in this case resulted in the Bank Merger Act of 1966. The Act that exempted bank mergers from the reach of the Clayton Act occurred before *Philadelphia National Bank* was decided. The Act also provides a defense for certain mergers: where the anticompetitive effects of a merger are outweighed by meeting a community's convenience and needs, the merger will not be illegal.

■==■

Quicknotes

CLAYTON ACT Legislation passed by the U.S. Congress in 1914 as an amendment to clarify and supplement the Sherman Antitrust Act of 1890. The act prohibited various anti-competitive business practices and gave labor certain rights in disputes with management. It declared that "the labor of a human being is not a commodity or article of commerce."

ENJOIN The ordering of a party to cease the conduct of a specific activity.

MERGER The acquisition of one company by another, after which the acquired company ceases to exist as an independent entity.

SHERMAN ACT Makes every contract or conspiracy in unreasonable restraint of commerce illegal.

■==■

United States v. General Dynamics Corp.

Federal government (P) v. Diversified corporation (D)

415 U.S. 486 (1974).

NATURE OF CASE: Divestiture action under § 7 of the Clayton Act.

FACT SUMMARY: General Dynamics Corp. (D) acquired a significant share of the regional coal market through a merger.

RULE OF LAW
A prima facie case based on a statistical showing of market dominance may be overcome by establishing that concentration is due to reduced demand and/or the ineffective ability to compete.

FACTS: General Dynamics Corp. (General) (D) owned a strip mine. General (D) acquired Material Services Corp. (Material) (D) through a merger. Material (D) owned United Electric Coal Companies (United) (D), whose regional coal holdings, when combined with those held by General (D), gave General (D) significant control in the regional coal market. The Government (P) brought an antitrust action under § 7 of the Clayton Act seeking divestiture on the grounds that the acquisition had an anticompetitive effect. The Government (P) alleged that the coal industry was already oligopolistic and the loss of even a single competitor had an anticompetitive effect by further centralizing control. The district court made extensive findings of fact and finally dismissed the action. It found that because of the presence of so many alternatives to coal, the relevant market was the energy market, which was not oligopolistic and which was highly competitive. It found that coal had declined in importance, and this was the major cause of the oligopolistic tendency in the market. Most coal was being purchased by utilities or under long-term leases. It found that United (D) had already committed most of its resources to long-term contracts, and it had insufficient reserves to compete with any other producer. Moreover, the distance between General's (D) mines and those owned by United (D) was too distant to allow for effective competition. Finding that these and other factors negated the anticompetitive effect inference raised by the Government's (P) statistical information, no violation of § 7 was found.

ISSUE: May a statistical case be overcome through a showing that a merger will not have an anticompetitive effect?

HOLDING AND DECISION: (Stewart, J.) Yes. A statistical case may be overcome through a showing that a merger will not have an anticompetitive effect. Statistical evidence is only valid insofar as it presents an accurate picture of the market. Such evidence may always be refuted to establish that no violation of antitrust law has occurred.

Since United's (D) coal was almost entirely committed to existing long-term contracts, it had no power to effect competition in the market since it could not compete for new business. Moreover, the decline in market competitors was almost solely related to natural causes rather than a concentration of ownership through merger and acquisition. Acquisition of a business which cannot compete should not produce an anticompetitive effect. We are not dealing with the "failing business" defense, only United's (D) market position and the effect of its acquisition on the relevant market. A purely speculative supposition that United (D) might have strengthened its market position by future acquisition is unpersuasive, and an anticompetitive effect cannot be created in such a manner. The Government's (P) prima facie case was overcome, and it failed to carry its burden of proof. We need not reach the question of what constitutes the relevant market since it is unnecessary to our decision. Affirmed.

ANALYSIS

General Dynamics delves quite deeply into defining the relevant market. Where transportation costs are a major factor in the price at which a commodity may be offered, the relevant market must be based on the location of a given plant or mine in relationship to its competitors. Where substitutes exit, there is a question of whether the product is part of a submarket or of the larger market. Anticompetitive effects may be found in specific cities in diverse parts of the country, and these may or may not be deemed the relevant market. Market determination is one of the most crucial factors in antitrust litigation. The result often hinges on this factor.

Quicknotes

CLAYTON ACT § 7 Prohibits the acquirement of stock or assets if the effect of such acquisition is to substantially lessen competition or create a monopoly.

DIVESTITURE The divestment of an interest in a corporation pursuant to court order.

OLIGOPOLISTIC A market condition in which the industry for a particular product is dominated by only a few companies.

PRIMA FACIE An action in which the plaintiff introduces sufficient evidence to submit an issue to the judge or jury for determination.

FTC v. Staples, Inc.

Federal agency (P) v. Corporation (D)

970 F. Supp. 1066 (D.C. Cir. 1997).

NATURE OF CASE: Motion for preliminary injunction.

FACT SUMMARY: The Federal Trade Commission (P) sought a preliminary injunction to enjoin the consummation of any acquisition of Office Depot (D) by Staples, Inc. (D).

RULE OF LAW
In a suit for a preliminary injunction to enjoin the consummation of a proposed merger, the court must first determine the Federal Trade Commission's likelihood of success on the merits in its case under § 7 of the Clayton Act and then balance the equities.

FACTS: Office Depot (D) and Staples, Inc. (D) are both corporations that sell office products through retail office supply superstores. Office Depot (D) is the largest such chain in the United States, and Staples (D) the second largest. The Federal Trade Commission (FTC) (P) sought a preliminary injunction to enjoin the consummation of any acquisition of Office Depot (D) by Staples (D).

ISSUE: In a suit for a preliminary injunction to enjoin the consummation of a proposed merger, must the court first determine the FTC's likelihood of success on the merits in its case under § 7 of the Clayton Act and then balance the equities?

HOLDING AND DECISION: (Hogan, J.) Yes. In a suit for a preliminary injunction to enjoin the consummation of a proposed merger, the court must first determine the FTC's likelihood of success on the merits in its case under § 7 of the Clayton Act and then balance the equities. Likelihood of success on the merits means the likelihood that the FTC (P) will succeed in proving after a full administrative trial on the merits, that the effect of a merger between Staples (D) and Office Depot (D) may be substantially to lessen competition or to tend to create a monopoly in violation of § 7 of the Clayton Act. The FTC (P) need only show there is a reasonable probability that the challenged transaction will substantially impair competition. The evidence provides a compelling showing that even where Staples (D) and Office Depot (D) charge higher prices, certain consumers will not go elsewhere for their supplies. Thus, there is a low cross-elasticity of demand between consumable office supplies sold by the superstores and those sold by other sellers. In addition, the concentration statistics in many of the geographic markets are at problematically high levels even before the proposed merger.

ANALYSIS

The court here also found that the balancing of equities favored the granting of a preliminary injunction. The defendants must rebut the presumption that the merger will substantially lessen competition by showing the FTC's (P) evidence gives an inaccurate prediction of the probable effect of the proposed transaction. Such evidence must, however, be credible. Here the court found that Staples (D) and Office Depot (D) failed to meet that burden.

Quicknotes

CLAYTON ACT Legislation passed by the U.S. Congress in 1914 as an amendment to clarify and supplement the Sherman Antitrust Act of 1890. The act prohibited various anti-competitive business practices and gave labor certain rights in disputes with management. It declared that "the labor of a human being is not a commodity or article of commerce."

PRELIMINARY INJUNCTION A judicial mandate issued to require or restrain a party from certain conduct; used to preserve a trial's subject matter or to prevent threatened injury.

Hospital Corp. of America v. FTC

Hospital chain (D) v. Federal agency (P)

807 F.2d 1381 (7th Cir. 1986), *cert. denied*, 481 U.S. 1038 (1987).

NATURE OF CASE: Appeal from an agency ruling that an acquisition violated federal antitrust law.

FACT SUMMARY: When Hospital Corp. of America (D) acquired two other hospital corporations in the Chattanooga, Tennessee area it became the second-largest provider of hospital services in the area.

🏛 RULE OF LAW
Acquisitions that create an appreciable danger of collusive practices in the future are unlawful.

FACTS: Hospital Corp. of America (Hospital Corp.) (D), initially owned, one hospital in Chattanooga, Tennessee. It then acquired two other hospital corporations in the Chattanooga area. Hospital Corp. (D) also assumed the contracts of one of the hospitals to manage two other Chattanooga-area hospitals. As a result of the acquisitions, Hospital Corp. (D) owned or managed five of the eleven hospitals in the area. The acquisitions reduced the number of competing hospitals in the Chattanooga market from eleven to seven. After a complaint, the Federal Trade Commission (FTC) (P) ruled that the acquisitions violated § 7 of the Clayton Act. Hospital Corp. (D) appealed.

ISSUE: Are acquisitions that create an appreciable danger of collusive practices in the future unlawful?

HOLDING AND DECISION: (Posner, J.) Yes. Acquisitions that create an appreciable danger of collusive practices in the future are unlawful. Section 7 does not require proof that an acquisition has actually caused higher prices. The fewer competitors there are in a market, the easier it is for them to coordinate their pricing without committing detectable violations of § 1 of the Sherman Act. As a result of the acquisitions, the four largest firms controlled 91 percent of the market, and the problem of coordination was therefore reduced to one of coordination among these four. It may be true that hospital services are complex and heterogeneous, and heterogeneity makes collusion more difficult. But the FTC (P) was not required to give this speculation any conclusive weight. Moreover, Hospital Corp.'s (D) nonprofit status does not necessarily affect its willingness to cooperate to reduce competition. Finally, Hospital Corp.'s (D) observation that the complainant who first contacted the FTC (P) was a competitor and was thus concerned about lower, not higher, prices does not advance Hospital Corp's (D) argument. Since the complainant was a nonprofit hospital, in attributing the complaint to fear of lower prices, Hospital Corp. (D) is contradicting its own argument that the nonprofit sector of the hospital industry does not obey the laws of economic self-interest. The FTC's (P) order is affirmed and enforced.

▶ ANALYSIS

When an economic approach is taken in a § 7 case, the ultimate issue is whether the challenged acquisition is likely to facilitate collusion aimed at pushing up the market price. Guidelines applicable to horizontal mergers only were issued in 1992 by the Department of Justice and the FTC jointly. However, since they are merely guidelines, no court is bound by them until an appropriate judge so holds.

■══■

Quicknotes

CLAYTON ACT, § 7 Prohibits the acquirement of stock or assets if the effect of such acquisition is to substantially lessen competition or create a monopoly.

COLLUSION An agreement between two or more parties to engage in unlawful conduct or in other activities with an unlawful goal, typically involving fraud.

■══■

FTC v. H.J. Heinz Co.

Federal agency (P) v. Food corporation (D)

246 F.3d 708 (D.C. Cir. 2001).

NATURE OF CASE: Appeal from denial of request for preliminary injunction of merger by the Federal Trade Commission (P).

FACT SUMMARY: H.J. Heinz Co. (Heinz) (D), the second-largest producer of jarred baby food in the U.S., entered into a merger agreement with Milnot Holding Corp. (Beech-Nut) (D), the third-largest producer of baby-food, to acquire all of Beech-Nut (D). The Federal Trade Commission (FTC) (P) sought a preliminary injunction of the planned merger.

🏛 RULE OF LAW
A merger must be preliminarily enjoined where the Federal Trade Commission makes out a prima facie case, which is not rebutted by sufficient evidence, that there is likelihood the merger may lessen competition.

FACTS: H.J. Heinz Co. (Heinz) (D), the second-largest producer of jarred baby food in the U.S., entered into a merger agreement with Milnot Holding Corp. (Beech-Nut) (D), the third-largest producer of baby-food, to acquire all of Beech-Nut (D). The jarred baby food market is dominated by Gerber Products Co. (Gerber), which enjoys a 65 percent market share, whereas Heinz (D) has 17.4 percent and Beech-Nut (D) has 15.4 percent. Gerber's products are sold in 90 percent of the nation's supermarkets, whereas Heinz (D) is sold in 40 percent of supermarkets. Beech-Nut (D) is carried in 45 percent of all grocery stores. The price difference between each brand is only a few cents. At the wholesale level, Heinz (D) and Beech-Nut (D) make lump-sum payments called "fixed trade spending" to supermarkets to obtain shelf placement. Gerber, with its strong name recognition and brand loyalty, does not make such payments. The Federal Trade Commission (FTC) (P) sought a preliminary injunction of the planned merger. The district court denied the requested injunction, and the court of appeals granted review.

ISSUE: Must a merger be preliminarily enjoined where the FTC makes out a prima facie case, which is not rebutted by sufficient evidence, that there is likelihood the merger may lessen competition?

HOLDING AND DECISION: (Henderson, J.) Yes. A merger must be preliminarily enjoined where the FTC makes out a prima facie case, which is not rebutted by sufficient evidence, that there is likelihood the merger may lessen competition. To prevail on its request, the FTC (P) must show that the merger would produce a firm controlling an undue percentage share of the relevant market, and would result in a significant increase in the concentration

of firms in that market. Such a showing establishes a "presumption" that the merger will substantially lessen competition. To rebut the presumption, the defendants must produce evidence that shows that the market-share statistics give an inaccurate account of the merger's probable effects on competition in the relevant market. If the defendant successfully rebuts the presumption of illegality, the burden of producing additional evidence of anticompetitive effect shifts to the government, and merges with the ultimate burden of persuasion, which remains with the government at all times.

II. a. Prima Facie Case

As to the FTC's (P) prima facie case, an increase in the concentration of a market raises the likelihood of anticompetitive conduct. Because the proposed merger will raise the concentration in the baby food market, as supported by statistics (HHI scores), the elimination of competition between two of three major competitors, and because of high barriers to market entry, the FTC (P) has made out its prima facie case—no court has ever approved a merger to duopoly under similar circumstances.

II. b. Rebuttal Arguments

1. Extent of Pre-Merger Competition

As to the defendants' rebuttal evidence, they make three arguments that the district court accepted. First, they argue that Heinz (D) and Beech-Nut (D) do not really compete against each other at the retail level, because consumers do not regard their products as substitutes, and generally only one of the two brands is available on the shelves of any given store. This argument is rejected because the two companies price against each other and depress each other's prices where they are both in the same area; because there is a single national market for jarred baby food and consumers will switch between them in response to small price increases; and because the merger will eliminate competition at the wholesale level between the only two competitors of the "second shelf" position—as to this argument, the district court committed clear legal error because it held that the elimination of such competition was irrelevant and because it ruled that the FTC (P) must prove with certainty the impact on consumers of such eliminated competition. There is no precedent that a reduction in competition for wholesale purchasers is not relevant unless the plaintiff can prove impact at the consumer level, and, in any event, the FTC (P) does not bear the burden of proving such impact with certainty. To the contrary, the antitrust laws assume that a retailer faced with an increase in costs of one of its

Continued on next page.

inventory items will try to pass that cost to consumers to the extent allowed by competition.

2. Post-Merger Efficiencies

Second, the defendants argue that any anticompetitive effects of the merger will be offset by post-merger efficiencies that will increase competition against Gerber. Although evidence of such efficiencies may constitute a valid defense, given the high market concentration in this case, to be sustained on rebuttal, there must be proof of "extraordinary efficiencies" which the defendants have failed to supply. The only cost reduction the district court quantified as a percentage of pre-merger costs, however, was the so-called "variable conversion cost": the cost of processing the volume of baby food now processed by Beech-Nut (D). The court accepted the claim that this cost would be reduced by 43 percent if the Beech-Nut (D) production were shifted to Heinz's (D) plant. However, "variable conversion cost" is only a percentage of the total variable manufacturing cost. A large percentage reduction in only a small portion of the company's overall variable manufacturing cost does not necessarily translate into a significant cost advantage to the merger. Thus, for cost reduction to be relevant, the percentage of Beech-Nut's (D) total variable manufacturing cost that would be reduced as a consequence of the merger must be considered. Using this method cuts the cost savings to 22.3 percent. Also, the relevant figures is not the percentage reduction in Beech-Nut's (D) costs, but the cost reductions measured across the new entity's combined production. Finally, any efficiencies must be merger-specific, i.e., not capable of being achieved by either company alone. However, there was no inquiry by the district court into why Heinz (D) could not, on its own, achieve efficiencies of the kind that allegedly would be created by the merger.

3. Innovation

Third, the defendants claim the merger is necessary to enable Heinz (D) to innovate, and, thus, improve its competitive position against Gerber. Given that Heinz (D) is actually the world's largest baby food manufacturer this is a difficult defense to prove, especially because the evidence presented on this point was highly speculative and not necessarily statistically significant. Accordingly, the district court had no basis to conclude that the FTC's (P) showing was rebutted by an innovation defense.

4. Structural Barriers to Collusion

As a final matter, the combination of a concentrated market and barriers to entry is a recipe for price coordination. Where rivals are few, firms will be able to coordinate their behavior, either by overt collusion or implicit understanding, in order to restrict output and achieve profits above competitive levels. The creation of a durable duopoly affords both the opportunity and incentive for both firms to coordinate to increase prices. Because the district court failed to specify any "structural market barriers to collusion" that are unique to the baby food industry, its

conclusion that the ordinary presumption of collusion in a merger to duopoly was rebutted is clearly erroneous. Because the FTC (P) succeeded in "raising questions going to the merits so serious, substantial, difficult and doubtful as to make them fair ground for thorough investigation, study, deliberation and determination," it is entitled to the preliminary injunction it requested. The court does not decide whether the FTC (P) will ultimately prove its case, but whether injunctive relief will be in the public interest. Weighing the equities in this case favors a preliminary injunction that will enable the FTC (P) to investigate the serious and substantial questions it has raised. Reversed and remanded.

▶ *ANALYSIS*

The most difficult mergers to assess are those that combine both negative and positive market effects. Such mergers create market power that increases the risk of oligopolistic pricing while at the same time creating efficiencies that reduce production or marketing costs. Here, the court determined that any potential positive effects would not outweigh any potential negative effects. Presumably, the merging parties agreed, because they abandoned the merger shortly after the court rendered its decision.

■■■■

Quicknotes

ENJOIN The ordering of a party to cease the conduct of a specific activity.

MERGER The acquisition of one company by another, after which the acquired company ceases to exist as an independent entity.

PRIMA FACIE An action in which the plaintiff introduces sufficient evidence to submit an issue to the judge or jury for determination.

■■■■

United States v. Sidney W. Winslow

Federal government (P) v. Shoemaking machine company (D)

227 U.S. 202 (1913).

NATURE OF CASE: Writ of error to determine if the counts in an indictment charged offenses under federal antitrust law.

FACT SUMMARY: After three manufacturers of shoemaking machinery, including Sidney W. Winslow (D), combined to form one company, the Government (P) filed suit, alleging violation of the Sherman Act.

🏛 RULE OF LAW
Where several companies that do not compete with one another combine in an effort to create greater efficiency, that combination is not unlawful.

FACTS: Three companies, including Sidney W. Winslow (Winslow) (D), made the majority of the machines used in making shoes worn in the nation. Each company made machines that performed different functions from the machines made by the other two, and the machines were patented. The three companies combined to form the United Shoe Machinery Company (United Shoe) (D), building a single new factory which then made all the machines which had previously been made by the three companies at different locations. The Government (P) filed suit, alleging that the combination was formed with the intent to extend the companies' monopolies, rights, and control over commerce in the states at the expense of the public and to discourage others from inventing and manufacturing machines for the work done by United Shoe (D), thus violating the Sherman Act. Winslow (D) and the others (D) argued the indictment did not charge offenses under the Sherman Act.

ISSUE: Where several companies that do not compete with one another combine in an effort to create greater efficiency, is that combination unlawful?

HOLDING AND DECISION: (Holmes, J.) No. Where several companies that do not compete with one another combine in an effort to create greater efficiency, that combination is not, unlawful. On its face, the combination here was an effort to achieve greater efficiency. The machines were patented, therefore making the machines a monopoly in any case. It was said that 70–80 percent of all the shoe machinery business was put into a single hand. This is inaccurate. But even one corporation making 70 percent of three noncompeting groups of patented machines is not more objectionable than three corporations making one group each. The Sherman Act does not extend to reducing all manufacture to isolated units of the lowest degree.

▌ ANALYSIS

As an analogy, Justice Holmes declared that it is as lawful (and far cheaper) for one corporation to make every part of a steam engine and to then put the machine together as it would be for one corporation to make the boilers and another to make the wheels. While Winslow (D) and the others were not actual competitors, Justice Holmes never considered that they were even potential competitors. There was a likely possibility that each of them might enter into the businesses run by the others.

■■■

Quicknotes

COMBINATION (ANTITRUST DEFINITION) Alliance of entities, for the purpose of impeding free trade, that results in a monopoly, suppression of competition, or affecting prices.

SHERMAN ACT Makes every contract or conspiracy in unreasonable restraint of commerce illegal.

WRIT OF ERROR A writ issued by an appellate court, ordering a lower court to deliver the record of the case so that it may be reviewed for alleged errors.

■■■

United States v. Continental Can Co.

Federal government (P) v. Metal container producer (D)

378 U.S. 441 (1964).

NATURE OF CASE: Appeal from a judgment for the defendant in an antitrust action involving a merger.

FACT SUMMARY: After Continental Can Co. (D) acquired Hazel-Atlas Glass Company, the Government (P) filed suit to obtain a divestiture order, alleging that the acquisition violated § 7 of the Clayton Act.

RULE OF LAW
The acquisition by one firm of another firm which is a potential competitor is likely to substantially lessen competition, thus violating federal antitrust law.

FACTS: Continental Can Co. (Continental) (D), the nation's second-largest producer of metal containers, acquired Hazel-Atlas Glass Company (Hazel-Atlas), the nation's third-largest producer of glass containers. Before the merger, Continental (D) had actively and vigorously sought to make inroads in the glass industry's hold on baby food, soft drink, and beer containers. The Government (P) brought suit, seeking a judgment that the acquisition violated § 7 of the Clayton Act and requesting an appropriate divestiture order. The district court held that the geographical market was the entire United States, while the product markets were metal containers, glass containers, and metal and glass beer containers. Trying the case without a jury, the district court found that the Government (P) had failed to prove reasonable probability of anticompetitive effect in any line of commerce and dismissed the complaint. The Government (P) appealed.

ISSUE: Is the acquisition by one firm of another firm which is a potential competitor likely to substantially lessen competition, thus violating federal antitrust law?

HOLDING AND DECISION: (White, J.) Yes. The acquisition by one firm of another firm which is a potential competitor is likely to substantially lessen competition, thus violating federal antitrust law. The district court was correct as to the geographical market but erred as to the product market. The record compellingly reveals the past competitive relationships between metal and glass containers. Based on that record, the relevant product market is the combined glass and metal container industries and all end uses for which they compete. Continental (D) was positioned as a major player in the relevant product market prior to the merger. When Continental (D) acquired Hazel-Atlas, it added significantly to its position in the relevant line of commerce. The acquisition of Hazel-Atlas by a company engaged in intense efforts to effect a change from glass to metal in the soft drink and baby food lines cannot help but diminish the likelihood of Hazel-Atlas' realizing its potential as a significant competitor in either line.

ANALYSIS

This decision clearly shows that the danger of any merger or acquisition is related to how the relevant markets are defined. Cross-elasticity of demand also indicates whether products are competitive or complementary, thus demonstrating the degree of actual competition that exists between any two companies. Comparing the instant case with the *United States v. Sidney W. Winslow*, 227 U.S. 202 (1913), it is apparent that the complementary products, i.e., machines that produce different shoe parts produced in *Winslow*, had a very low cross-elasticity of demand, as opposed to the products produced by Continental Can (D) and Hazel-Atlas, which had a high cross-elasticity of demand.

Quicknotes

CLAYTON ACT § 7 Prohibits the acquirement of stock or assets if the effect of such acquisition is to substantially lessen competition or create a monopoly.

DIVESTITURE The divestment of an interest in a corporation pursuant to court order.

MERGER The acquisition of one company by another, after which the acquired company ceases to exist as an independent entity.

FTC v. Procter & Gamble Co.

Federal agency (P) v. Corporation (D)

386 U.S. 568 (1967).

NATURE OF CASE: Action to compel divestment of merged company.

FACT SUMMARY: Procter & Gamble Co. (D) purchased Clorox, the leading company in the bleach market.

RULE OF LAW

Where a giant corporation diversifies by merging with the leading producer in a related field, there is an anticompetitive effect which violates § 7.

FACTS: Clorox was the leading bleach producer in the nation. It controlled nearly 50 percent of the market and, in certain geographic areas, controlled a much larger share. Eighty percent of the market was controlled by four firms. In many areas of the country, the other three firms did not even compete with Clorox. Other than Purex, Clorox was the only firm with more than one plant. The low mark-up and high transportation cost limited effective marketing to a radius of 300 miles from the plant. Procter & Gamble Co. (Procter) (D), a giant in the household products field, had been looking for areas in which to diversify and purchased Clorox. The Federal Trade Commission (FTC) (P) found that the merger had an anticompetitive effect. First, it removed Procter (D) as a potential entrant into the market. Secondly, it would tend to suppress competition for fear that Procter (D) would retaliate by selling Clorox at a loss while making it up with its other products. Thirdly, since all bleach has the same chemical formula, advertising is the key to success in the area. In 1957, Clorox spent $5.4 million on advertising. Procter (D) spent $127 million. With this large of an advertising budget, Procter (D) could further dominate an already oligopolistic market. The court of appeals reversed.

ISSUE: Where a giant corporation diversifies by merging with the leading producer in a related field, is there an anticompetitive effect that violates § 7?

HOLDING AND DECISION: (Douglas, J.) Yes. Where a giant corporation diversifies by merging with the leading producer in a related field, there is an anticompetitive effect that violates § 7. Clorox could not exert its maximum market control for fear of entry by one of the financial giants of a related field. Its control was further limited by a fairly small advertising budget. It did not command preferred treatment by retailers. Procter & Gamble's (D) acquisition of Clorox changed all of this because Procter (D) had a large advertising budget, did not fear new entrants, and controlled a preferred mode of treatment by retailers. Fear of retaliation diminishes existing competitors and the movement of new entrants into the market. The findings of the FTC (P) were more than warranted by these facts. The order is reinstated.

ANALYSIS

The rationale in *Procter* is limited to situations where entry would become more difficult or the oligopolistic market would be further centralized. Where the acquiring financial giant cannot make effective use of its size, no violation will probably be present. Where advertising is of minimal value and economies of size have already been reached, there is little potential for the acquiring of additional market control. When this is added to a highly competitive market which may be easily entered, no antitrust violations occur from acquisitions. Beatrice Food Co., 1972 Trade Reg. Rep. 1120121.

■===■

Quicknotes

CLAYTON ACT, § 7 Prohibits the acquirement of stock or assets if the effect of such acquisition is to substantially lessen competition or create a monopoly.

MONOPOLY A privilege or right conferred upon an individual or entity granting it the exclusive power to manufacture, sell and distribute a particular service or commodity; a market condition in which one or a few companies control the sale of a product or service thereby restraining competition in respect to that article or service.

OLIGOPOLISTIC A market condition in which the industry for a particular product is dominated by only a few companies.

■===■

Citizen Publishing Co. v. United States

Publishing company (D) v. Federal government (P)

394 U.S. 131 (1969).

NATURE OF CASE: Appeal from a ruling for the plaintiff in an antitrust action.

FACT SUMMARY: After the *Citizen* (D), a daily newspaper, acquired its competitor, the *Star* (D), the *Citizen* (D) asserted the failing company doctrine as a defense to the Government's (P) charge of a violation of the Clayton Act.

🏛 RULE OF LAW
The failing company defense can be applied only if the resources of one company are so depleted that the business failure is probable and no other prospective purchaser is available.

FACTS: Tucson, Arizona, had two daily newspapers which competed vigorously with each other. However, the *Star* (D) operated at a profit, while the *Citizen* (D) operated at a loss. Despite its losses, the *Citizen* (D) was purchased by two men, one of whom was prepared to finance the paper's losses for a while. They did not seek to sell the *Citizen* (D), nor was it about to go out of business. They did, however, negotiate a joint operating agreement between the papers, except for their news and editorial departments. Thus, all commercial rivalry between the papers ceased. Competing publishing operations were also foreclosed. The Government (P) filed suit, alleging violation of the Clayton Act. *Citizen* (D) asserted the "failing company" defense. The district court rejected the defense, finding that *Citizen* (D) was not on the verge of going out of business at the time of the agreement. *Citizen* (D) appealed.

ISSUE: May the failing company defense be applied where business failure is probable and no other prospective purchaser is available?

HOLDING AND DECISION: (Douglas, J.) Yes. The failing company defense may be applied where business failure is probable and no other prospective purchaser is available. Acquisition of a company faced with the grave probability of a business failure does not substantially lessen competition within the meaning of federal antitrust law. However, in this case, there is no evidence that the joint operating agreement was the last straw at which *Citizen* (D) grasped. Indeed, it continued to be a significant threat to the *Star* (D). The *Star* (D) would hardly be willing to enter into an agreement to share its profits with the *Citizen* (D) if it were truly on the brink of collapse, as the *Star* (D) now claims. Furthermore, the failing company doctrine plainly cannot be applied unless it is established that the acquiring company is the only available purchaser. *Citizen* (D) has not carried its burden of proof.

▶ *ANALYSIS*

The Court noted that the record was silent on what the market, if any, for the *Citizen* (D) might have been, since it was not offered for sale. Further, experience had demonstrated that companies reorganized under Chapters X or XI of the Bankruptcy Act often emerge as strong competitive companies. The prospects of reorganization of the *Citizen* (D) at the time of the agreement would have had to be dim or nonexistent to make the failing company doctrine applicable to this case.

■=■

Quicknotes

CLAYTON ACT Legislation passed by the U.S. Congress in 1914 as an amendment to clarify and supplement the Sherman Antitrust Act of 1890. The act prohibited various anti-competitive business practices and gave labor certain rights in disputes with management. It declared that "the labor of a human being is not a commodity or article of commerce."

FAILING COMPANY DOCTRINE Exemption, from Clayton Act, that permits an otherwise unlawful merger if it is shown that the failing company was bankrupt or in danger of becoming bankrupt.

■=■

CHAPTER 8

Secondary-Line Differential Pricing and the Robinson-Patman Act

Quick Reference Rules of Law

FTC v. Morton Salt Co.

Federal agency (P) v. Salt manufacturer (D)

334 U.S. 37 (1948).

NATURE OF CASE: Action against quantity discount rates.

FACT SUMMARY: Morton Salt Co. (D) sold its products to retailers and wholesalers at a standard price. Discounts were offered to all volume purchasers.

🏛 RULE OF LAW
Quantity discounts may be justified only if actual savings result to the manufacturer; e.g., freight costs.

FACTS: Morton Salt Co. (Morton) (D) sold its products to wholesalers and retailers. It offered discounts based on the quantity purchased. Only five large retail chains were able to take advantage of the lowest discount rate. The Federal Trade Commission (FTC) (P) entered a cease and desist order for price discrimination under § 2 of the Robinson-Patman Act. Morton (D) appealed on the basis that its discounts were available to all purchasers on an equal basis.

ISSUE: Are uniform quantity discounts unlawful?

HOLDING AND DECISION: (Black, J.) Yes. Uniform quantity discounts reward those who are large enough to take advantage of them at the expense of smaller competitors. Section 2 of the Robinson-Patman Act makes this an illegal practice unless actual savings to the manufacturer are being passed along to the volume purchaser. If large quantities can be manufactured and shipped more cheaply, this type of savings can be passed along. Morton (D) had the burden of justifying its discount policy. This it failed to meet. The Act does not require a finding of actual injury. It may be invoked if there is a reasonable possibility that injury may result from the practice. Affirmed.

▶ ANALYSIS

A discount on a product having a small retail price which involves only a small percentage of the retailer's business may have no anticompetitive effect. However, if each of the many products sold by the retailer could be obtained less expensively, the aggregate savings when passed on to customers would injure smaller retailers who could not buy in large quantities. For another case in this area, see *Goodyear Tire and Rubber Co. v. FTC*, 101 F.2d 620 (6th Cir. 1939).

■══■

Quicknotes

CEASE AND DESIST ORDER An order from a court or administrative agency prohibiting a person or business from continuing a particular course of conduct.

ROBINSON-PATMAN ACT § 2 Makes price discrimination unlawful if the intent is to harm competition.

■══■

Volvo Trucks North America, Inc. v. Reeder-Simco GMC, Inc.

Truck manufacturer (D) v. Authorized dealer (P)

546 U.S. 164 (2006).

NATURE OF CASE: Appeal from affirmance of judgment for plaintiff in discriminatory pricing action under § 2 of the Clayton Act as amended by the Robinson-Patman Price Discrimination Act.

FACT SUMMARY: Volvo Trucks North America, Inc. (Volvo) (D), a truck manufacturer, contended that Reeder-Simco GMC, Inc. (Reeder) (P), one of Volvo's (D) authorized regional dealers, suffered no competitive injury under § 2 of the Clayton Act as amended by the Robinson-Patman Price Discrimination Act when it gave Reeder (P) lower price concessions than it gave to other Volvo (D) dealers vis-à-vis non-Volvo dealers, but did not discriminate against Reeder (P) when Reeder (P) and another Volvo (D) dealer were seeking concessions with regard to the same ultimate customer.

> ### 🏛 RULE OF LAW
> A manufacturer may not be held liable for second-ary-line price discrimination under § 2 of the Clayton Act as amended by the Robinson-Patman Price Discrimination Act in the absence of a showing that the manufacturer discriminated between dealers competing to resell its product to the same retail customer.

FACTS: Reeder-Simco GMC, Inc. (Reeder) (P), an authorized dealer of heavy-duty trucks manufactured by Volvo Trucks North America, Inc. (Volvo) (D), generally sold those trucks through an industrywide competitive bidding process, whereby the retail customer describes its specific product requirements and invites bids from dealers it selects based on such factors as an existing relationship, geography, and reputation. Once a Volvo (D) dealer receives the customer's specifications, it requests from Volvo (D) a discount or "concession" off the wholesale price. Volvo (D) decides on a case-by-case basis whether to offer a concession. The dealer then uses its Volvo (D) discount in preparing its bid; it purchases trucks from Volvo (D) only if and when the retail customer accepts its bid. Reeder (P) was one of many regional Volvo (D) dealers. Although nothing prohibited a Volvo (D) dealer from bidding outside its territory, Reeder (P) rarely bid against another Volvo (D) dealer. In the atypical case in which a retail customer solicited a bid from more than one Volvo (D) dealer, Volvo's (D) stated policy was to provide the same price concession to each dealer. Volvo (D) eventually announced a program it called "Volvo Vision," which had as its goal to enlarge the size of its dealers' markets and to reduce by almost half the number of its dealers. After Volvo Vision went into effect, Reeder (P) learned that Volvo (D) had given another dealer a price concession greater than the discounts Reeder (P) typically received. Reeder (P) suspected that it was one of the dealers Volvo (D) sought to eliminate, and filed suit

under § 2 of the Clayton Act, as amended by the Robinson-Patman Price Discrimination Act alleging that its sales and profits declined because Volvo (D) offered other dealers more favorable price concessions. At trial, Reeder (P) presented evidence of two instances when it bid against another Volvo (D) dealer for a particular sale. In the first, although Volvo (D) initially offered Reeder (P) a lower concession, Volvo (D) ultimately matched the concession offered to the competing dealer. Neither dealer won the bid. In the second, Volvo (D) initially offered the two dealers the same concession, but increased the other dealer's discount after it, rather than Reeder (P), was selected. Reeder (P) primarily relied on comparisons between concessions it received on four occasions when it bid successfully against non-Volvo dealers (and thus purchased Volvo (D) trucks), with more favorable concessions other successful Volvo (D) dealers received in bidding processes in which Reeder (P) did not participate. Reeder (P) also compared concessions Volvo (D) offered it on several occasions when it bid unsuccessfully against non-Volvo dealers (and therefore did not purchase Volvo (D) trucks), with more favorable concessions accorded other Volvo (D) dealers who gained contracts on which Reeder (P) did not bid. The jury found a reasonable possibility that discriminatory pricing may have harmed competition between Reeder (P) and other Volvo (D) dealers, and that Volvo's (D) discriminatory pricing injured Reeder (P). The district court entered judgment for Reeder (P), and the court of appeals affirmed. The U.S. Supreme Court granted certiorari.

ISSUE: May a manufacturer be held liable for secondary-line price discrimination under § 2 of the Clayton Act as amended by the Robinson-Patman Price Discrimination Act in the absence of a showing that the manufacturer discriminated between dealers competing to resell its product to the same retail customer?

HOLDING AND DECISION: (Ginsburg, J.) No. A manufacturer may not be held liable for secondary-line price discrimination under § 2 of the Clayton Act as amended by the Robinson-Patman Price Discrimination Act in the absence of a showing that the manufacturer discriminated between dealers competing to resell its product to the same retail customer. Under the Clayton Act and Robinson-Patman Act, price discrimination is proscribed only to the extent that it threatens to injure competition. A hallmark of the requisite competitive injury is the diversion of sales or profits from a disfavored purchaser to a favored purchaser. A permissible inference of competitive injury may arise from evidence that a favored competitor received a significant price reduction over a substantial period of time. Here,

Continued on next page.

however, Reeder (P) cannot establish the competitive injury required under the Act, since it did not actually compete with a favored Volvo (D) dealer. Reeder (P) presented the following comparisons at trial: (1) comparisons of concessions Reeder (P) received for four successful bids against non-Volvo dealers, with larger concessions other successful Volvo (D) dealers received for different sales on which Reeder (P) did not bid (purchase-to-purchase comparisons); (2) comparisons of concessions offered to Reeder (P) in connection with several unsuccessful bids against non-Volvo dealers, with greater concessions accorded other Volvo (D) dealers who competed successfully for different sales on which Reeder (P) did not bid (offer-to-purchase comparisons); and (3) comparisons of two occasions on which Reeder (P) bid against another Volvo (D) dealer (head-to-head comparisons). Because the purchase-to-purchase and offer-to-purchase comparisons fail to show that Volvo (D) sold at a lower price to Reeder's "competitors," those comparisons do not support an inference of competitive injury. In none of the discrete instances on which Reeder (P) relied did it compete with beneficiaries of the alleged discrimination for the same customer. Nor did Reeder (P) even attempt to show that the compared dealers were consistently favored over it. Reeder simply paired occasions on which it competed with non-Volvo dealers for a sale to Customer A with instances in which other Volvo (D) dealers competed with non-Volvo dealers for a sale to Customer B. The compared incidents were tied to no systematic study and were separated in time by as many as seven months. An inference of competitive injury from evidence of such a mix-and-match, manipulable quality will not be made, since there is no evidence of a discrete "favored" dealer here, as contemplated by the Robinson-Patman Act, and the evidence has left open the possibility that Reeder (P), on occasion, might have gotten a better deal vis-à-vis one or more of the dealers in its comparisons. While Reeder (P) may have competed with other Volvo dealers for the opportunity to bid on potential sales in a broad geographic area, competition at that initial stage is based on a variety of factors, including the existence *vel non* of a relationship between the potential bidder and the customer, geography, and reputation. Once the customer has chosen the particular dealers from which it will solicit bids, the relevant market becomes limited to the needs and demands of the particular end user, with only a handful of dealers competing for the sale. Volvo (D) dealers' bidding for sales in the same geographic area does not mean that they in fact competed for the same customer-tailored sales. As to the head-to-head comparisons, when multiple dealers bid for the business of the same customer, only one dealer will win the business and thereafter purchase the supplier's product to fulfill its contractual commitment. Even assuming the Act applies to head-to-head transactions, Reeder (P) did not establish that it was disfavored vis-à-vis other Volvo (D) dealers in the rare instances in which they competed for the same sale—let alone that the alleged discrimination was substantial. The Robinson-Patman Act signals no large departure from antitrust law's primary concern, interbrand competition, and

should not be construed as geared more to the protection of existing *competitors*, than to the stimulation of *competition*. There is no evidence here that any favored purchaser possesses market power, the allegedly favored purchasers are dealers with little resemblance to large independent department stores or chain operations, and the supplier's selective price discounting fosters competition among suppliers of different brands. By declining to extend Robinson-Patman's governance to such cases, the Court continues to construe the Act consistently with antitrust law's broader policies. Reversed and remanded.

DISSENT: (Stevens, J.) Reeder's (P) theory of the case was that Volvo (D) offered Reeder (P) worse prices that it offered to other regional dealers in an effort to eliminate Reeder (P). For decades, juries have inferred the requisite injury to competition under the Robinson-Patman Act from the fact that a manufacturer sells goods to one retailer at a higher price than to its competitors—which are those who sell in the same interstate retail market. Reeder (P) clearly would prevail under this longstanding approach. Under Volvo's (D) approach, and the one erroneously adopted by the majority, each transaction involving Reeder (P) and another Volvo (D) dealer seeking concessions with regard to the same ultimate customer was a separate market, defined by the customer and the bidding dealers. Under this approach, for each specific customer who solicited bids, Reeder's (P) only "competitors" were the other dealers making bids. Accordingly, if none of these other dealers were Volvo (D) dealers, then Reeder (P) suffered no competitive harm (relative to other Volvo (D) dealers) when Volvo (D) gave it a discriminatorily high price. There is nothing in the Act, precedent, or reason that supports this approach. Every time Reeder (P) managed to sell a Volvo (D) truck, it either had to accept a lower profit margin than available to favored Volvo (D) dealers, or it had to pass the higher cost on to the customer and thereby lose potential future sales. Such lost profits long have been held to constitute a proper basis for inferring competitive injury. Thus, the majority's holding seems to be that absent head-to-head bidding with a favored dealer, a dealer in a competitive bidding market can suffer no competitive injury. There is no support for this result in the statute.

▶ ANALYSIS

There are three categories of competitive injury that may give rise to a Robinson-Patman Act claim: primary line, secondary line, and tertiary line. Primary-line cases entail conduct—most conspicuously, predatory pricing—that injures competition at the level of the discriminating seller and its direct competitors. Secondary-line cases, of which this case is one, involve price discrimination that injures competition among the discriminating seller's customers (here, Volvo's

Continued on next page.

(D) dealerships); cases in this category typically refer to "favored" and "disfavored" purchasers. Tertiary-line cases involve injury to competition at the level of the purchaser's customers. To establish a secondary-line injury, Reeder (P) had to show that (1) the relevant Volvo (D) truck sales were made in interstate commerce; (2) the trucks were of "like grade and quality"; (3) Volvo (D) discriminated in price between Reeder (P) and another purchaser of Volvo (D) trucks; and (4) "the effect of such discrimination may be . . . to injure, destroy, or prevent competition" to the advantage of a favored purchaser, i.e., one who "receive[d] the benefit of such discrimination." It was undisputed that Reeder (P) satisfied the first and second requirements. The issue was thus whether it could satisfy the other two requirements. Volvo (D) argued that Reeder (P) could not satisfy the third and fourth requirements because Reeder (P) had not identified any differentially priced transaction in which it was both a "purchaser" under the Act and "in actual competition" with a favored purchaser for the same customer.

■══■

Quicknotes

PRICE DISCRIMINATION   Charging one buyer more or less than that charged another buyer for the same product or service.

ROBINSON-PATMAN ACT   Makes price discrimination unlawful if the intent is to harm competition.

■══■

J. Truett Payne Co. v. Chrysler Motors Corp.

Automobile dealer (P) v. Automobile company (D)

451 U.S. 557 (1981).

NATURE OF CASE: Appeal from directed verdict in action for damages under § 2(a) of the Robinson-Patman Act.

FACT SUMMARY: J. Truett Payne Co. (P), a Chrysler dealer, claimed that Chrysler Motors Corp.'s (D) incentive programs constituted discrimination and thus caused it to go out of business.

🏛 RULE OF LAW
In order to receive damages under the Robinson-Patman Act a plaintiff must show an actual violation of § 2(a) and that the violation caused an actual antitrust injury.

FACTS: J. Truett Payne Co. (Payne) (P) was a Chrysler-Plymouth dealer. Chrysler Motors Corp. (Chrysler) (D) granted a bonus to their dealers based on how many sales they made above set objectives. Sales were determined by how many automobiles the dealer purchased from Chrysler (D). Chrysler (D) set Payne's (P) sales objectives higher than those of its competitors. Because of this, Payne (P) received fewer bonuses than its competitors. Payne (P) claimed that, because it did not get these bonuses, the prices it paid for automobiles were higher than that of its competitors. Payne (P) brought suit against Chrysler (D) under § 2(a) of the Sherman Act, alleging that Chrysler's (D) incentive program resulted in price discrimination. The trial court granted Chrysler's (D) motion for a directed verdict, and Payne (P) appealed.

ISSUE: To receive damages under the Robinson-Patman Act, must a plaintiff show an actual violation of § 2(a) and that the violation caused an actual antitrust injury?

HOLDING AND DECISION: (Rehnquist, J.) Yes. In order to receive damages under the Robinson-Patman Act a plaintiff must show an actual violation of § 2(a) and that the violation caused an actual antitrust injury. While § 2(a) is violated merely by showing that price discrimination may have harmed competition, private actions for damages must show actual damages in order to succeed. Payne (P) did not present any evidence showing the effect of the price discrimination on retail price. Since the lower court did not address the question of liability, a determination of damages would be premature. Remanded for a determination as to whether the evidence supports a finding of a violation of § 2(a).

▶ ANALYSIS

The Fifth Circuit, on remand, dismissed because the evidence did not support a finding of a violation of the Act. When it examined the evidence, it found that sales had actually increased during the period of alleged price discrimination. Under *Brunswick v. Pueblo Bowl-O-Mat, Inc.*, 429 U.S. 477 (1977), an activity only gives rise to damages if it causes injury of the type the antitrust laws are designed to prevent. Clearly, the sort of intensification of competition that occurred in this case would not qualify.

Quicknotes

DIRECTED VERDICT A verdict ordered by the court in a jury trial.

ROBINSON-PATMAN ACT § 2 Makes price discrimination unlawful if the intent is to harm competition.

FTC v. Henry Broch & Co.

Federal agency (P) v. Broker (D)

363 U.S. 166 (1960).

NATURE OF CASE: Action against price discrimination through the acceptance of lower broker's fees.

FACT SUMMARY: Henry Broch & Co. (D) agreed to accept a three percent brokerage fee in lieu of its normal 5 percent fee in order to accommodate Smuckers' demand for a lower price.

🏛 RULE OF LAW
Section 2(c) makes it unlawful for any person to discriminate in granting price reductions. This includes the reduction of brokerage fees.

FACTS: Canada Foods paid Henry Broch & Co. (Broch) (D) a five percent fee to act as its broker. Canada Foods authorized Broch (D) and its other brokers to sell its apple concentrate at $1.30 a gallon. Smuckers refused to pay more than $1.25 per gallon on a 500-gallon order. Both Broch (D) and another broker working for Canada Foods attempted to convince Smuckers to buy at the higher price. Finally, in order to secure the business, Broch (D) agreed to reduce its commission to three percent. Smuckers agreed to this price reduction. Broch (D) made this concession only to Smuckers; all other customers were charged five percent. The Federal Trade Commission (FTC) (P) claimed that this practice violated § 2(c) of the Robinson-Patman Act.

ISSUE: May a broker agree to accept less commission in order to obtain a lower price for a customer?

HOLDING AND DECISION: (Douglas, J.) No. Section 2(c) makes the granting of a price concession by any person an unlawful method of competition. The broker's actions, when he is acting for the manufacturer, fall within this proscription. The Robinson-Patman Act was passed to prevent such practices. It prevents manufacturers, or those working for them, from yielding to the economic pressure of large buyers. No unfair preferences may be justified. The end result of Broch's (D) action was that Smuckers received a lower price for Canada Foods product. If the brokerage fee is reduced to reflect actual savings and these are passed on to all similar customers, § 2(c) is not violated. Here, however, only Smuckers was given the preference and it was given solely to obtain the sale. Affirmed.

▌ANALYSIS

The payment of a commission where no services are performed is in the nature of a discount. However, such a "discount" could be rationalized as a direct sale to a buyer. The cost savings being passed along were the saved brokerage fees. Case law has held such discounts do not violate antitrust law. The dissent's position seems to have merit. The majority seemed to have engaged in a semantics argument based on the parties having labeled the payment as a commission.

Quicknotes

ROBINSON-PATMAN ACT Makes price discrimination unlawful if the intent is to harm competition.

FTC v. Borden Co.

Federal agency (P) v. Milk producer (D)

383 U.S. 637 (1966).

NATURE OF CASE: Appeal from judgment setting aside a Federal Trade Commission order applying § 2(a) of the Robinson-Patman Act.

FACT SUMMARY: The Borden Co. (D) produced and sold the identical evaporated milk under its own national brand, as well as under private labels at lower prices.

🏛 RULE OF LAW
Brand names and consumer preferences are not factors to be considered when determining if a product is of "like grade and quality" for the purposes of § 2(a) of the Robinson-Patman Act.

FACTS: Borden Co. (D) produced and sold chemically and physically identical evaporated milk under its own label, as well as under several private labels. The Borden (D) label is nationally recognized, and thus milk they sold under that label was priced higher than milk sold under the private labels. The Federal Trade Commission (FTC) (P) ordered that § 2(a) of the Robinson-Patman Act applied to the Borden brand since it was of "like grade and quality" as the private brands. The court of appeals found that the brand name of and customer preference for the Borden brand made it a different grade as a matter of law and set aside the FTC's (P) order. The FTC (P) appealed.

ISSUE: Are brand name and consumer preference factors to be considered when determining if a product is of "like grade and quality" for the purposes of § 2(a) of the Robinson-Patman Act?

HOLDING AND DECISION: (White, J.) No. Brand name and consumer preference are not factors to be considered when determining if a product is of "like grade and quality" for the purposes of § 2(a) of the Robinson-Patman Act. Section 2(a) makes it unlawful to discriminate in price between different purchasers of commodities of "like grade and quality." The purpose of the Act is to prevent the distortion of competition through disparate treatment of consumers completing the same transaction. In order to achieve this goal the term "like grade and quality" must refer solely to the physical characteristics of the goods and not to consumers' perceptions of the good. Consumer preference is too easily manipulated by marketing and advertising to be a valid measure of a good's quality since it would allow the producers themselves to determine when § 2(a) would apply. Reversed.

▶ ANALYSIS

The holding of the Court, denying the value of name recognition, rejects advertising costs as a legitimate expense. The

FTC (P) is invested with the power to regulate the content of advertising. Such regulation may be enough to protect the consumer from misrepresentation without completely devaluing the importance of name recognition and consumer confidence.

■■■

Quicknotes

ROBINSON-PATMAN ACT § 2 Makes price discrimination unlawful if the intent is to harm competition.

■■■

United States v. Borden Co.
Federal government (P) v. Milk producer (D)
370 U.S. 460 (1962).

NATURE OF CASE: Action to enjoin price discrimination.

FACT SUMMARY: Borden Co. (D) attempted to justify its use of discount prices for quantity purchases by showing that they led to actual cost savings.

RULE OF LAW
Discounts which are based on cost savings may not be passed on to arbitrarily drawn classes of customers.

FACTS: Borden Co. (D) and Bowman (D) sold milk in the Chicago area. They granted volume discounts to independent grocers on a sliding scale. All retail chains were given a flat discount. The Federal Trade Commission (FTC) (P) entered a cease-and-desist order enjoining the practices as a form of price discrimination. Borden (D) and Bowman (D) appealed on the basis that the discounts were the result of actual savings resulting to them from volume sales. They established that their delivery costs were much less to chain stores. The district court found that the facts justified the discount and dismissed the order. The FTC (P) appealed on the basis that the blanket discount given to all chain stores had not been justified.

ISSUE: May arbitrary classes, be established for the granting of differing discount rates allegedly justified by cost savings?

HOLDING AND DECISION: (Clark, J.) No. Where a manufacturer deals with numerous customers, it may pass on discounts by reasonably drawn classes. It need not analyze actual cost savings resulting from volume purchases by each class member. However, each member of a class must purchase a similar quantity and effect a similar cost savings. Arbitrarily granting the same discount to all chain stores regardless of the quantity purchased results in an arbitrary classification. Finally, not all independents received additional services which led to the imposition of a higher cost rate. These stores should not have been grouped with those receiving such extra services. Such practices do not justify Bowman (D) and Borden's (D) claim that their discount system was based on cost savings. The FTC's (P) order is reinstated.

▶ ANALYSIS

The court places a heavy burden on companies who wish to justify price discrimination through cost savings. However, it is clear that Congress wished to make such practices illegal. Those seeking an exemption must be prepared to convincingly establish that actual cost savings were indeed passed on to the volume purchaser. See also *In the Matter of Champion Spark Plug Co.*, 50 FTC 30 (1953).

Quicknotes

CEASE AND DESIST ORDER An order from a court or administrative agency prohibiting a person or business from continuing a particular course of conduct.

PRICE DISCRIMINATION Charging one buyer more than another for the same product or service.

United States v. United States Gypsum Co.

Federal government (P) v. Gypsum board manufacturer (D)

438 U.S. 422 (1978).

NATURE OF CASE: Criminal action for antitrust violations.

FACT SUMMARY: The Government (P) brought an indictment against United States Gypsum Co. (D) and others alleging violations of § 1 of the Sherman Act.

🏛 RULE OF LAW
A good-faith belief, rather than absolute certainty, that a price concession is being offered to meet an equally low price offered by a competitor is sufficient to satisfy the Robinson-Patman Act's § 2(b) meeting-competition defense.

FACTS: The Government (P) brought a criminal indictment against United States Gypsum Co. (Gypsum) (D) and others alleging violations of § 1 of the Sherman Act. The allegations consisted of price-fixing. The focus was interseller price verification. This was the practice allegedly followed by the gypsum board manufacturers of telephoning a competing producer to determine the price currently being offered on gypsum board to a specific customer. Gypsum (D) contended that the exchanges of price information which did occur were for the purposes of complying with the Robinson-Patman Act's § 2(b) meeting-competition defense and preventing customer fraud. The trial court found Gypsum (D) guilty, and the court of appeals reversed. In this portion of the appeal, the U.S. Supreme Court discussed the meeting-competition defense as a "controlling circumstance" precluding liability under § 1 of the Sherman Act.

ISSUE: Is a good-faith belief, rather than absolute certainty, that a price concession is being offered to meet an equally low price offered by a competitor sufficient to satisfy the Robinson-Patman Act's § 2(b) meeting-competition defense?

HOLDING AND DECISION: (Burger, C.J.) Yes. A good-faith belief, rather than absolute certainty, that a price concession is being offered to meet an equally low price being offered by a competitor is sufficient to satisfy the Robinson-Patman Act's § 2(b) meeting-competition defense. Section 2(b) does not require the seller to justify price discriminations by showing that in fact they met a competitor's price. But it does place on the seller the burden of showing that the price was made in good faith to meet a competitor's. The concept of good faith lies at the core of the meeting-competition defense. Good faith is flexible and pragmatic, not technical and doctrinaire. The good faith standard can be satisfied by efforts falling short of interseller verification in most circumstances where the seller has only vague, generalized doubts about the reliability of its commercial adversary—the buyer. This Court cannot go so far as to recognize even a limited "controlling circumstances" exception for interseller verification, for that would be to remove from scrutiny under the Sherman Act conduct falling near its center with no assurance, and indeed with serious doubts, that competing antitrust policies would be served thereby. Exchanges of price information, even when putatively for purposes of Robinson-Patman Act compliance must remain subject to close scrutiny under the Sherman Act.

▶ ANALYSIS

In a footnote to the case discussed above, the Court wrote, ". . . (A) Purpose of complying with the Robinson-Patman Act by exchanging price information is not inconsistent with knowledge that such exchanges of information will have the probable effect of fixing or stabilizing prices. Since we hold knowledge of the probable consequences of conduct to be the requisite mental state in a criminal prosecution like the instant one where an effect on prices is also alleged, a defendant's purpose in engaging in the proscribed conduct will not insulate him from liability unless it is deemed of sufficient merit to justify a general exception to the Sherman Act's proscriptions."

■=■

Quicknotes

INDICTMENT A formal written accusation made by the prosecution to the grand jury under oath, charging an individual with a criminal offense.

PRICE-FIXING An illegal combination in violation of the Sherman Act entered into for the purpose of setting prices below the natural market rate.

ROBINSON-PATMAN ACT § 2 Makes price discrimination unlawful if the intent is to harm competition.

SHERMAN ACT § 1 Prohibits price-fixing.

■=■

Falls City Industries v. Vanco Beverage, Inc.

Brewery (D) v. Wholesaler (P)

560 U.S. 428 (1983).

NATURE OF CASE: Appeal from finding of liability in action under § 2(a) of the Robinson-Patman Act claiming price discrimination.

FACT SUMMARY: Vanco Beverage, Inc. (Vanco) (P), a distributor of Falls City's Industries' (Falls City) (D) beer in Indiana, brought suit against Falls City (D), claiming it discriminated in price against Vanco (P) by charging a distributor, who competed in the same geographic area, less than it charged Vanco (P).

🏛 **RULE OF LAW**
The "meeting competition" defense may be used by a defendant who in good faith raises its price on a territorial basis in response to the competition.

FACTS: Falls City Industries (Falls City) (D), a brewery, sold beer to wholesalers in Indiana and Kentucky. Vanco Beverage, Inc. (Vanco) (P) and Dawson Springs were the sole wholesalers for their counties in Indiana and Kentucky, respectively, even though the entire area was considered one metropolitan area. Because of Indiana's regulation of beer sales, the two companies did not compete directly with each other. Falls City (D) sold beer to Dawson at a cheaper price than it sold beer to Vanco (P). Vanco (P) sued Falls City (D), claiming its pricing policy prevented Vanco (P) from competing in the market since consumers could go to Kentucky to purchase the same beer at lower prices. Falls City (D) exerted the defense of "meeting competition" under § 2(b) of the Robinson-Patman Act. Both the district court and the court of appeals concluded that Falls City's (D) higher Indiana price was not set in good faith and rejected its defense. Falls City (D) appealed.

ISSUE: May the "meeting-competition" defense be used by a defendant who in good faith raised its prices on a territorial basis in response to the competition?

HOLDING AND DECISION: (Blackmun, J.) Yes. The "meeting-competition" defense may be used by a defendant who in good faith raised its price on a territorial basis in response to the competition. The purpose of the defense is to allow a seller to respond to different competitive situations differently. Allowing sellers to invoke it only when they have lowered their prices on a customer-by-customer basis, as suggested by the lower courts, would defeat this purpose. The price change, however, must be made in a good-faith response to the competition. Falls City's (D) higher price in Indiana was set in response to particular market conditions in that state. There is no evidence that Falls City's (D) lower price in Kentucky was not a good-faith attempt to compete with the lower prices of its competitors there. Reversed.

▶ **ANALYSIS**

The seminal case on the "meeting competition" defense is *FTC v. A.E. Staley Mfg. Co.*, 324 U.S. 746 (1945). In *Staley*, the defense argued unsuccessfully that it had tried to "meet competition" by meeting a competitor's price schedule that was itself in violation of the Robinson-Patman Act. The *Vanco* decision interprets the *Staley* decision to say only that the "meeting-competition" defense can't be used when the competitor's price schedule has itself been found illegal.

▪▬▪

Quicknotes

PRICE DISCRIMINATION Charging one buyer more than another for the same product or service.

ROBINSON-PATMAN ACT § 2 Makes price discrimination unlawful if the intent is to harm competition.

▪▬▪

Great Atlantic & Pacific Tea Co. v. FTC

Supermarket (D) v. Federal agency (P)

440 U.S. 69 (1979).

NATURE OF CASE: Action alleging violations of the Federal Trade Commission and Robinson-Patman Acts.

FACT SUMMARY: The Great Atlantic & Pacific Tea Co. (D) told Borden that the latter's bid was not competitive with other bids.

🏛 RULE OF LAW
If a seller has a valid meeting-competition defense, there is no prohibited price discrimination.

FACTS: The Great Atlantic & Pacific Tea Co. (A&P) (D) told Borden that the latter's bid, in connection with the purchase of milk from Borden, was not competitive with other bids. A&P's (D) buyer stated to Borden: "I have a bid in my pocket. You people are so far out of line it is not even funny. You are not even in the ballpark." When the Borden representative asked for more details, he was told nothing except that a $50,000 improvement in Borden's bid "would not be a drop in the bucket." Borden decided to submit a new bid which doubled the estimated annual savings to A&P (D) from $410,000 to $820,000. Borden emphasized that it needed to keep A&P's (D) business and was making the new offer to meet another bid. A&P (D) then accepted Borden's bid. The Federal Trade Commission (FTC) (P) filed a complaint against A&P (D). The Administrative Law Judge found that this conduct violated Section 2(f) of the Robinson-Patman Act. The FTC (P) affirmed and rejected A&P's (D) defenses that the Borden bid had been made to meet competition and was cost justified. The Court of Appeals for the Second Circuit held that substantial evidence supported the findings of the FTC (P) and that as a matter of law A&P (D) could not successfully assert a meeting-competition defense because it, unlike Borden, had known that Borden's offer was better than another competitor's. Finally, the court held that the FTC (P) had correctly determined that A&P (D) had no cost justification defense. The U.S. Supreme Court granted certiorari.

ISSUE: Is there prohibited price discrimination if a seller has a valid meeting-competition defense?

HOLDING AND DECISION: (Stewart, J.) No. If a seller has a valid meeting-competition defense, there is no prohibited price discrimination. The test for determining when a seller has a valid meeting-competition defense is whether a seller can show the existence of facts which would lead a reasonable and prudent person to believe that the granting of a lower price would in fact meet the equally low price of a competitor. A good-faith belief, rather than absolute certainty, that a price concession is being offered to meet an equally low price offered by a competitor is sufficient to satisfy the Robinson-Patman's Section 2(b) defense. Here, Borden exercised good faith. Borden was told that its first offer was "not even in the ball park" and that a $50,000 improvement "would not be a drop in the bucket." In light of Borden's established business relationship with A&P (D), Borden could have justifiably concluded that A&P's (D) statements were reliable and that it was necessary to make another bid offering substantial concessions to avoid losing its account with A&P (D). Faced with a substantial loss of business and unable to find out the precise details of the competing bid, Borden made another offer stating that it was doing so in order to meet competition. Borden, in short, was entitled to a meeting-competition defense. Since Borden had a meeting-competition defense and thus could not be liable, A&P (D), who did no more than accept that offer, could not be liable either. Reversed.

DISSENT: (Marshall, J.) The Court's holding does not address the situation where a buyer accidentally receives a lower bid. The standard for liability for buyers under § 2(f) of the Robinson-Patman Act should allow the buyer to use the "meeting competition" defense if he induces the seller to meet the competitor's price in good faith, regardless of whether the price in fact beats the competition.

▶ ANALYSIS

A price discrimination provision was contained in the Clayton Act of 1914. Section 2 of the Clayton Act, the price discrimination provision, was revised by the Robinson-Patman Act of 1936. The former Section 2 was not very clear; the Robinson-Patman version is no better. Gellhorn, *Antitrust Nutshell* at 30-31.

Quicknotes

CERTIORARI A discretionary writ issued by a superior court to an inferior court in order to review the lower court's decisions; the Supreme Court's writ ordering such review.

ROBINSON-PATMAN ACT § 2 Makes price discrimination unlawful if the intent is to harm competition.

Other Forms of Regulation and Exemptions

Quick Reference Rules of Law

Credit Suisse Securities v. Billing

Underwriter investment bank (D) v. Securities investor (P)

127 S. Ct. 2383 (2007).

NATURE OF CASE: Appeal from reversal of dismissal of class action asserting antitrust law violations related to the sale of securities.

FACT SUMMARY: Investment bank underwriters (D) contended that their conduct during the course of an initial public offering (IPO), which investors (P) alleged violated antitrust laws, was not actionable under the antitrust laws because the securities law impliedly precluded application of the antitrust laws to such conduct.

RULE OF LAW

The securities laws implicitly preclude the application of the antitrust laws to conduct of securities underwriters during the course of initial public offering (IPO) that includes requiring investors to: buy additional shares of a security at escalating prices in the future; to pay unusually high commissions on subsequent security purchases; and to purchase from the underwriters other less desirable securities.

FACTS: Securities investors (P) brought suit, alleging that investment banks, acting as underwriters (D), violated antitrust laws when they formed syndicates to help execute initial public offerings (IPOs) for several hundred technology-related companies. The investors (P) claimed that the underwriters (D) unlawfully agreed that they would not sell newly issued securities to a buyer unless the buyer committed (1) to buy additional shares of that security later at escalating prices (known as "laddering"), (2) to pay unusually high commissions on subsequent security purchases from the underwriters, or (3) to purchase from the underwriters (D) other less desirable securities (known as "tying"). The underwriters (D) moved to dismiss, claiming that federal securities law impliedly precludes application of antitrust laws to the conduct in question. The district court dismissed the complaints, but the court of appeals reversed. The U.S. Supreme Court granted certiorari.

ISSUE: Do the securities laws implicitly preclude the application of the antitrust laws to conduct of securities underwriters during the course of initial public offering (IPO) that includes requiring investors to: buy additional shares of a security at escalating prices in the future; to pay unusually high commissions on subsequent security purchases; and to purchase from the underwriters other less desirable securities?

HOLDING AND DECISION: (Breyer, J.) Yes. The securities laws implicitly preclude the application of the antitrust laws to conduct of securities underwriters during the course of initial public offering (IPO) that includes requiring investors to: buy additional shares of a security at

escalating prices in the future; to pay unusually high commissions on subsequent security purchases; and to purchase from the underwriters other less desirable securities. Where regulatory statutes are silent in respect to antitrust, courts must determine whether, and in what respects, they implicitly preclude the antitrust laws' application. Taken together, three of the Court's cases make clear that a court deciding this preclusion issue is deciding whether, given context and likely consequences, there is a "clear repugnancy" between the securities law and the antitrust complaint, i.e., whether the two are "clearly incompatible." These cases, in finding sufficient incompatibility to warrant an implication of preclusion, treated as critical four conditions: (1) the existence of regulatory authority under the securities law to supervise the activities in question; (2) evidence that the responsible regulatory entities exercise that authority; and (3) a resulting risk that the securities and antitrust laws, if both applicable, would produce conflicting guidance, requirements, duties, privileges, or standards of conduct. In addition, (4) the possible conflict affects practices that lay squarely within an area of financial market activity that securities law seeks to regulate. Applying these principles here, it is clear that several of these four conditions exist here and lead to the conclusion that the securities laws preclude application of the antitrust laws. These include the underwriters' (D) efforts jointly to promote and sell newly issued securities is central to the proper functioning of well-regulated capital markets; the fact that the law grants the Securities and Exchange Commission (SEC) authority to supervise such activities; and the fact that the SEC has continuously exercised its legal authority to regulate this type of conduct. These show that the first, second, and fourth conditions are satisfied in this case. This leaves the third condition: whether there is a conflict rising to the level of incompatibility. The complaint does not attack the bare existence of IPO underwriting syndicates or any of the joint activity that the SEC considers a necessary component of IPO-related syndicate activity. Instead, the complaint here can be read as attacking the manner in which the underwriters (D) jointly seek to collect "excessive" commissions through the practices of laddering, tying, and collecting excessive commissions, which according to the investors (P) the SEC itself has already disapproved and, in all likelihood, will not approve in the foreseeable future. Nonetheless, certain considerations, taken together, lead to the conclusion that securities law and antitrust law are clearly incompatible in this context. First, to permit antitrust actions such as this threatens serious securities-related harm. For one thing, a fine, complex, detailed line separates activity that the SEC

Continued on next page.

permits or encourages from activity that it forbids. Also, the SEC has the expertise to distinguish what is forbidden from what is allowed. For another thing, reasonable but contradictory inferences may be drawn from overlapping evidence that shows both unlawful antitrust activity and lawful securities marketing activity. Further, there is a serious risk that antitrust courts, with different nonexpert judges and different nonexpert juries, will produce inconsistent results. Together these factors mean there is no practical way to confine antitrust suits so that they challenge only the kind of activity the investors (P) seek to target, which is presently unlawful and will likely remain unlawful under the securities law. Rather, these considerations suggest that antitrust courts are likely to make unusually serious mistakes in this respect, which in turn means that underwriters (D) must act to avoid not simply conduct that the securities law forbids, but also joint conduct that the securities law permits or encourages. Thus, allowing an antitrust lawsuit would threaten serious harm to the efficient functioning of the securities market. Second, any enforcement-related need for an antitrust lawsuit is unusually small. For one thing, the SEC actively enforces the rules and regulations that forbid the conduct in question. For another, investors (P) harmed by underwriters' (D) unlawful practices may sue and obtain damages under the securities law. Finally, the fact that the SEC is itself required to take account of competitive considerations when it creates securities-related policy and embodies it in rules and regulations makes it somewhat less necessary to rely on antitrust actions to address anticompetitive behavior. In sum, an antitrust action in this context is accompanied by a substantial risk of injury to the securities markets and by a diminished need for antitrust enforcement to address anticompetitive conduct. Together these considerations indicate a serious conflict between application of the antitrust laws and proper enforcement of the securities law. Reversed.

▶ ANALYSIS

The three decisions on which the Court relied in reaching its decision were: *Silver v. New York Stock Exchange*, 373 U.S. 341 (1963); *Gordon v. New York Stock Exchange, Inc.*, 422 U.S. 659 (1975); and *United States v. National Assn. of Securities Dealers, Inc.*, 422 U.S. 694 (1975) (*NASD*). In *Silver* the Court considered a dealer's claim that, by expelling him from the New York Stock Exchange, the Exchange had violated the antitrust prohibition against group "boycotts." The Court indicated that, where possible, courts should "reconcil[e] the operation of both [i.e., antitrust and securities] statutory schemes . . . rather than holding one completely ousted." It also set forth the standard that repeal of the antitrust laws is to be regarded as implied only if necessary to make the Securities Exchange Act work, and even then only to the minimum extent necessary. It also held that the securities law did not preclude application of the antitrust laws to the claimed boycott insofar as the Exchange denied the expelled dealer a right to fair procedures. In *Gordon*, the

Court considered an antitrust complaint that essentially alleged "price fixing" among stockbrokers. Congress and the SEC both subsequently disapproved the price fixing practices. Even though there was likely compatibility of the laws in the future, the Court nonetheless expressly found conflict, which arose from the fact that the law permitted the SEC to supervise the competitive setting of rates and to reintroduce fixed rates under certain conditions. The Court consequently wrote that "failure to imply repeal would render nugatory the legislative provision for regulatory agency supervision of exchange commission rates." The upshot was that, in light of potential future conflict, Court found that the securities law precluded antitrust liability even in respect to a practice that both antitrust law and securities law might forbid. Finally, in *NASD*, the Court considered a Department of Justice antitrust complaint claiming that mutual fund companies had entered various agreements with securities broker-dealers that were anticompetitive. The Court again found "clear repugnancy," and it held that the securities law, by implication, precluded all parts of the antitrust claim. In reaching this conclusion, the Court found that antitrust law (e.g., forbidding resale price maintenance) and securities law (e.g., permitting resale price maintenance) were in conflict. In deciding that the latter trumped the former, the Court relied upon the same kinds of considerations it found determinative in *Gordon*.

Quicknotes

ANTITRUST LAW Body of federal law prohibiting business conduct that constitutes a restraint on trade.

PUBLIC OFFERING The offer to sell securities to the public.

Verizon Communications, Inc. v. Law Offices of Curtis V. Trinko, LLP

Incumbent local telephone company (D) v. Local telephone service customer (P)

540 U.S. 398 (2004).

NATURE OF CASE: Appeal from reversal of dismissal for failure to state a claim of action under § 2 of the Sherman Act.

FACT SUMMARY: Verizon Communications, Inc. (Verizon) (D), the incumbent local exchange carrier (LEC) serving New York State, contended that Law Offices of Curtis V. Trinko, LLP (P), a local telephone service customer of AT&T, failed to state a claim under § 2 of the Sherman Act when it alleged that Verizon (D) denied interconnection services to rivals in order to limit entry and had filled rivals' orders on a discriminatory basis as part of an anticompetitive scheme to discourage customers from becoming or remaining customers of competitive LECs.

🏛 RULE OF LAW
A complaint alleging breach of an incumbent local exchange carrier's duty under the Telecommunications Act of 1996 to share its network with competitors does not state a claim under § 2 of the Sherman Act.

FACTS: The Telecommunications Act of 1996 imposes upon an incumbent local exchange carrier (LEC) the obligation to share its telephone network with competitors, including the duty to provide access to individual network elements on an "unbundled" basis. New entrants, so-called competitive LECs, combine and resell these unbundled network elements (UNEs). Verizon Communications, Inc. (Verizon) (D) was the incumbent local exchange carrier (LEC) serving New York State. To foster increased competition, Verizon (D) had signed interconnection agreements with rivals such as AT&T, detailing the terms on which it would make its network elements available. Verizon (D) also entered the long-distance market. Competitive LECs complained that Verizon (D) was violating its obligation to provide access. A consent decree and orders issued from the state regulatory agency (PSC) and the Federal Communications Commission (FCC), which led to the imposition of financial penalties, remediation measures, and additional reporting requirements on Verizon (D). Law Offices of Curtis V. Trinko, LLP (P), a local telephone service customer of AT&T, then filed a class action alleging, inter alia, that Verizon (D) had filled rivals' orders on a discriminatory basis as part of an anticompetitive scheme to discourage customers from becoming or remaining customers of competitive LECs in violation of § 2 of the Sherman Act. The district court dismissed the complaint, concluding that the allegations of deficient assistance to rivals failed to satisfy § 2's requirements. The court of appeals reversed and reinstated the antitrust claim, and the U.S. Supreme Court granted certiorari.

ISSUE: Does a complaint alleging breach of an incumbent local exchange carrier's duty under the Telecommunications Act of 1996 to share its network with competitors state a claim under § 2 of the Sherman Act?

HOLDING AND DECISION: (Scalia, J.) No. A complaint alleging breach of an incumbent local exchange carrier's duty under the Telecommunications Act of 1996 to share its network with competitors does not state a claim under § 2 of the Sherman Act. Antitrust analysis must always be attuned to the particular structure and circumstances of the industry at issue. When there exist a regulatory structure designed to deter and remedy anticompetitive harm, the additional benefit to competition provided by antitrust enforcement will tend to be small, and it will be less plausible that the antitrust laws contemplate such additional scrutiny. Here, Verizon (D) was subject to oversight by the FCC and the PSC, both of which responded to certain deficiencies raised in the complaint by imposing fines and other burdens on Verizon (D). Thus, the regulatory regime was an effective steward of the antitrust function. Against the slight benefits of antitrust intervention here must be weighed a realistic assessment of its costs. Allegations of violations of § 251(c)(3) duties are both technical and extremely numerous, and hence difficult for antitrust courts to evaluate. Applying § 2's requirements to this regime can readily result in "false positive" mistaken inferences that chill the very conduct the antitrust laws are designed to protect. One false-positive risk is that an incumbent LEC's failure to provide a service with sufficient alacrity might have nothing to do with exclusion. This cost counsels against expanding § 2 liability unduly, especially since allegations of violations of § 251(c)(3) duties are difficult for antitrust courts to evaluate, not only because they are highly technical, but also because they are likely to be extremely numerous, given the incessant, complex, and constantly changing interaction of competitive and incumbent LECs implementing the sharing and interconnection obligations. Reversed and remanded.

▶ ANALYSIS

This portion of the decision in *Trinko* shows that the Court has assumed a very modest—almost deferential—position as to the scope of antitrust law's role in regulated markets, even where those markets are being deregulated, where regulations in those markets already address competition.

Allied Tube & Conduit Corp. v. Indian Head, Inc.

Conduit producer (P) v. Conduit producer (D)

486 U.S. 492 (1988).

NATURE OF CASE: Appeal from reversal of j.n.o.v. in action for unreasonable restraint of trade.

FACT SUMMARY: The National Fire Protection Association convened to vote on Indian Head Inc.'s (D) proposal that plastic conduit be an "approved" type of electrical conduit in the National Electric Code, but Allied Tube & Conduit Corp. (P), the nation's largest producer of steel conduit, "stacked" the meeting with its supporters so that Indian Head's (D) proposal was defeated.

🏛 RULE OF LAW
Where an economically interested party exercises decision-making authority in formulating a product standard for a private association made up of market participants, that party enjoys no *Noerr* immunity from antitrust liability for anticompetitive effects the standard exerts on the marketplace.

FACTS: The National Fire Protection Association (NFPA), made up of industry, labor, academia, insurers, doctors, firefighters and government officials, through "consensus standard making" published the National Electric Code, which established product and performance requirements for the design and installation of electrical wiring systems. The Code was influential in the marketplace: electricians worked according to Code, underwriters insure only structures built according to Code, and many state and local governments adopted the Code into law without change. The Code covered conduits, hollow tubes used to carry electrical wiring through walls and floors. Indian Head Inc. (D) developed a plastic conduit and applied to the NFPA for its inclusion on the Code's "approved" list. When Allied Tube & Conduit Corp. (Allied Tube) (P), the nation's largest producer of steel conduits, learned of Indian Head's (D) application, it recruited hundreds of supporters to join NFPA so that they could vote against Indian Head's (D) proposal at the next annual meeting. These Allied Tube (P) recruits did not actively participate in the NFPA meeting or even understand what was going on, but their votes defeated Indian Head's (D) proposal. Indian Head (D) then filed an antitrust lawsuit under the Sherman Act § 1, alleging that Allied Tube (P) had unreasonably restrained trade in the electrical conduit market. The jury found Allied Tube (P) liable and awarded treble damages, but the district court granted j.n.o.v., arguing that *Noerr* immunity applied to Allied Tube (P) because NFPA was "akin to a legislature" which Allied Tube (P) had tried to influence by the "use of methods consistent with acceptable standards of political action . . . ." The court of appeals reversed, holding *Noerr* immunity inapplicable, and Allied Tube (P) appealed.

ISSUE: Where an economically interested party exercises decision-making authority in formulating a product standard for a private association made up of market participants, does that party enjoy *Noerr* immunity from antitrust liability for anticompetitive effects the standard exerts on the market for that product?

HOLDING AND DECISION: (Brennan, J.) No. Where an economically interested party exercises decision-making authority in formulating a product standard for a private association made up of market participants, the party enjoys no *Noerr* immunity from antitrust liability for anti-competitive effects the standard exerts on the market for that product. Concerted efforts to restrain or monopolize trade by petitioning government officials are protected from antitrust liability under the *Noerr* immunity doctrine. Immunity can arise either from direct urging of government action or private action "incidental" to valid efforts to influence government action. Here, the restraint of trade on which liability was predicated is the NFPA's exclusion of Indian Head's (D) product from the Electric Code; thus the "source, context and nature" of the anticompetitive restraint to be examined is the standard-setting process of a private association. Although the NFPA National Electric Code is adopted into law by many governments, the NFPA is not a "quasi-legislative" body because no official authority has been conferred on it by any government. Nor was it an "incidental" action because it consisted of "rounding up" economically interested persons to set private standards and did not involve an essentially political activity, such as a publicity campaign to influence public opinion, as in *Eastern R.R. Presidents Conf. v. Noerr Motor Freight, Inc.*, 365 U.S. 127 (1961). Rather, the NFPA members were exercising market power in a private context, and Allied Tube (P) influenced that exercise of market power in such a way as to exclude trading in plastic conduit. The defeat of Indian Head's (D) proposal to include plastic conduit as an "approved" type in the National Electric Code constituted an implicit agreement among NFPA members not to trade in that particular type of conduit and thus constituted a restraint of trade. Affirmed.

▶ ANALYSIS

The intent to actually lessen competition in a particular product appears to be at the core of the Supreme Court's decision here. Compare *NAACP v. Claiborne Hardware Co.*, 458 U.S. 886 (1982), in which the Court held that the First Amendment protected the nonviolent elements of a boycott of white merchants organized by the NAACP and designed

Continued on next page.

to make white government and business leaders comply with a list of demands for racial equality. Although the boycotters intended to inflict a generalized economic injury on the merchants, the Court held that the boycott was not motivated by any desire to lessen competition or to reap economic benefits; the boycotters were ordinary consumers who did not stand to profit financially from a lessening of competition in the boycotted market.

■══■

Quicknotes

J.N.O.V. (JUDGMENT NOTWITHSTANDING THE VERDICT) A judgment entered by the trial judge reversing a jury verdict if the jury's determination has no basis in law or fact.

RESTRAINT OF TRADE Agreement between entities, for the purpose of impeding free trade, that results in a monopoly, suppression of competition, or affecting prices.

SHERMAN ACT § 1 Prohibits price-fixing.

■══■

FTC v. Superior Court Trial Lawyers Assn.

Federal agency (P) v. Professional association (D)

493 U.S. 411 (1990).

NATURE OF CASE: Appeal from remand of action for violation of the FTC Act § 5.

FACT SUMMARY: Members of the Superior Court Trial Lawyers Association (D) who provided most of the representation in the District of Columbia for indigent criminal defendants agreed to refuse to provide legal services until they received an hourly wage increase.

> ## 🏛 RULE OF LAW
> Horizontal agreements between market competitors to price-fix or to conduct a boycott are per se violations of the Sherman Act § 1 prohibition against restraints of trade even if they contain an expressive component suggestive of First Amendment protection.

FACTS: About one hundred lawyers regularly provided legal representation to indigent criminal defendants in the District of Columbia. By federal act they were paid from $20–30 per hour. These lawyers were members of the Superior Court Trial Lawyers Association (SCTLA) (D), and when SCTLA efforts to pass federal bills to raise this wage failed, the affected lawyers formed a "strike committee" which voted not to accept any new cases if legislation was not immediately passed providing for an increase in their fees. The SCTLA (D) members publicized their proposed boycott in the news media, and when their fees were not increased, began the boycott, which had a severe impact on the District's criminal justice system. The system, with no lawyers to replace the SCTLA (D) "regulars," was on the brink of collapse, forcing the District's mayor to meet with the "strike committee" and to arrive at a compromise agreement which would raise the fees on an interim basis to $35 per hour and eventually to $45–55 per hour in return for an end to the boycott. The Federal Trade Commission (FTC) (P) sued SCTLA (D) under § 1 of the Sherman Act and § 5 of the Federal Trade Commission Act for, respectively, restraint of trade and unfair competition, and won in the administrative law court and the court of appeals. The court of appeals, however, rejected application of the per se rule invalidating the boycott, holding that the "expressive component" of the SCTLA (D) boycott raised First Amendment concerns which required courts to apply the antitrust laws "prudently and with sensitivity"; it remanded to the FTC for a finding of whether the SCTLA (D) had market power and whether its boycott had anticompetitive effects. The FTC (P) appealed.

ISSUE: Are horizontal agreements between market competitors to price-fix or to conduct a boycott per se violations of the Sherman Act § 1 prohibition against restraints of trade even if they contain an expressive component suggestive of First Amendment protection?

HOLDING AND DECISION: (Stevens, J.) Yes. Horizontal agreements between market competitors to price-fix or to conduct a boycott are per se violations of the Sherman Act § 1 prohibition against restraints of trade even if they contain an expressive component suggestive of First Amendment protection. Here, the agreement among SCTLA (D) lawyers was designed to obtain higher prices for their services and was implemented by a concerted refusal to serve the only customer in the market, the District of Columbia, for the particular services. The constriction on supply is the essence of price-fixing, and thus the horizontal arrangement was a "naked" restraint on price and output. Such price-fixing is per se invalid under the Sherman Act § 1. The rationale for application of a per se rule here—to avoid complicated and prolonged investigations into market definition and market power in every case—outweighs whatever incidental expressive component the SCTLA (D) boycott may have had and which may have raised First Amendment implications. The creation of a new standard of review by the court of appeals based on such an expressive component was misplaced because all boycotts are the product of at least some communication; boycotts depend on the support of the public or third parties for their success; and SCTLA's (D) boycott was not "uniquely expressive." Reversed [insofar as the court of appeals held per se rules inapplicable to the SCTLA (D) boycott].

▌ANALYSIS

Other Supreme Court cases support the minority position in this case that "broad prophylactic rules (i.e., per se rules of Sherman Act antitrust violation) in the area of free expression are suspect." *NAACP v. Button,* 371 U.S. 415, 438 (1963). In one case, for example, the Supreme Court invalidated a state program under which taxpayers applying for a certain exemption had to prove they did not advocate the overthrow of the U.S. government. *Speiser v. Randall,* 357 U.S. 513 (1958) ("no ... compelling interest at stake as to justify a short-cut procedure which ... suppress[es] protected speech.") In another, the Supreme Court decided that the First Amendment prohibited a state from imposing liability on a newspaper for publishing embarrassing but truthful information on a "negligence per se" theory. The *Florida v. Star v. B.J.F.,* 491 U.S. 557 (1989) ("case-by-case findings" required rather than "liability [which] follows automatically from publication").

■=▪

Quicknotes

BOYCOTT A concerted effort to refrain from doing business with a particular person or entity.

Continued on next page.

HORIZONTAL AGREEMENTS Agreement entered into by entities at the same level of production for the purpose of restraining trade.

PER SE VIOLATION Business transactions that in themselves constitute restraints on trade, obviating the need to demonstrate an injury to competition in making out an antitrust case.

RESTRAINT OF TRADE Agreement between entities, for the purpose of impeding free trade, that results in a monopoly, suppression of competition, or affecting prices.

SHERMAN ACT Makes every contract or conspiracy in unreasonable restraint of commerce illegal.

UNFAIR COMPETITION Any dishonest or fraudulent rivalry in trade and commerce, particularly imitation and counterfeiting.

Professional Real Estate Investors, Inc. v. Columbia Pictures Industries, Inc.

Resort hotel owner (D) v. Motion picture studio (P)

508 U.S. 49 (1993).

NATURE OF CASE: Appeal from summary judgment denying damages in counterclaim for Sherman Act antitrust violations.

FACT SUMMARY: Professional Real Estate Investors, Inc. (D) alleged that a copyright infringement action filed against it by Columbia Pictures Industries, Inc. (P) was a mere sham that cloaked underlying acts of monopolization and conspiracy to restrain trade.

RULE OF LAW
Litigation cannot be deprived of immunity as a sham unless the litigation is objectively baseless.

FACTS: Professional Real Estate Investors, Inc. (PRE) (D) rented videodiscs to the guests in its hotel for in-room viewing. Columbia Pictures Industries, Inc. (Columbia) (P) held copyrights to the films recorded on PRE's (D) videodiscs. Columbia (P) also owned a wired cable system that competed with the videodisc players by transmitting movies to hotel rooms. Columbia (P) sued PRE (D) for alleged copyright infringement. PRE (D) counter-claimed, charging Columbia (P) with restraint of trade and attempt to monopolize in violation of the Sherman Act. PRE (D) alleged that Columbia's copyright action was a mere sham to cover its antitrust violations. The trial court granted summary judgment to PRE (D) on the copyright claim, and the court of appeals affirmed on the grounds that a hotel was not a "public place" and that PRE (D) was not "transmitting" Colombia's (P) movies. On remand, Columbia (P) argued that its infringement action was not a sham and was therefore entitled to immunity. The court agreed and granted Columbia's (P) motion for summary judgment on PRE's (D) antitrust claims. The court of appeals affirmed. PRE (D) appealed, and the U.S. Supreme Court granted certiorari.

ISSUE: Can litigation be deprived of immunity as a sham if the litigation is not objectively baseless?

HOLDING AND DECISION: (Thomas, J.) No. Litigation cannot be deprived of immunity as a sham unless the litigation is objectively baseless. The Sherman Act does not punish "political activity," and consequently, those who petition government for redress are generally immune from antitrust liability. Immunity does not extend, however, to those who seek litigation as a cover for their attempts to destroy their competitors. In order to rise to the level of "sham" litigation, the lawsuit must be objectively baseless in the sense that no reasonable litigant could realistically expect success on the merits. Only if the challenged litigation is objectively without merit may a court then look to the litigant's subjective motivation. In other words, an objectively reasonable effort to litigate cannot be sham, regardless of actual subjective intent on the part of the litigant to interfere with the business relationships of a competitor. Here, any reasonable copyright owner in Columbia's (P) position could have believed that it had some chance of winning an infringement suit against PRE (D). Thus, PRE (D) failed to establish the objective prong of the sham exception to immunity. Affirmed.

CONCURRENCE: (Stevens, J.) The Court's holding is broader than need be. There are numerous cases in which a reasonable litigant could expect to succeed on the merits, yet bringing the suit would be unreasonable and a sham.

ANALYSIS

A "sham" is the use of the governmental process—not the outcome of that process—as an anticompetitive weapon. Where the plaintiff is indifferent to the outcome of the litigation itself but is attempting to impose a collateral harm on the defendant by impairing his credit, abusing the discovery process, or interfering with his access to governmental agencies, he may be perpetrating a "sham."

Quicknotes

CERTIORARI A discretionary writ issued by a superior court to an inferior court in order to review the lower court's decisions; the Supreme Court's writ ordering such review.

CONSPIRACY Concerted action by two or more persons to accomplish some unlawful purpose.

COPYRIGHT Refers to the exclusive rights granted to an artist pursuant to Article I, section 8, clause 8 of the United States Constitution over the reproduction, display, performance, distribution, and adaptation of his work for a period prescribed by statute.

MONOPOLY A privilege or right conferred upon an individual or entity granting it the exclusive power to manufacture, sell and distribute a particular service or commodity; a market condition in which one or a few companies control the sale of a product or service thereby restraining competition in respect to that article or service.

RESTRAINT OF TRADE Agreement between entities, for the purpose of impeding free trade, that results in a monopoly, suppression of competition, or affecting prices.

Continued on next page.

SHERMAN ACT Makes every contract or conspiracy in unreasonable restraint of commerce illegal.

SUMMARY JUDGMENT Judgment rendered by a court in response to a motion by one of the parties, claiming that the lack of a question of material fact in respect to an issue warrants disposition of the issue without consideration by the jury.

Fisher v. City of Berkeley

Landlord (P) v. City (D)

475 U.S. 260 (1986).

NATURE OF CASE: Appeal from denial of damages under antitrust laws.

FACT SUMMARY: Fisher (P) and other landlords contended a rent control ordinance violated antitrust laws.

> 🏛 **RULE OF LAW**
> Rent control ordinances do not conflict with federal antitrust laws unless they involve concerted action in price-fixing.

FACTS: The City of Berkeley (Berkeley) (D) enacted a statute setting maximum rent charges. Landlords sued, contending, among other things, the ordinance was preempted by the Sherman Act. The trial court upheld the ordinance on its face, and the appellate court reversed. The California Supreme Court held the ordinance was not an undue burden on trade and upheld the ordinance. The U.S. Supreme Court granted certiorari.

ISSUE: Do rent control ordinances violate antitrust laws even in the absence of concerted action?

HOLDING AND DECISION: (Marshall, J.) No. Rent control ordinances do not conflict with federal antitrust laws in the absence of concerted action. The rent controls in this case were unilaterally set by Government (P) and imposed upon landlords. Thus, no concerted action to limit competition or fix prices was involved. As a result, the ordinance did not conflict with the Sherman Act, whose application is contingent upon the presence of concerted action. Because no conflict existed, the ordinance was not preempted. Affirmed.

▶ **ANALYSIS**

The California Supreme Court made its determination of the validity of the ordinance based on a test it devised. It was based upon the U.S. Supreme Court's Commerce Clause cases dealing with the impact of state regulation on interstate commerce. The majority opinion bases its conclusion on an interpretation of the antitrust laws rather than embarking upon a new method of analysis. The majority thus upheld the result on different grounds. This case is unusual in that the majority opinion is written by Justice Marshall with a dissent by Justice Brennan. These two justices rarely take opposing views.

■≡■

Quicknotes

BURDEN ON TRADE Agreements between entities, for the purpose of impeding free trade, that results in a monopoly, the suppression of competition, or affecting prices.

CERTIORARI A discretionary writ issued by a superior court to an inferior court in order to review the lower court's decisions; the Supreme Court's writ ordering such review.

PRICE-FIXING An illegal combination in violation of the Sherman Act entered into for the purpose of setting prices below the natural market rate.

RENT CONTROL A municipal ordinance limiting the maximum rent that may be lawfully charged for rental property.

SHERMAN ACT Makes every contract or conspiracy in unreasonable restraint of commerce illegal.

■≡■

California Retail Liquor Dealers Assn. v. Midcal Aluminum, Inc.

Dealer's association (D) v. Wine distributor (P)

445 U.S. 97 (1980).

NATURE OF CASE: Appeal from judgment granting injunctive relief against a state wine pricing system.

FACT SUMMARY: Midcal Aluminum Inc. (P) challenged California's wine pricing program after being charged with selling wine below the price set by the producer's schedule.

🏛 RULE OF LAW
A state policy is immune from antitrust regulation if it is "clearly articulated" and "actively supervised" by the state.

FACTS: California law required that all wine prices be set by a fair trade contract or schedule. The wine producers must set a price schedule and file it with the state. No wholesaler may sell wine to a retailer at other than the price set by the wine producer. The state enforced the price but in no way controlled or reviewed the schedules. Midcal Aluminum, Inc. (Midcal) (P), a wholesaler of controlled wine, was charged with selling wine below the set price. Midcal (P) admitted the allegations and then filed a writ of mandate in the appellate court, contending that the state's wine price scheme restrained trade in violation of the Sherman Act. The appellate court agreed and issued an injunction. The California Retail Liquor Dealers Assn. (D) appealed.

ISSUE: Is a state policy which is "clearly articulated" and "actively supervised" by the state immune from antitrust regulation?

HOLDING AND DECISION: (Powell, J.) Yes. A state policy is immune from antitrust regulation if it is "clearly articulated" and "actively supervised" by the state. California's regulation and purpose, i.e., to permit resale price maintenance, was clearly stated in the legislation. However, the pricing system is subject to the antitrust laws since the state did not regulate the pricing system. The prices were set solely at the discretion of private parties and were never reviewed by the state. Affirmed.

▶ ANALYSIS

As described in *Midcal*, the "state action" doctrine is extremely deferential to state regulation. Not only does it allow continued enforcement of laws clearly in violation of federal antitrust laws, it describes the manner in which a state may draft anti-competitive regulation so as to be sheltered from the antitrust laws. Opponents of such federal deference argue that state regulation is inappropriate if it is ineffective relative to federal oversight or if spillover effects from the regulation adversely impact out-of-state parties.

■■■■

Quicknotes

INJUNCTIVE RELIEF A court order issued as a remedy, requiring a person to do, or prohibiting that person from doing, a specific act.

RESTRAINT OF TRADE Agreement between entities, for the purpose of impeding free trade, that results in a monopoly, suppression of competition, or affecting prices.

WRIT OF MANDATE The written order of a court directing a particular action.

■■■■

Hallie v. City of Eau Claire

Unincorporated township (P) v. City (D)

471 U.S. 34 (1985).

NATURE OF CASE: Appeal from denial of injunctive relief.

FACT SUMMARY: The Towns (P) appealed from a court of appeals decision finding that the City of Eau Claire (D) did not violate the Sherman Act by acquiring a monopoly over the treatment provision of sewage treatments/services and by tying the provision of such services to the provision of sewage collection and transportation services.

🏛 RULE OF LAW
A municipality's anticompetitive activities are protected by the state action exemption to the federal antitrust laws when the activities are authorized but not compelled by the state and the state does not actively supervise the anticompetitive conduct.

FACTS: After obtaining federal funds, the City of Eau Claire (the City) (D) built a sewage treatment facility within the Eau Claire Service Area, which included the Towns (P). The facility was the only one in the market available to the Towns (P). The City (D) had refused to supply sewage treatment services to the Town (P), supplying services to individual areas in the Towns (P) if those areas voted to annex themselves to the City (D) and voted to use the City's (D) sewage collection and transportation services. The Towns (P), alleging that they were potential competitors in the collection and transportation of sewage, sued for violations of the Sherman Act. The Towns (P) contended that the City (D) had used its monopoly over sewage treatment to gain an unlawful monopoly in the provision of sewage collection and transportation services. The district court ruled for the City (D), and the court of appeals affirmed. From this decision, the Towns (P) appealed.

ISSUE: Are a municipality's anticompetitive activities protected by the state action exemption to the federal antitrust laws when the activities are authorized but not compelled by the state and the state does not actively supervise the anticompetitive conduct?

HOLDING AND DECISION: (Powell, J.) Yes. A municipality's anticompetitive activities are protected by the state action exemption to the federal antitrust laws when the activities are authorized but not compelled by the state and the state does not actively supervise the anticompetitive conduct. In order to reach a decision in the present case, it must be determined how clearly a state policy must be articulated in order for a municipality to take advantage of the state action exemption and whether action by a municipality must be actively supervised by the state. In the present case, the City (D) acted pursuant to statutes that authorized the City (D) to provide treatment services and to determine the areas to be served. It is clear that anticompetitive effects would logically result from the broad authority to regulate. It is not required that the statute expressly state that the delegated activity was intended to have anticompetitive effects. These statutes cannot be construed as neutral; they specifically authorize activity that will likely result in anticompetitive effects. The clear articulation requirement of the state action test has been satisfied. Compulsion has never been required with respect to municipalities and is unnecessary as an evidentiary matter to prove that certain practices constitute state action. Finally, the requirement of state supervision mainly serves as evidentiary function, to ensure that the activity is engaged in pursuant to state policy. Once it is clear that state authorization exists, there is no need to require the state to supervise actively the municipality's activities. Affirmed.

▶ ANALYSIS

The dropping of the requirement of active state supervision creates a sort of rebuttable presumption that the municipality is acting in conformity with the state goals underlying the delegation of authority to the municipality. In the proper case, however, a plaintiff may be able to show that the municipality, acting pursuant to state policy, may be serving its own interests at the expense of state goals. In such a case, active state supervision may be imposed on the municipality in order to ensure that the activity can be truly considered state action.

■■■

Quicknotes

INJUNCTIVE RELIEF A court order issued as a remedy, requiring a person to do, or prohibiting that person from doing, a specific act.

MONOPOLY A privilege or right conferred upon an individual or entity granting it the exclusive power to manufacture, sell and distribute a particular service or commodity; a market condition in which one or a few companies control the sale of a product or service thereby restraining competition in respect to that article or service.

SHERMAN ACT Makes every contract or conspiracy in unreasonable restraint of commerce illegal.

TYING Selling a specified product to a buyer only if the buyer also agrees to purchase another product.

■■■

City of Columbia & Columbia Outdoor Advertising, Inc. v. Omni Outdoor Advertising, Inc.

City and billboard advertiser (D) v. Billboard advertiser (P)

499 U.S. 365 (1991).

NATURE OF CASE: Appeal of reversal of judgment n.o.v., reinstating award of damages for antitrust violations.

FACT SUMMARY: Omni Outdoor Advertising, Inc. (P) contended that the city government of Columbia, South Carolina (D) had, through regulation, given Columbia Outdoor Advertising, Inc. (D) a de facto monopoly on billboard advertising.

🏛 **RULE OF LAW**
A city may, through regulation, give a business concern a de facto monopoly on a business activity.

FACTS: Columbia Outdoor Advertising, Inc. (Columbia Outdoor) (D) had long been the near-exclusive provider of billboard advertising in the city of Columbia, South Carolina (City) (D). Columbia Outdoor (D) had considerable influence in the municipal governing structure due to both personal and business affiliations. In 1981, Omni Outdoor Advertising, Inc. (Omni) (P) began erecting billboards. The City (D) responded with various forms of restrictive ordinances. The final ordinance created spacing restrictions which had the practical effect of ending the erection of new billboards, a result that essentially locked-in Columbia Outdoor's (D) near-monopoly. Omni (P) filed an action under the Sherman Act. A jury returned a verdict of $1 million, but the district court gave Columbia Outdoor (D) and the City (D) judgment notwithstanding the verdict. The Fourth Circuit reversed and reinstated the jury verdict. The U.S. Supreme Court granted review.

ISSUE: May a city, through regulation, give a business concern a de facto monopoly on a business activity?

HOLDING AND DECISION: (Scalia, J.) Yes. A city may, through regulation, give a business concern a de facto monopoly on a business activity. This Court has held that principles of federalism mandate that a sovereign state may impose anticompetitive restraints within it territory. With respect to political subdivisions such as cities, such restraints may be imposed if authorized by statute. The statute need not specifically authorize such restraints; all that must be delegated is the power used to create the restraint, such as zoning. Such authority was given here. Omni (P) urges a "conspiracy" exception to this rule. This Court is not inclined to create such an exception, as it would probably swallow the rule; any governmental regulation in response to constitutionally protected lobbying could be seen as a "conspiracy." For this reason, such an exception will not be recognized. Beyond this, no liability can accrue to a private party who urges anticompetitive regulation, largely

for reasons just explained. Such urging is part of the political process, and as long as improper tactics (e.g., bribery) are not used, such activity cannot constitute an antitrust violation. Reversed and remanded.

▶ **ANALYSIS**

The rule here extended to cities was announced as to states in *Parker v. Brown*, 317 U.S. 341 (1943), and is called the *Parker* rule. The rule does have on important exemption, called the "market participant" exception. When a state elects not to regulate but to enter a market as a participant, it must play by the same rules as other participants. It cannot give itself a monopoly.

■■■

Quicknotes

JUDGMENT N.O.V. (NOTWITHSTANDING THE VERDICT) Judgment entered by the trial judge reversing a jury verdict if the jury's determination has no basis in law or fact.

MONOPOLY A privilege or right conferred upon an individual or entity granting it the exclusive power to manufacture, sell and distribute a particular service or commodity; a market condition in which one or a few companies control the sale of a product or service thereby restraining competition in respect to that article or service.

■■■

FTC v. Ticor Title Insurance Co.

Federal agency (P) v. Insurance Co. (D)

504 U.S. 621 (1992).

NATURE OF CASE: Appeal from judgment dismissing administrative complaint filed by the Federal Trade Commission (FTC).

FACT SUMMARY: After Ticor Title Insurance Co. (D) had its rates set by a title insurance rating bureau licensed by the state the FTC (P) filed a complaint alleging that the rating system constituted price-fixing.

> **RULE OF LAW**
> In order to receive immunity from the application of antitrust laws, a state price regulatory system must be under the active supervision of the state.

FACTS: Four states established title insurance rating bureaus which jointly filed insurance rates for Ticor Title Insurance Co. (Ticor) (D) and other insurance companies (D). Under the system in question, the bureau would file the rates, and, if the state did not reject them within thirty days, the rates would go into effect. Although the mechanisms for review of rates were in place, any review that did occur was cursory. The Federal Trade Commission (FTC) (P) filed a complaint against the insurance companies (D), alleging that the system constituted price-fixing. The insurance companies (D) claimed that they were entitled to state-action immunity from federal antitrust rules since they were acting pursuant to a government regulatory scheme. The FTC (P) rejected this defense. The court of appeals allowed the defense. The FTC (P) appealed.

ISSUE: Must a state price regulatory system be under the active supervision of the state to be exempt from the application of antitrust laws?

HOLDING AND DECISION: (Kennedy, J.) Yes. In order to be exempt from the application of antitrust laws, a state price regulatory system must be under the active supervision of the state. The purpose of immunity for state action is to allow the state to restrict competition when necessary to achieve important goals without undermining the federal goals of antitrust. That purpose is achieved by adequate state control over regulatory schemes that justify price-fixing by private parties. Approval by failure to act, i.e., the mere potential for state supervision as provided by the regulatory schemes in this case, does not constitute active supervision. Reversed and remanded.

▶ *ANALYSIS*

This case raises the question of the efficacy of the supervision requirement when a municipality places the economic decision-making power given to it by the state into the hands of private individuals. Who must do the supervising: the state or the municipalities? In *Englert v. City of McKeesport*, 637 F. Supp. 930 (W.D. Pa. 1986), the court held that it is the municipality which is responsible for supervising the conduct of the private parties.

■■■

Quicknotes

PRICE-FIXING An illegal combination in violation of the Sherman Act entered into for the purpose of setting prices below the natural market rate.

■■■

Glossary

Common Latin Words and Phrases Encountered in the Law

A FORTIORI: Because one fact exists or has been proven, therefore a second fact that is related to the first fact must also exist.

A PRIORI: From the cause to the effect. A term of logic used to denote that when one generally accepted truth is shown to be a cause, another particular effect must necessarily follow.

AB INITIO: From the beginning; a condition which has existed throughout, as in a marriage which was void ab initio.

ACTUS REUS: The wrongful act; in criminal law, such action sufficient to trigger criminal liability.

AD VALOREM: According to value; an ad valorem tax is imposed upon an item located within the taxing jurisdiction calculated by the value of such item.

AMICUS CURIAE: Friend of the court. Its most common usage takes the form of an amicus curiae brief, filed by a person who is not a party to an action but is nonetheless allowed to offer an argument supporting his legal interests.

ARGUENDO: In arguing. A statement, possibly hypothetical, made for the purpose of argument, is one made arguendo.

BILL QUIA TIMET: A bill to quiet title (establish ownership) to real property.

BONA FIDE: True, honest, or genuine. May refer to a person's legal position based on good faith or lacking notice of fraud (such as a bona fide purchaser for value) or to the authenticity of a particular document (such as a bona fide last will and testament).

CAUSA MORTIS: With approaching death in mind. A gift causa mortis is a gift given by a party who feels certain that death is imminent.

CAVEAT EMPTOR: Let the buyer beware. This maxim is reflected in the rule of law that a buyer purchases at his own risk because it is his responsibility to examine, judge, test, and otherwise inspect what he is buying.

CERTIORARI: A writ of review. Petitions for review of a case by the United States Supreme Court are most often done by means of a writ of certiorari.

CONTRA: On the other hand. Opposite. Contrary to.

CORAM NOBIS: Before us; writs of error directed to the court that originally rendered the judgment.

CORAM VOBIS: Before you; writs of error directed by an appellate court to a lower court to correct a factual error.

CORPUS DELICTI: The body of the crime; the requisite elements of a crime amounting to objective proof that a crime has been committed.

CUM TESTAMENTO ANNEXO, ADMINISTRATOR (ADMINISTRATOR C.T.A.): With will annexed; an administrator c.t.a. settles an estate pursuant to a will in which he is not appointed.

DE BONIS NON, ADMINISTRATOR (ADMINISTRATOR D.B.N.): Of goods not administered; an administrator d.b.n. settles a partially settled estate.

DE FACTO: In fact; in reality; actually. Existing in fact but not officially approved or engendered.

DE JURE: By right; lawful. Describes a condition that is legitimate "as a matter of law," in contrast to the term "de facto," which connotes something existing in fact but not legally sanctioned or authorized. For example, de facto segregation refers to segregation brought about by housing patterns, etc., whereas de jure segregation refers to segregation created by law.

DE MINIMIS: Of minimal importance; insignificant; a trifle; not worth bothering about.

DE NOVO: Anew; a second time; afresh. A trial de novo is a new trial held at the appellate level as if the case originated there and the trial at a lower level had not taken place.

DICTA: Generally used as an abbreviated form of obiter dicta, a term describing those portions of a judicial opinion incidental or not necessary to resolution of the specific question before the court. Such nonessential statements and remarks are not considered to be binding precedent.

DUCES TECUM: Refers to a particular type of writ or subpoena requesting a party or organization to produce certain documents in their possession.

EN BANC: Full bench. Where a court sits with all justices present rather than the usual quorum.

EX PARTE: For one side or one party only. An ex parte proceeding is one undertaken for the benefit of only one party, without notice to, or an appearance by, an adverse party.

EX POST FACTO: After the fact. An ex post facto law is a law that retroactively changes the consequences of a prior act.

EX REL.: Abbreviated form of the term "ex relatione," meaning upon relation or information. When the state brings an action in which it has no interest against an individual at the instigation of one who has a private interest in the matter.

FORUM NON CONVENIENS: Inconvenient forum. Although a court may have jurisdiction over the case, the action should be tried in a more conveniently located court, one to which parties and witnesses may more easily travel, for example.

GUARDIAN AD LITEM: A guardian of an infant as to litigation, appointed to represent the infant and pursue his/her rights.

HABEAS CORPUS: You have the body. The modern writ of habeas corpus is a writ directing that a person (body) being detained (such as a prisoner) be brought before the court so that the legality of his detention can be judicially ascertained.

IN CAMERA: In private, in chambers. When a hearing is held before a judge in his chambers or when all spectators are excluded from the courtroom.

IN FORMA PAUPERIS: In the manner of a pauper. A party who proceeds in forma pauperis because of his poverty is one who is allowed to bring suit without liability for costs.

INFRA: Below, under. A word referring the reader to a later part of a book. (The opposite of supra.)

IN LOCO PARENTIS: In the place of a parent.

IN PARI DELICTO: Equally wrong; a court of equity will not grant requested relief to an applicant who is in pari delicto, or as much at fault in the transactions giving rise to the controversy as is the opponent of the applicant.

IN PARI MATERIA: On like subject matter or upon the same matter. Statutes relating to the same person or things are said to be in pari materia. It is a general rule of statutory construction that such statutes should be construed together, i.e., looked at as if they together constituted one law.

IN PERSONAM: Against the person. Jurisdiction over the person of an individual.

IN RE: In the matter of. Used to designate a proceeding involving an estate or other property.

IN REM: A term that signifies an action against the res, or thing. An action in rem is basically one that is taken directly against property, as distinguished from an action in personam, i.e., against the person.

INTER ALIA: Among other things. Used to show that the whole of a statement, pleading, list, statute, etc., has not been set forth in its entirety.

INTER PARTES: Between the parties. May refer to contracts, conveyances or other transactions having legal significance.

INTER VIVOS: Between the living. An inter vivos gift is a gift made by a living grantor, as distinguished from bequests contained in a will, which pass upon the death of the testator.

IPSO FACTO: By the mere fact itself.

JUS: Law or the entire body of law.

LEX LOCI: The law of the place; the notion that the rights of parties to a legal proceeding are governed by the law of the place where those rights arose.

MALUM IN SE: Evil or wrong in and of itself; inherently wrong. This term describes an act that is wrong by its very nature, as opposed to one which would not be wrong but for the fact that there is a specific legal prohibition against it (malum prohibitum).

MALUM PROHIBITUM: Wrong because prohibited, but not inherently evil. Used to describe something that is wrong because it is expressly forbidden by law but that is not in and of itself evil, e.g., speeding.

MANDAMUS: We command. A writ directing an official to take a certain action.

MENS REA: A guilty mind; a criminal intent. A term used to signify the mental state that accompanies a crime or other prohibited act. Some crimes require only a general mens rea (general intent to do the prohibited act), but others, like assault with intent to murder, require the existence of a specific mens rea.

MODUS OPERANDI: Method of operating; generally refers to the manner or style of a criminal in committing crimes, admissible in appropriate cases as evidence of the identity of a defendant.

NEXUS: A connection to.

NISI PRIUS: A court of first impression. A nisi prius court is one where issues of fact are tried before a judge or jury.

N.O.V. (NON OBSTANTE VEREDICTO): Notwithstanding the verdict. A judgment n.o.v. is a judgment given in favor of one party despite the fact that a verdict was returned in favor of the other party, the justification being that the verdict either had no reasonable support in fact or was contrary to law.

NUNC PRO TUNC: Now for then. This phrase refers to actions that may be taken and will then have full retroactive effect.

PENDENTE LITE: Pending the suit; pending litigation under way.

PER CAPITA: By head; beneficiaries of an estate, if they take in equal shares, take per capita.

PER CURIAM: By the court; signifies an opinion ostensibly written "by the whole court" and with no identified author.

PER SE: By itself, in itself; inherently.

PER STIRPES: By representation. Used primarily in the law of wills to describe the method of distribution where a person, generally because of death, is unable to take that which is left to him by the will of another, and therefore his heirs divide such property between them rather than take under the will individually.

PRIMA FACIE: On its face, at first sight. A prima facie case is one that is sufficient on its face, meaning that the evidence supporting it is adequate to establish the case until contradicted or overcome by other evidence.

PRO TANTO: For so much; as far as it goes. Often used in eminent domain cases when a property owner receives partial payment for his land without prejudice to his right to bring suit for the full amount he claims his land to be worth.

QUANTUM MERUIT: As much as he deserves. Refers to recovery based on the doctrine of unjust enrichment in those cases in which a party has rendered valuable services or furnished materials that were accepted and enjoyed by another under circumstances that would reasonably notify the recipient that the rendering party expected to be paid. In essence, the law implies a contract to pay the reasonable value of the services or materials furnished.

QUASI: Almost like; as if; nearly. This term is essentially used to signify that one subject or thing is almost analogous to another but that material differences between them do exist. For example, a quasi-criminal proceeding is one that is not strictly criminal but shares enough of the same characteristics to require some of the same safeguards (e.g., procedural due process must be followed in a parole hearing).

QUID PRO QUO: Something for something. In contract law, the consideration, something of value, passed between the parties to render the contract binding.

RES GESTAE: Things done; in evidence law, this principle justifies the admission of a statement that would otherwise be hearsay when it is made so closely to the event in question as to be said to be a part of it, or with such spontaneity as not to have the possibility of falsehood.

RES IPSA LOQUITUR: The thing speaks for itself. This doctrine gives rise to a rebuttable presumption of negligence when the instrumentality causing the injury was within the exclusive control of the defendant, and the injury was one that does not normally occur unless a person has been negligent.

RES JUDICATA: A matter adjudged. Doctrine which provides that once a court of competent jurisdiction has rendered a final judgment or decree on the merits, that judgment or decree is conclusive upon the parties to the case and prevents them from engaging in any other litigation on the points and issues determined therein.

RESPONDEAT SUPERIOR: Let the master reply. This doctrine holds the master liable for the wrongful acts of his servant (or the principal for his agent) in those cases in which the servant (or agent) was acting within the scope of his authority at the time of the injury.

STARE DECISIS: To stand by or adhere to that which has been decided. The common law doctrine of stare decisis attempts to give security and certainty to the law by following the policy that once a principle of law as applicable to a certain set of facts has been set forth in a decision, it forms a precedent which will subsequently be followed, even though a different decision might be made were it the first time the question had arisen. Of course, stare decisis is not an inviolable principle and is departed from in instances where there is good cause (e.g., considerations of public policy led the Supreme Court to disregard prior decisions sanctioning segregation).

SUPRA: Above. A word referring a reader to an earlier part of a book.

ULTRA VIRES: Beyond the power. This phrase is most commonly used to refer to actions taken by a corporation that are beyond the power or legal authority of the corporation.

Addendum of French Derivatives

IN PAIS: Not pursuant to legal proceedings.

CHATTEL: Tangible personal property.

CY PRES: Doctrine permitting courts to apply trust funds to purposes not expressed in the trust but necessary to carry out the settlor's intent.

PER AUTRE VIE: For another's life; during another's life. In property law, an estate may be granted that will terminate upon the death of someone other than the grantee.

PROFIT A PRENDRE: A license to remove minerals or other produce from land.

VOIR DIRE: Process of questioning jurors as to their predispositions about the case or parties to a proceeding in order to identify those jurors displaying bias or prejudice.

Casenote Legal Briefs